The Murder of Mr. Grebell

The Murder of Mr. Grebell

Madness and Civility in an English Town

Paul Kléber Monod

Yale University Press   New Haven and London

Published with assistance from the Annie Burr Lewis Fund.
Set in Caslon type by Tseng Information Systems, Inc.
Printed in the United States of America.

Library of Congress Cataloging-in-Publication Data
Monod, Paul Kléber.
The murder of Mr. Grebell : madness and civility in an English town /
Paul Kléber Monod.— 1st ed.
p. cm.
ISBN 0-300-09985-1 (alk. paper)
1. Murder—England—Rye—Case studies.   2. Grebell, Allen, d. 1743.
3. Breads, John, d. 1743.   I. Title.
HV6535.G6R696   2003
364.15'23'094225—dc21
2003009882

A catalogue record for this book is available from the British Library.

The paper in this book meets the guidelines for permanence and
durability of the Committee on Production Guidelines for Book
Longevity of the Council on Library Resources.

10   9   8   7   6   5   4   3   2   1

To Jan and Evan
and my students on both sides of the Atlantic

Contents

Acknowledgments

This book is an expression of my affection for the whole county of Sussex, east and west. In 1990-91, my wife, Jan Albers, and I spent a happy year there, teaching at the University of Sussex and living in Lewes. For that opportunity, I am grateful to the Leverhulme Trust, the University of Sussex, and Middlebury College. Most of the research for the book was done that year in the East Sussex Record Office, whose staff made up for their cramped quarters with a congeniality and helpfulness beyond all expectations. It was there that I discovered the remarkable records of the town of Rye. The members of the Rye Local History Group, who kindly invited me to speak to them about their favourite murder in 1991, must have expected my work to appear in print many years ago, but another project intervened, and it took a decade to complete what I had begun. The final draft was completed while I was a visiting fellow at Oxford University in 2001-2, for which I give heartfelt thanks to the principal and fellows of Harris Manchester College as well as to Middlebury College.

The individuals who have assisted me along the long path to completion are so numerous that I will surely forget some (and some whom I encountered briefly along the way may well have forgotten me). At Lewes, they included Judy Brent, Graham Mayhew, Christopher Whittick, and all the staff at the East Sussex Records Office (surely, the hardest-working people in the archive business); in Chichester, Tim McCann of the West Sussex Records Office; and at the Rye Castle Museum, Rosemary Bagley, the late Geoffrey Bagley, and Allan Downend. Among my colleagues at the University of Sussex I must single out Colin Brooks, who made it all possible, and that happy warrior Willy Lamont. The students who took courses in early modern British history with me at Sussex were a great inspiration, and I remember them fondly. Michael Hunter and Stephen Hipkin helped me with inquiries, as did Colin Brent, who has an incomparable knowledge of Sussex history. Alan Dickinson invited me to talk on my research at Rye. My cousin Margaret Monod (despite loud groans every time I called) and her partner Joyce Chester gave me a place to stay in Brighton whenever I needed it. Back in the United States, Derek Hirst organized a panel at the North American Conference on British Studies at which I presented material from Chapter Three. Dan Szechi made many useful comments on my presentation. My interest in Sussex was sustained at Middlebury by my undergraduate students, who kept reminding me of why this might be an interesting book to write. I am particularly grateful to one Middlebury student, Hope Stege, who produced the map of Rye.

In 1995 I received a letter from M. V. Saville, a local historian who had attended my talk at Rye and was interested in my work. He has since done more research than anyone, including me, into the Grebell murder. After meeting at last in 2001, we began a correspondence in which he shared his findings and challenged many points in my account. He reminded me that professional historians ignore local experts at their own peril. I hope that Mike will be moderately satisfied with my amendments; my debt to him is greater than it is possible to express here.

Another big debt is to David Underdown, who showed enormous generosity in reading an early, awkward draft of the book. Thankfully, his comments did not release fire from heaven. Another merciful reader was Perry Gauci, who provided me with a big moral boost as I was finishing up the book in 2002. For the kindness they showed me while I was on leave at Oxford, I would like to thank Rowena Archer, Robin Briggs, John Robertson, Maxine Berg, Margot Finn, Judith Maltby, Diarmaid MacCulloch, and Felicity Heal. I could not have asked for a better editor than Lara Heimert of Yale University Press.

My dear wife, Jan Albers, has liked this best of all the books on which I have worked. Because of her support, it has been a pleasure to write. I have learned a great deal from her own work on Vermont. What else I owe her is simply everything. My son, Evan, liked this book, too, because it entailed several trips to places he enjoys as much as I do. The three of us drove around in an old Saab that an uncle of mine once owned. After his death, it passed on to my cousin, who sold it to my mother (who bought it on another uncle's advice), who then gave it to us. That car summed up the joy of having an extended family. To my mother, who introduced me to small-town English life, and to all the Donovan clan, I give a loud beep of thanks.

The exquisite town of Rye has sustained my interest for a decade, and my final acknowledgements must go to its citizens. They made me believe that they never resented my intrusions. Not least among them was the mayor, Peter Dyce, who let me see John Breads's skull and gibbet in February 2002. Because I had mixed feelings about its being shown, I had deliberately avoided seeing the skull until the book was almost finished. What I found was the weathered top part of a human cranium, enclosed in a small frame of rusty iron straps, and kept unobtrusively in a rather cluttered upstairs room. For the curious, I have included a photograph of it. I hope that readers of this book will be encouraged to spend time in Rye and visit its splendid Court Hall, but they will not be missing much if they pass up a trip to the upstairs room. The last remains of Breads's body will continue to be exposed, but the harsh justice meted out to him does not oblige us to disturb his rest.

I

Spook Stories

And I want to be in Rye at twilight and lean *myself* by
the wall of the ancient town — *myself,* like ancient wall and
dust and sky, and the purple dusk, grown old, grown old
in heart.

—Malcolm Lowry to Conrad Aiken, 13 March 1929

This is the story of a violent murder that happened in 1743 in a
town on the south coast of England. No mystery surrounds the
identity of the killer, but his motives have never been clear. He
may have been insane, he may have been possessed by devils, or
he may have been seeking revenge against the leading men of the
town. Whatever the explanation for his crime, he was tried very
irregularly, by a judge who was brother-in-law to the murdered
man and was allegedly the intended victim. After his execution,
the murderer's body was put on display in a gibbet, where it was
left to rot. His skull is still in the gibbet, now kept in a small
upstairs room in the town hall, where it can be seen by visitors.
He is one of the last British criminals of the eighteenth century
who is still being punished.

This is also the story of the town where the murder happened:
Rye, in East Sussex. The killing and the subsequent trial connect to broader issues in the history of the Sussex port, issues
that affected other small towns in early modern England. We
can see the events of 1743 as emblematic of the social and political relationships that existed in many parts of the kingdom.
The isolation of Rye does not trivialize the case, because the

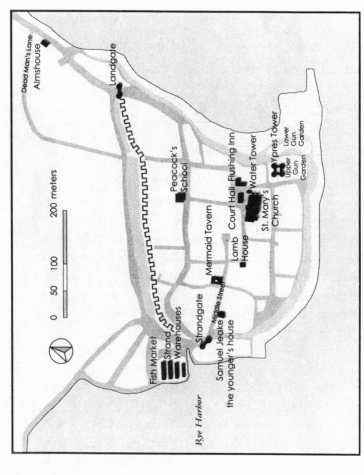

The town of Rye, from a ground plot drawn by Samuel Jeake the elder in 1667 and redrawn in 1728 by the surveyor William Wybourn (ESRO, Rye 132/15).

map of early modern England was dotted with scores of little urban backwaters of which we know very little, from Lyme Regis to Cromer, Stamford to Morpeth, Kendal to Leominster. The murder may lead us to question just how detached they were from national trends. Were they stuck in a grim and impoverished past, or were they moving, along with the larger cities, into an eighteenth-century British version of social modernity, marked by the commercial values and consumer culture of the "middling sort"?

The Rye murder cannot provide a single full answer, but it can direct us towards possible answers. It is a story of personal violence and judicial vengeance. As such, it gives us access to the tensions and animosities that existed among people who jostled up against one another in the restricted space of a small urban community. It casts a harsh light on the transition from the narrowly focused community norms of the Reformation period to the more expansive ideals of a commercial society. The older values of English towns and villages stressed "good neighbourliness," which has been defined as "a mutual recognition of reciprocal obligations of a practical kind."[1] In other words, there was a general consensus about how neighbours should behave towards one another. Good neighbourliness supposedly thrived in tight-knit, inward-looking communities like seventeenth-century Rye, where personal security depended on the support and assistance of other people. This kind of community support was notably lacking in the 1743 murder trial. We should not assume, of course, that neighbourly values were always benign. Anyone's behaviour could be closely monitored, and deviance was strictly punished, so as to promote secular and religious harmony.

By contrast, the urban values of the eighteenth century tended to emphasize what was called "civility" by some and "politeness" by others. Civility began as a courtly code of good manners, practiced by aristocrats who did not want to be associated with the "rude" or "barbarous" behaviour of the lower classes. It also separated the English, and others who claimed a connection with the culture of classical Rome, from "savages" like the Irish and North American Indians. Eventually, it became "a sign of a gentleman's membership of 'civil society,'" and was adopted by people of the middling sort—merchants, shopkeepers, tradesmen, and their families—who did not wish to be identified with the plebeian multitude. In this broader, less exclusive form it was often dubbed politeness. It rested more on the internal regulation of one's actions than on the outward approval of the community. While it was not anti-religious, politeness tended to emphasize worldly models of proper behaviour rather than the rewards and punishments of the afterlife. Because of its connections with city life and commerce, politeness has been associated with a "consumer revolution" and an "urban renaissance" in eighteenth-century England.[2] If Rye and other small towns gloried in a polite modernity, however, we will have to explain how this was compatible with poverty, oligarchical control, and the horrors of the public scaffold or the gibbet.

This study poses some broad questions, but it has a narrow focus, and it can be called a "microhistory." Microhistories centre on a particular narrative or story, usually derived from the records of legal proceedings.[3] The purpose of microhistory is to penetrate to an individual level of experience, so as to show how historical circumstances were felt or perceived. Microhistories therefore tend to integrate background or context into the retelling of the story. However, the legal case that is retold in this chapter does not easily lend itself to such an approach, because there is no complete first-hand narrative. If we want to understand what happened, we have to fill the gaps in the legal record by using a range of additional sources. They are sometimes confusing and often provide less information than we would like to know. Yet perhaps the tentative, fragmentary kind of history that is offered here reflects the complexity and ambiguity of human experience more closely than would a single coherent narrative, presented with the assumption that text and context, narrative and background, can be joined together in a harmonious whole. In the end, reconstructing the crime and its setting in bits and pieces, without finality or certainty, may give a truer picture of the judge, James Lamb, the victim, Allen Grebell, and John Breads, the man who brutally murdered him. It may also allow a truer picture of the contrasting textures of life in a small English town.

A Tale Sufficiently Recorded

The best way to enter Rye today is as a passenger in the little train that heaves and rattles between Hastings and Ashford. Catch the train at Hastings and you will have a glimpse of what Rye definitely is *not:* a sprawling, bustling Victorian seaside resort, "very gray and sober and English," in the carefully chosen words of Henry James. Beyond the narrow limits of the old town at its eastern end, Hastings is a place without pretence or mystery. For Henry James, it offered "a kind of *résumé* of middleclass English civilisation."[4] Today that *résumé*, from the seafront parade and sweeping terraces to the cafes and jellied eel stands, may be discoloured with age and frayed at the edges, but the town still prides itself on the mixture of posh facades and low pleasures that marked the culture of leisure among the Victorian middle classes.

None of this exists at Rye. It is smaller, and stranger, and redolent not of middle-class values, but of the older culture of the middling sort, an early modern culture that elsewhere passed away with the rise of mass society. Approaching the town, you seem to leave behind the noisy legacy of the nineteenth century. The train lurches through woodlands and meadows on the eastern edge of the Weald, the isolated hill country that was famed in earlier times for iron foundries fuelled by its plentiful timber. The train finally breaks into a more open landscape, moving towards the two green bumps on the landscape that are topped by tiny Winchelsea and its bigger neighbour, Rye. Beyond them, out of sight but already in the consciousness of the expectant visitor, stretches the flat, tranquil expanse of Romney Marsh. The Marsh has largely been reclaimed from the sea, and is now dotted with farms and scattered villages. Yet it is still self-enclosed enough, still peculiar enough, to merit its old reputation as "the sixth continent."

At the junction of three great solitudes—the Weald, the Marsh, and the sea—Winchelsea and Rye defend their own terrain and their own separateness. "Little hilltop communities sensibly even yet," Henry James mused about them at the end of the nineteenth century. By then, their maritime commerce was almost dead, and it was hard to imagine that the two towns had once been thriving ports. Yet as James pointed out, "with the memory of their tight walls and stiff gates not wholly extinct, Rye and Winchelsea hold fast to the faint identity which remains their least fragile support, their estates as 'Ancient Towns.'" He meant that both were members of the exclusive medieval mercantile confederation known as the Cinque Ports, which included most of the chief harbours along the Channel coasts of East Sussex and Kent. The Charters and Customals of the Ports appointed a warden over them all, but gave each of them the right to govern itself through an assembly of freemen. Every year, the freemen elected a mayor, who chose up to twelve jurats to assist him. The mayor and jurats made ordinances for the Port; they held their own court of sessions, in which civil and criminal causes could be tried; and they sent representatives to joint meetings of the Ports, known as Brotherhoods and Guestlings. In exchange for these privileges, the Portsmen had been expected to provide fully manned ships for the king's navy, although Rye was able to avoid this onerous duty by the mid-sixteenth century. Even today, the Cinque Ports have preserved their warden, some of their ceremonies, and a strong sense of their own uniqueness.[5]

At Rye, the "faint identity" of a Cinque Port is physically enshrined in cobbled streets, black-stained warehouses, clapboard cottages, and half-timbered alehouses. The town forms what James called a "compact little pyramid . . . crowned with its big but stunted church."[6] Yet it is not simply a charming open-air museum. All of its architectural remains are vital selling-points in the tourist trade. The place is full of shops and hostelries and small businesses that cater to the "trippers." Some locals resent putting on this commercial face. The resident poet Patric Dickinson expressed contempt for the visitors, who "lurch on the cobbles / Gawping and peering"; but he knew as well as anyone that these "morons . . . / Asking for Woolworths" (which, incidentally, is still open for business) have provided the life-blood for what would otherwise be an anaemic economy.[7]

Dickinson admitted the contribution of "the first tourist to settle, / Also the greatest," the American novelist and "almost-Ryer," Henry James.[8] In 1897, James took a long lease on Lamb House, an eighteenth-century brick building that stands near the top of the hill. He revelled in the history of his house, "George the Second having passed a couple of nights there and so stamped it for ever. . . . Likewise the Mayors of Rye have usually lived there! Or the persons usually living there have usually *become* mayors!"[9] For James, everything about Lamb House and Rye was "old-world" and safe and familiar—not unlike a nostalgic fantasy of the English ports from which the original European settlers of New England came. The precise details of his antiquarian daydream did not matter much to James, and he probably would not have been dismayed to learn that it was George I, not George II, who spent four nights in Lamb House in January 1726. In any case, he was quite right that all but one of the house's previous owners had at some time been mayors of Rye.

Although he eventually bought Lamb House and lived there until 1913, there is no evidence that Henry James was ever interested in the historical horror story connected with it: the brutal murder of Allen Grebell in 1743. His friend Ford Madox Ford turned up his nose at the local popularity of the tale, sniffing that "Rye was prouder of its murderer than of its two literary lights, [John] Fletcher and Henry James."[10] The latter luminary never wrote about the murder in his letters nor mentioned it in his journals. It inspired no incidents or characters in his fiction. It was not, after all, a Jamesian type of story—it was too vulgar and unsubtle. Its seemingly banal motives had no resonance for the upper-middle-class psychology that was his favourite domain. Perhaps the Rye murder story also violated the feelings of safety and introspection that James tried to cultivate at Lamb House.

Surprisingly, none of Rye's many resident writers gave fictional attention to the Grebell murder—not even E. F. Benson, who succeeded Henry James as occupant of Lamb House. A lower-brow writer than James, Benson was the creator of genteel comedies, some of them set in a fictionalized Rye, and of scores of short, popular "spook stories" that appeared in the 1920s and 1930s. He penned one ghostly tale that takes place in a town near Romney Marsh, recognizable as Rye. Its main protagonist is called "James Lamp." The name is only one letter removed from that of the builder of Lamb House, James Lamb, who was brother-in-law to the murdered Allen Grebell. Benson's Lamp, however, is a servant who has shot his wife and is finally brought to justice by her ghost.[11] As will be seen, Benson did take an interest in retelling the Grebell murder, but he passed his effort off as history, and so became responsible for perpetuating the literary fictions that have plagued later reconstructions.

Joan Aiken's 1991 novel *The Haunting of Lamb House,* a psychological "spook story" in the tradition of Henry James, is set in the same time period as the murder case. Allen Grebell figures in the book (erroneously, albeit engagingly) as a much-travelled misanthrope with an Indian servant. In fact, there is no evidence that he ever left England. As for his murder, it "has been sufficiently recorded elsewhere," the narrator tells us, "so I will only allude to it briefly."[12] Evidently, the story has become such a cliché that no self-respecting novelist would wish to rehash it today.

Who was responsible for "sufficiently recording" the tale? Anybody who visits Rye can give an answer. The murder is described in every town guidebook, from the venerable *Adams' Historical Guide to Rye Royal,* first published in 1934, to the glossy *Rye Colour Guide.* Its details also appeared in H. Montgomery Hyde's *The Story of Lamb House, Rye: The Home of Henry James,* which was the National Trust's guide to the house for almost thirty years after its publication in 1966. The killing was revisited in 1975 in Kenneth Clark's *Murder by Mistake,* a pamphlet based partly on archival sources and issued by the Rye Museum. In 1997, the story was retold in pictures by John Ryan, the famous author and illustrator of children's books. There have been many more retellings in various ephemeral forms over the past decades, including a relatively accurate stage version of the trial. Visitors today may hear the traditional story from the voiceover that accompanies the beautiful town model, or see it alluded to on the town's webpage.[13]

In short, the Rye murder is part of the experience of the place, for tourists as well as locals. Its grim memory has been attached to Lamb House, to the churchyard, to Grebell's monument within the church, and to the town hall, where the skull of the murderer Breads (or at least the top part of it) can be viewed in the gibbet-cage in which it has been kept for more than two and a half centuries. The murder has become part of the strangeness and uniqueness of Rye. It has become a powerful draw for tourists, who quickly learn about it and are usually intrigued by it. It has done a lot of financial good for the inhabitants of Rye; but it belongs to the trippers more than to the residents, and it has often been just a little embarrassing to those who value the beauty and quietude of the place.

The pamphlets and guidebooks are not completely consistent about the facts of the murder, but they generally repeat the same outline. This is what most of them tell us: in 1743, James Lamb was mayor of Rye and owner of Lamb House. In the house opposite lived Allen Grebell, his brother-in-law, who had also served as mayor on numerous occasions. The fifty-year-old Grebell was the scion of one of the leading merchant families in Rye. Between them, Lamb and Grebell controlled the town with a firm hand. A few years earlier, Lamb had levied a fine for using short weights on John Breads, a butcher who owned the Flushing Inn in Market Street. Breads resented this treatment. Since then, his wife had died, which had apparently intensified the butcher's irrational hatred of James Lamb.

On the night of 16 March 1743 (1742 by the old calendar, which changed on March 25 rather than January 1), Lamb was invited to dinner on a revenue sloop, to celebrate the recent appointment to the customs service of his third son, John. Feeling unwell, he asked his brother-in-law Allen Grebell to go in his place, and lent him his red mayoral cloak to keep him warm. Grebell returned from the dinner around midnight, having made merry and imbibed a great deal. As he walked through the churchyard, he felt something knock him from behind. He did not realize that he had been stabbed by John Breads, who was lying in wait for James Lamb, but who mistook Grebell for his enemy on account of the red cloak. Grebell stumbled home, sent his manservant off to bed, and sat down in a chair by the fire. There he bled to death, never knowing what had hit him in the churchyard.

Meanwhile, James Lamb spent a restless night. His late wife appeared to him in a dream, warning him that something terrible had happened to her brother. Lamb ignored the dream, but it was repeated twice more that night. At daybreak, he went to Grebell's house, where he found the corpse of his brother-in-law, still sitting upright in his chair. Although suspicion fell at first on the manservant, the real killer soon made himself obvious. Breads had been dancing around the town, drunk and half-naked, shouting "butchers should kill lambs!" He was duly arrested and arraigned for murder on May 25 before a court that sat at Lamb's warehouse in the Strand, as the town hall was then under construction. Presiding over the court were the mayor himself and three jurats. Breads was found guilty of murder. Before sentencing, he cried out at Mayor Lamb, "I did not mean to kill Mr. Grebell. It was you I meant it for and I would murder you now, if I could!"

Breads was hanged on June 8 outside the Strandgate on the west side of the town. His body was suspended in a gibbet-cage near the scaffold, and later in the parish church, until old women stole the bones to make a cure for rheumatism. His estate was forfeited to the corporation, which also took charge of the education of his two sons, one of whom became an innkeeper. Breads's gibbet and skull finally went on display in the town hall, where they still provide a ghastly thrill for visitors. As for the chair in which Grebell died, it could be seen in the Garden Room at Lamb House until it was destroyed in a bombing raid during the Second World War.

The guidebooks and pamphlets are never too sure as to whether the story has a moral. They all accept that Breads was not in his right senses, but they tend to stress his bitter malevolence and drunkenness rather than the state of his mental health or his social condition. They characterize Lamb as a local boss, but nobody goes so far as to suggest that the murder might have had a political rather than a personal motive. Lamb's role in the trial of his would-be murderer may have been irregular, but the guidebook writers want us to know that he acted in accordance with the law, as it was then understood. Breads was a violent man, motivated by revenge, who clearly deserved his fate.

How accurate is this retelling? Some historians would argue that the question is pointless, inasmuch as any attempt to assess historical "accuracy" must end in failure. For them, history is a palimpsest of narratives, each with its own significance. None is less "true" or "accurate" than any other, and there is no convincing way to distinguish "fact" from fiction. Historians can only offer explanations of why narratives were written in a specific way. This approach reminds us of our own fallibility in reconstructing history, but it also turns its back on the purpose of historical investigation, which is to recover some of what actually happened in the past. An absolute certainty about history is not possible, but we can at least try to discern what is probable; and there are cases in which probability is strong enough to constitute a fact. It is a fact, for example, that Allen Grebell was killed by John Breads on 17 March 1743. No evidence contradicts it; no reliable account challenges it. It can also be said that, judging by contemporary sources, the conventional narrative of the Rye murder consists of a few facts sprinkled amidst a very great deal of fiction.

THE CRUEL STAB OF A SANGUINARY BUTCHER

To reconstruct the history of the murder, we can turn to a handful of contemporary sources for information. The most extensive of them are the town records, which are in general well preserved and remarkably complete. The records of the sessions court, however, are exceptionally thin, reflecting both the infrequency of its meetings and the triviality of most of its business. Rye, like the other Cinque Ports, had the right to indict felons in its own court. Cases of homicide and capital larceny had been tried regularly in the Rye sessions in the sixteenth and early seventeenth centuries.[14] Yet for at least sixty years before 1743, the sessions had dealt exclusively with minor offences like undersized measures ("small potts" and false weights), defective pavements, and Sabbath breaking. A man named John Breads, who may have been the future murderer, paid a heavy fine of £1.1s to the town chamberlain in November 1730, but we do not know for what offence. In January 1737, a butcher named "John Breads junior" was presented for using three light weights. Local historians have usually assumed that this was also the murderer. It is more likely that he was another, younger man of the same name who practiced butchering in the town. John Breads junior appeared in court, but no fine was recorded. It was a petty infraction, and many local tradesmen were charged with it.[15]

As for graver crimes during the same period, no trials for homicide are mentioned after 1656 in the Rye sessions court records. The last surviving examination in a capital larceny case was taken in 1683; the next known case was in 1754. Murder, serious theft, and other crimes punishable by hanging must have happened in the town during those decades, but they were probably sent to the Sussex Assizes. Evidence for this assumption can be found in the town clerk's bills for 1737, which mention two horse thieves who were arrested at Rye, then removed to the county gaol to await trial.[16] By 1740, the pages of the Rye sessions book become dull reading, and it is increasingly hard to imagine that serious felonies were ever tried in the town court.

How surprising, then, suddenly to find in the sessions book

a full trial report, dated 25 May 1743, for a "Court of Gaol Delivery"—the first time that epithet had been used in a century! The court was held before Mayor James Lamb and jurats Ralph Norton, John Slade and Henry Carleton. Because none of the presiding magistrates was trained in criminal law, and the town counsel was (deliberately?) absent, legal assistance was provided by John Knowler, the recorder of Canterbury. The court heard only one case: a bill of indictment preferred against John Breads the elder, butcher, "for the Willful Murder of Allen Grebell." Unfortunately, no depositions or recorded testimonies exist for the case, and no witnesses are named, so we do not know what evidence was given. A fourteen-member grand jury was sworn, and it found the indictment to be a true bill. The grand jurymen included William Rockett, proprietor of the Mermaid Tavern, which is still a local landmark. Defending himself without a lawyer, Breads pleaded not guilty to the arraignment.

A petty jury of twelve men was then sworn. One of them was Nathaniel Pigram junior, the son of a jurat. They found Breads guilty, but ruled "that he had no Goods or Chattells Lands or Tenements at the Time of the said murder committed nor at any time since to their Knowledge." This did not necessarily mean that he was destitute; it may have signalled the jury's wish that whatever property he possessed would not be forfeit to the town, as was the custom in felony cases that ended with execution. The mayor and jurats duly sentenced Breads to death. A memorandum in the sessions book adds that on June 8, "[t]he said John Breads in pursuance of his Sentence was executed upon the Salts without the Strand Gate of the Town and hanged in Chaines there."[17]

The town records also contain various bills arising from the trial that were paid by the chamberlain. From these hastily scrawled scraps of paper, we learn that the judges and jurymen were not deprived of food and drink on that long day. Five shillings' worth of wine was served during the trial, and afterwards a splendid dinner for forty gentlemen and twenty-five servants was held at the Red Lion inn, at a cost of £14.11.10. The chamberlain's neatly kept account book also includes small payments for expenses made to those who participated in the trial. Stephen Fryman, who seems to have chaired the grand jury, was given 6s.8d, while John Knowler was awarded the handsome sum of £21 for his role at the trial. The most enigmatic entry in the account book is the two shillings paid to the innkeeper William Rockett, marked as being for "Breed's wife." Was this woman married to the murderer? Probably not; it is more likely that she was the wife of the other John Breads, who had married Elizabeth Baker in 1738. She may have provided Rockett with food and drink during the trial. As for the murderer's wife, Mary Breads, mother of his two sons, John and Richard, she had been buried in February 1739, four years before the murder. No further marriage of John Breads is recorded in the Rye parish register, and there is no mention of a second wife in the town records.[18]

Breads was kept in prison for three months, a long period of time to wait for trial in the eighteenth century. Information relating to his imprisonment can be found in the chamberlain's vouchers, small slips of paper that record payments for various services. They show that Breads was kept in the Ypres Tower, a venerable pile of medieval stones that was in poor repair and had not housed a long-term prisoner for many years. In March and April 1743, payment vouchers were issued "for Cleaning the Gole twise," "for constant attendance upon the prisoner for three months," "for a ring to a Chaien to the Jayel," and "for a payer of feters and 4 Stapels to hould Breads." Evidently, the prisoner was kept in irons and under close watch before he was condemned—an indication that he was thought to be dangerous, to himself if not to others. Leg irons were common in eighteenth-century prisons, but chains, staples, and fetters were mainly used on prisoners who had already been sentenced, unless there was a fear of escape or self-inflicted harm.

The vouchers also reveal that the gibbet was constructed on June 5 and cost fifteen shillings, although only 8s.2d had been allowed for it. Francis Jewhurst, a local jack-of-all-trades who would himself come to trial seven years later for illicitly practicing the "Art, mistery or occupation of a Baker," was given 10s.6d "for Carring John Breads to Exicution." Finally, a voucher for £1.16.6 was marked "paide the man that hong him & his assistance."[19] This was probably the same executioner who "dropped" criminals condemned to death by the county Assizes.

The most extensive and complicated set of town records pertaining to the case deals with Breads's estate, in which the corporation was very interested. As was noted above, the petty jury's pronouncement about the murderer's lack of goods, chattels and lands was formulaic. In an Assize case, it would not have prevented the county sheriff from making an inquiry into a condemned criminal's estate, which was legally forfeit to the crown. Breads did in fact own property, namely the Flushing Inn, although in the absence of deeds, his ownership has to be reconstructed from recognizances (promises to pay) and licenses that were taken out by alehouse keepers. The presence of two John Breads in the town confuses matters. The younger man seems to have been a butcher throughout his career, living at the west end of the churchyard. His older namesake, "John Breads, victualler," entered into recognizances for alehouse licenses in May 1735, October 1735, and October 1737. A license was paid for "John Breads at the fflushing" in September 1735, so we know where his place of business was. In January 1738, the two John Breads were each assessed for the parish rates, meaning that they both owned or leased property in the town. Eleven months later, however, "John Breads butcher" appears as surety on a recognizance for an alehouse license taken out by John Igglesdon. The former victualler had now become a butcher, like his younger namesake, probably using premises that still exist, at the back of the Flushing Inn. As for the alehouse, he seems to have been leasing it to Igglesdon. On 2 March 1743, a few days before the murder, the parish overseers listed in the rate book only one John Breads, the lifelong butcher, but John Igglesdon paid a rate commensurate to what the victualler John Breads had paid in 1738.[20]

The town magistrates may have assumed that Breads had sold his property, but if so, they were wrong. Their interest in the estate was suddenly revived late in 1743 by a lawsuit brought against John Igglesdon by a man named Pearson and his wife. The Pearsons seem to have had custody of the murderer's two sons and may have been living with them in the adjacent property. While the substance of the lawsuit is unclear, it is likely that the Pearsons claimed that they were the legitimate tenants of the Flushing Inn, rather than Igglesdon. They were represented by a local lawyer, Henry Dodson, who will appear again later in this chapter. The town at first tried to make a "compromise" between the litigants, then sided with Igglesdon and paid for his plea to be prepared by a lawyer. Taking no chances, the town clerk, Edwin Wardroper, consulted two of the leading barristers in England, Nicholas Fazakerly and the former solicitor general Sir John Strange, about the innkeeper's plea. That such eminent lawyers should be consulted on a very minor lawsuit gives a hint of the corporation's ultimate intention: to claim the Breads estate for itself.

By declaring that he had no property, the jury at Breads's trial had been merciful to his family. The Rye magistrates did not share those sentiments. On 27 February 1744, Mayor Lamb, meeting with jurats Nathaniel Pigram senior and Samuel Jeake III, decided that an inquisition was to be taken to find the estate of John Breads, "a Felon," which might escheat to the corporation on his being attainted and executed, in accordance with a royal charter of 1465. The chamberlain, James Lamb junior, was to begin the inquiry. Meanwhile, the case of Igglesdon versus Pearson and his wife was heard at King's Bench in Easter Term 1744. Sir John Strange had advised the town "to plead double ffee," meaning that the Pearsons should be compelled to pay twice the rent that they might owe (presumably on the Shambles) if they lost the case. Apparently, they did lose. By June 15, the town clerk had prepared the inquisition into Breads's property and drawn up an attornment or transfer of John Igglesdon's tenancy to the chamberlain, meaning that the town had taken over responsibility for leasing the Flushing Inn. The records of the King's Bench lawsuit were transferred to Rye by a *mittimus* order in January 1745 (they have since disappeared). The victorious Igglesdon enjoyed the further patronage of the corporation in the following June, when it paid for bell-ringers to drink at the Flushing Inn.[21]

The mayor and jurats soon set up a committee to make a list of Breads's debts and "to take care of the Children of the said John Breads and to provide them proper Masters for putting them out Apprentices or otherwise as they shall think proper with the Rents and Profits of their late Fathers Estate." This is the first mention in the town records of the children, John and Richard. They were placed in the care of Edward Pierson, without doubt the same man as the litigant Pearson, with whom they may have been living since the death of their father. The corporation must have feared that with their family property in its hands, the Breads boys would become a charge to the parish. As for the murderer's debts, the chamberlain's committee reported in February 1745 that Breads had owed £9.13.8 at his death, a relatively small sum. From then until Michaelmas 1748, the chamberlain kept meticulous accounts of what was received and paid out on the estate of the late criminal, including annual rental payments from John Igglesdon. The receipts amounted to £97.18.6, the payments (including school fees and room and board for the two Breads boys) to £82.04.9 1/2. What happened to the remaining £15.13.8 1/2 is anyone's guess. Richard Breads eventually took out an alehouse license for the Two Brewers Inn, which still stands in the Landgate, now called the Queen's Head. His education had not done him much good, for he was illiterate and marked the license rather than signing it.[22]

The almost obsessive concern of the corporation with the forfeiture of John Breads's property is a theme that runs through the town records of the mid-1740s. What about the circumstances and motives of his crime? The town archives are silent. Nobody within the corporation thought fit to record even the slightest explanation of what had happened. To fill in the details, we have to turn to two London newspapers, *The General Evening Post* and *The Daily Post*, and to a Canterbury paper, *The Kentish Post*. It is a sign of the deep cultural changes brought about by the eighteenth century that national and regional periodicals reveal more about a local event than town records do. In spite of its geographical isolation, Rye had become part of a nation-wide network of information, centred on the capital. That network depended on unpaid correspondents who sent letters to the London press about noteworthy incidents in their localities. The murder must have been of interest in the capital, especially to the merchants and investors who read daily or twice-weekly papers to find out the shipping and stock-market news, and who had commercial ties to the small ports of the south coast. At Rye, newspapers were kept in the court hall, and their circulation among the leading men of the town was regarded as a civic responsibility by the corporation.

Both *The General Evening Post* and *The Daily Post* carried reports of the Rye murder in March and May 1743. The *Daily Post* added an update on Breads's execution in June. The reports were reprinted in the *Kentish Post,* along with briefer notices of the trial, so they reached a wide audience in the southeast. The main reports are worth quoting in full. Here is the first:

> Extract of a Letter from Rye, dated March 17: As Mr. Allen Grebell, of this Place, was coming home between Two and Three o'Clock this Morning, after having been to take Leave of his Nephew, who was just then embark'd for France, he was attack'd in coming thro' the Church-yard by one John Breads, a Butcher, who with a naked Knife met and stabb'd the unhappy Gentleman in two Places in the left Breast; one of the Wounds, which was above the Pap, perforated into the Thorax, quite thro' the Lobe of the Lungs; the other, which was a little lower, and nearer his Arm, penetrated the Lungs also, whence, in a short time issued out so great a Quantity of Blood that he died. The Wounds, upon the Examination of several Surgeons, were both adjudg'd to be mortal; and the Coroner's Jury, who finished their Enquiry this Evening, have brought in their Verdict Wilful Murder. The Criminal, upon Examination, confess'd the Fact, and said, he was mistaken, for that he believ'd the Person he met with was Mr. Lamb, the Mayor. He attack'd another Person a little time before this happen'd, whom, he said, he mistook for Mr. Norton, and wounded him in the Arm. The Wretch is confin'd close in this Gaol, and 'tis hoped will meet with his Deserts.[23]

No red cloak, no blow from behind, no hidden wound, no slow death in a chair by the fire: Grebell was struck from the front, and he cannot have been unaware of it. The forensic detail suggests that the writer was present when the coroner's jury presented its verdict. Unfortunately, the records of the inquest, in which Mayor Lamb served as coroner, have not survived; but vouchers dated March 17 show that the coroner's jury spent 6s.8d "for Licker" at the Red Lion, and that a further 2s of "Licker" was "had by the Dockters," meaning that there was a medical examination of the corpse. The coroner's jury did not present an indictment against Breads, as the grand jury had to draw up its own indictment on May 25.[24]

The newspaper also mentions a previous attack on a person Breads mistook for Mr. Norton. The intended victim was Ralph Norton, a jurat who sat on the bench at John Breads's trial. Judging by the parish rate books, he was one of the richest men in Rye.[25] Norton later became an opponent of the Lamb faction, as will be seen in Chapter Four, but his political attitude at this time is unknown. The murderer's claim that he had wanted to kill Mr. Norton suggests that he did not have a personal grudge against James Lamb alone. Breads was not tried for the other attack, but by allowing Norton to sit on the bench at his trial, the mayor further ensured a conviction.

The second newspaper report damages the conventional account of Breads's defiant behaviour at his trial:

> They write from Rye in Sussex, that last Wednesday came on, before the Right Worshipful the mayor, Jurats and Common Council, the Trial of John Breads, a Butcher, for the barbarous Murder of Mr. Allen Grebell of that Town, Merchant (as mention'd in this Paper some time since). The Criminal pleaded not guilty; and said, if he had committed the Fact, he knew nothing of it, for it was done when he was in Distraction: He also said, that the Night he met William Fowl in a Lane, call'd

the Dead-Man's Lane, just without the Town, he thought he was then among a Parcel of Devils: In short, he affected Madness, but it avail'd little, for after a Trial of eleven Hours and a half he was capitally convicted, and receiv'd Sentence of Death. After his Conviction, he begg'd of the Mayor to let him have Time to make his Peace with God before his Execution, the Day for which is not yet fix'd.[26]

In this version, no threats are made in the courtroom against Mayor Lamb. Instead, Breads argues that at the time of the murder, he was "in Distraction"—that is, he was temporarily insane. For the first time, the possibility of Breads's madness arises. The writer of the report clearly did not believe it, but no other explanation for his deed is given.

The meeting with William Fowl in Dead-Man's Lane, the former site of public hangings on the northeast edge of the town, may refer to the first attack, in which Breads mistook someone for Ralph Norton. The Fowl family were fishermen, and apparently very poor, as they do not appear in parish rate books. In the 1720s, William Fowl had been a student at Sanders' School, a non-denominational, charitable institution. He may have been a religious Dissenter. Like other sons of fishermen at the school, Fowl must have left classes early in the summers to go "on the Mackeril Season." He was a man of no consequence in the town, so it is not surprising that he appeared in none of the later retellings of the murder story. It is hard to imagine how Breads mistook him for Norton, unless he was hallucinating; so the attack on Fowl gives strength to the argument that the butcher was "Distracted." No wonder it was not prosecuted.

What is perhaps the most extraordinary information given in the second newspaper report is that the trial lasted eleven and a half hours, in an era when the average length of a criminal trial was half an hour. Did some members of the jury think the butcher's madness was not "affected," and did that prolong their discussions? The writer tells us nothing about this.

The final newspaper bulletin concerns the execution of John Breads. It turns his dying words into a confession of guilt, albeit with an odd twist, as the condemned man claims to the end that he had not meant to commit murder. The writer, who may not be the same person responsible for the earlier reports, shows more sympathy to the claim of madness, and seems non-committal about Mayor Lamb's defence of Rye's legal privileges:

> Yesterday about Eleven o'Clock John Breads, pursuant to his Sentence, for the Murder of Mr. Grebell, was convey'd, amidst a numerous Crowd of Spectators, from Prison to the Place of Execution, where he behav'd with great Penitence and Resignation, and to the last declar'd that he had no premeditated Design against the Deceas'd, or any other Person whatsoever, attributing the Fact to his Distraction only; but acknowledg'd he had been a very wicked Liver, and deserv'd the Punishment he was subjected to by Law. He desir'd all People to take Warning by his unhappy End, and was turn'd off the Ladder about Twelve, praying to the Lord to receive his Soul. He was afterward hang'd in Chains, as a proper Spectacle to deter the Practicers of Wickedness, and (if possible) to reclaim every Evil-doer in this Corporation.
>
> It is observable that no one has receiv'd Sentence for Execution from this Court before for above a hundred Years past; and had not the present Mayor, who is ever watchful to prefer, as well as preserve, our ancient Privileges, over-rul'd it, it is suppos'd

that this Wretch would have been remov'd to have
taken his Trial at the Assizes for the County.[27]

The legal wrangling that is referred to here accounts for the
two month delay between Breads's arrest and his trial. Lamb's
decision to try Breads at Rye may not have pleased other legal
authorities. The absence from the trial of the town's legal counsel, Joseph Kirke, is noteworthy. The town magistrates were
obliged to bring in a counsellor from Canterbury, John Knowler.
Like the Cinque Ports, Canterbury had its own sessions court.
Special jurisdictions such as these required the presence of a
legally qualified recorder, who was usually paid a salary. Knowler
seems to have filled that position in the courtroom at Rye, as he
did at Canterbury. He was handsomely remunerated.[28]

The final newspaper report hints that not everybody supported James Lamb's decision to put Breads on trial before the
hitherto moribund sessions court. Somebody was "over-rul'd"
by the mayor, but the reporter does not tell us who it was.
Further details are provided by two local observers who wrote
privately about the case, James Collier and Henry Dodson. Interestingly, both writers were critical of Mayor Lamb. James
Collier was the son of John Collier, mayor and customs collector
at Hastings. The Colliers knew Rye well and were friendly with
its leading families. James Collier referred to the Breads case in
a letter to his father, written from London on 9 June 1743:

> Yesterday being the day appointed for Breads's Exe-
> cution I suppose he suffered, I heard on Munday he
> was to be hanged in Chains; Mr. [Robert] Money-
> penny informed me before the Tryal that Mr. [Phil-
> lips] Gybbon had made use of his utmost Endeav-
> ours to perswade mr. Lamb to send the Prisoner to
> the County Gaol, & have him tryed at the Assizes;
> & that the Ld. Chancellour [the Earl of Hardwicke]

had told young [Thomas?] Lamb that considering the Cirumstances he wou'd not have his Father try this affair at Rye. Mr. [Peter] Burrel since his return has often declared that any Unprejudiced Jury in England woud have found the Prisoner Guilty of the Indictment.[29]

Evidently, the murder trial had caused a stir at London, where the government was still in a state of upheaval in the wake of the fall of Sir Robert Walpole's administration a year before. Robert Moneypenny, the source of Collier's information, was legal counsel for Dover and later for Rye. It is remarkable that, according to Moneypenny, both Phillips Gybbon, the long-standing Whig member of Parliament for Rye, and Lord Chancellor Hardwicke, the highest judge in England, tried to dissuade James Lamb from presiding over the trial at Rye. Gybbon may have been worrying about how he could steer another bill to improve Rye harbour through the House of Commons, if the mayor was perceived as abusing his power. Hardwicke may have had his mind on the possibility of a petition for a mistrial or *nolli prosequi* on procedural grounds. Peter Burrell, the member of Parliament for Haslemere and a wealthy Portugal merchant, was more supportive of Mayor Lamb, but he had recently been accused of corruption himself, in connection with contracts for paying the forces in Jamaica. A close associate of Walpole, Burrell no doubt felt solidarity with the much criticized mayor of Rye.[30]

The other observer who recorded a contemporary reaction to Breads's trial and execution was the lawyer Henry Dodson, former town clerk of Hastings and a resident of Rye in the 1740s and 1750s. He wrote frequent letters to John Collier, with whom he had trained as a lawyer, about land transactions around Rye, as well as about local politics. Dodson's father and brother were rectors of Hurstpierpoint, a rural parish whose local squire, Henry Campion, was a Tory politician. It is possible that Henry Dodson had similar political leanings, as he was a close friend of the Tory squire John Fuller of Brightling. That might explain why he was so hostile to the Whig magistrates of Rye. He certainly annoyed the Hastings jurats in 1736, when he testified against them in a lawsuit by a man who was trying to obtain the freedom of the town by parental right. Dodson was well acquainted with James Lamb, from whom he rented a house, and he represented the Pearsons in their lawsuit against John Igglesdon.[31]

Four days after Breads's execution, Dodson wrote a brief note about the trial into a family Bible. It was a very unusual place to set down this kind of information. Normally, family Bibles were inscribed with birthdates and lineages, not comments on contemporary events. Apparently, Dodson wanted to keep his strong views about the trial private, while at the same time preserving them for posterity. The note was published (with some errors) in the 1860s, but the Bible was not found again by researchers until the 1990s, when its owner was traced through some clever detective work by two local historians. The note reveals nothing new about the murder, but it implies that the court proceedings were unfair to the defendant:

> Mr Greble was Murdered in our Churchyard, by John Breads a Butcher of this place, the 17th day of March, 1742/3, for which Crime he was tried, On Wednesday the 25th day of May 1743, in this Town, in A Warehouse, belonging to James Lamb Esqr. the present Mayor, at the Strand; when, he was found Guilty, after a Tryall of Ten hours, and recev'd Sentence of death, which, was passed on him by the above Mayor, who sat as Judge, with

Mr. Knowler a Councellour, of Canterbury in Kent, his Assistant, on that Occasion, on Wednesday, the Eighth day of this Instant June, between Eleven and Twelve of the Clock in the forenoon, the unhappy Wretch was Executed on the Salts, westward, of the Town, and when dead, was forthwith hung up in Chaines.

how fair a Tryal, the Prisoner had, I leave the Reader, to determine after he is informed, the above Mr. Lamb, was Mayor, Coroner, Party Prosecuting, Judge, Witness, and Sheriff, in Presenting, Trying, and Executing the said John Breads.

I suppose, he was Mayor, Coroner, and Sheriff, as essentiall, to the office of Mayoralty. Party and prosecutor, as Brother in Law to the Unfortunate good Gentleman, that was killed, and Judge, and Witness out of Zeal, in getting the Prisoner proved Sane, tho on the Tryall, he acknowledged, he had Caused the Prisoner to be Confined, some Years ago, for feigned Madness.

As to feigned Madness, I do not Understand it, but I verily beleive, the Prisoner was mad in the afternoon, of the day, before the Unhappy Catastrophe happened.[32]

Apparently, the murder trial was not the first time Breads had claimed to be insane. Unfortunately, nothing is known about Breads's imprisonment "for feigned madness." Was it connected to his £1.1s fine in 1730? Dodson also implies that he witnessed Breads's mad behaviour on the afternoon of March 16. This may have been the attack on William Fowl, although the newspaper account suggested that it took place at night rather than in the afternoon.

Because the trial records are so scanty and the newspaper reports reveal nothing about Lamb's conduct in the courtroom, Dodson's assertions cannot easily be denied. As Lord Hardwicke and others familiar with the law must have realized, it was extremely unusual, perhaps unprecedented, for a judge to preside over the trial of someone who had murdered a member of his family, and it violated the appearance of fairness that was a central concern of the eighteenth-century system of justice. Judges routinely interrogated witnesses and made comments on testimony, but they were also expected to give the accused every opportunity to prove innocence.[33] Precisely how James Lamb may have acted as judge at Breads's trial is hard to assess, but his relationship to the deceased must have aroused suspicions of bias, and it is significant that no account credits him with impartiality.

Dodson goes further in accusing Lamb of being the prosecutor in the case. Trials for homicide required an accuser, but this responsibility often fell on the coroner's jury or the grand jury, because the victim was dead and no relative or friend wanted to take on the expense of prosecution. As noted earlier, the coroner's jury did not proffer an indictment, which lends credence to Dodson's allegation that Lamb was the prosecutor. If so, the mayor was in clear violation of the accepted practices of English common law, under which a judge could not initiate proceedings in his own court. It is strange that his assistant John Knowler did not point this out to him, and it raises the question of what the counsellor's role was at the trial. It would have been improper for Knowler to direct the prosecution while also serving as recorder, but no evidence supports the hypothesis that he acted for the defence. It was becoming more common for those accused of crimes to employ lawyers, and Knowler himself served as defence counsel in at least one later trial at Surrey Assizes.

Any interventions he made in the Breads case, however, were not recorded and did no apparent good for the defendant.[34]

Dodson also claims that Lamb appeared as a witness to prove that Breads was sane. Again, if this is accurate, it breached common-law precedent, which prevented judges from giving sworn testimony in cases over which they were presiding. Interestingly, neither the trial record nor the newspaper reports makes any mention of witnesses. The chamberlain's accounts and vouchers include no allowances for feeding or transporting witnesses, which might have been expected in a trial that lasted ten or eleven hours. Names of witnesses would normally be written on the back of the indictment, but unfortunately it is missing, as are the depositions. Their absence among the well-kept records of the Rye corporation suggests that they were deliberately suppressed. Whatever the case, we can assume that if witnesses other than Mayor Lamb appeared at all, they were called upon only to establish matters of fact, not to explain the motivation of the accused. Otherwise, Dodson or the newspapers would probably have referred to their testimony.

Lamb's characterization of Breads's previous madness as "feigned" was crucial, because it could be used to dismiss Breads's explanation of his state of mind at the time of the crime. Breads, of course, maintained that he had been "in Distraction" or temporarily insane when he killed Allen Grebell. The butcher may have had some knowledge of the law. Insanity was a legitimate defence in the eighteenth century, especially in cases of homicide. As William Blackstone argued in 1769, there could be no criminal intent, and therefore no conviction, in cases where "a defective or vitiated understanding" was proven. "In criminal cases therefore idiots and lunatics are not chargeable for their own acts, if committed when under these incapacities; no, not even for treason itself." Homicide in particular "must be com-

mitted by a *person of sound memory and discretion:* for a luna-
tic . . . [is] incapable of committing any crime; unless in such
cases where they shew a consciousness of doing wrong, and of
course a discretion, or discernment, between good and evil."[35]
Juries had long shared his opinion, and there were some notable
cases of acquittal on the basis of insanity in the late seventeenth
and early eighteenth centuries. Even after conviction, a claim of
madness was good grounds for requesting a royal pardon. Defendants who were thought to be mad could be committed by
the court to the care of relatives, or sent to prison, but they were
seldom hanged.[36]

Blackstone and other legal writers also maintained that homicide required "malice aforethought." "This is the grand crite-
rion, which now distinguishes murder from other killing: and
this malice prepense, *malitia praecognita,* is not so properly spite
or malevolence to the deceased in particular, as any evil design in
general; the dictate of a wicked, depraved, and malignant heart."
A case that lacked malice was either manslaughter or excusable.
Blackstone maintained that malice could be implied in many instances where it was not plainly expressed, and by placing it in
the "heart" rather than the "head," he suggested that it might be
felt rather than thought. Juries, however, often adopted a stricter
view of what constituted malicious intent, demanding that it be
proven rather than implied. As a result of this and other forms
of judicial mercy, most accused murderers were not put to death
in the eighteenth century. The ratio of hangings to indictments
for homicide at Surrey Assizes, for example, ranged from 1:11 in
1720–40, to 1:3 in 1740–60, and 1:9 in 1760–80.[37] The reputation for ferocity of eighteenth-century justice is not unmerited,
but it has more to do with the infliction of capital punishment
for petty crimes like theft than with the numbers of men who
actually "dropped."

In cases where an insanity plea was made, juries usually wanted some further proof of madness—for example, frantic energy, fits of laughter or rage, restless wandering, or unusual strength—in order to reject the possibility of malice. Even this might not prove convincing, as in the case of "Mad Ned" Arnold, convicted at Surrey Assizes in 1723 for shooting at Lord Onslow, or that of the famous Lord Ferrers, who killed his estate manager and was hanged for it in 1760, despite claiming "occasional insanity of mind."[38] Arnold and Ferrers were both thought to have reasonable motives for their deeds. John Breads may have offered similar proofs of his own insanity to the jury, as Henry Dodson implies; we simply do not know. As for malicious intent, he explicitly denied it in both his trial and his dying speech. Neither the newspaper reports nor Dodson's note mention any reasonable motive for his deed, and none has been offered since. In the end, it made little difference; the testimony of Mayor Lamb denied that he was "in Distraction," and "malice aforethought" must have been implied by the jury as well as by the magistrates.

Dodson's allegations of unfairness against James Lamb and his colleagues on the bench were not groundless, and they were strengthened by the decision to make the death penalty exceptionally severe by gibbeting. A few years later, the Murder Act of 1752 would encourage judges to use the gibbet, an iron or leather cage in which bodies were exposed until they rotted. Before the Murder Act, however, gibbeting was a punishment usually imposed after sentencing, not by the judge but by royal order. It was generally reserved for smugglers, pirates, and the most brutal killers, those who had broken community norms as well as legal codes.[39] Gibbeting was not always viewed favourably by the public, however. In London, the crowds who attended executions sometimes expressed strong disapproval when the authorities refused to give proper burial to the body of a hanged criminal, even when the deceased was thought to be guilty. Exposing the body—or worse, selling it to the surgeons for dissection—could be offensive to religious, moral and social principles. Evidently, it caused great distress to the families of the condemned. "Felons wanted to be buried *decently*, preferably in the home churchyard," notes V. A. C. Gatrell, adding that "bodies on gibbets were never safe from nocturnal raids by family and friends."[40]

We do not know whether the people of Rye had a negative reaction to the humiliating treatment of Breads's body. No friends or family cut him down. Gibbeting marked him as an outcast and an outsider, a man who had no place in the community, which was a very severe condemnation in the insular world of a Cinque Port. That this was precisely the court's intention can be deduced from another celebrated case of gibbeting that had recently occurred in East Sussex, and may have had an impact on the treatment of John Breads. Its details give us some insight into how the judges wanted Breads and his crime to be perceived by the public. In 1734, a Jewish peddler named Jacob Harris was hanged and gibbeted at Horsham. Harris had been convicted of cutting the throats of three people at Ditchling Common. He killed a publican in whose house he was staying, a maid who discovered the crime, and the publican's wife, who was sick in bed. The publican lived long enough to identify his attacker. Harris was captured nearby. Tried and found guilty at Sussex Assizes, the peddler was hanged on August 31, and his body was placed in a gibbet on the turnpike near the scene of his crime.

The hanging and gibbeting of Jacob Harris was not soon forgotten in the neighbourhood. "Many went to see him hanging," a local diarist recorded, and Reverend William Hayley of Brightling "preached an impressive sermon upon it the Sunday following." Local folk continued to sing about "Jacob's Post" in a gruesome ditty that concluded:

And where he did the crime, they took the pains
To bring him back and hang him up in chains;
It is a dismal sight for to behold,
Enough to make a heart of stone run cold.

As late as the mid-nineteenth century, five or six feet of the gibbet remained above the ground. Like John Breads's cage at Rye, it was "imagined to possess a power of enchantment." Pieces of it were broken off and carried around in pockets because they were thought to offer "a peculiar preventive virtue against aching teeth."[41]

Although the evidence definitely pointed to Harris as the perpetrator of the crime, the severity of his treatment cannot be separated from his religion and ethnicity. Prejudice against Jews was still strong in England, as the failure of the Jewish Naturalization Bill of 1753 would show. Minor regulations all over the kingdom discriminated against them. At Rye, for example, Jews were required by an ordinance of 1721 to pay 7d per head to the water bailiff as passengers entering the port, while Christians paid only 2d.[42] It is unlikely that Harris's body would have been exposed on a gibbet if he had not been a Jew, and therefore ineligible for Christian resurrection at the Last Judgement. Besides, an itinerant Jewish peddler would not have had friends or relations in the Sussex countryside who might have tried to rescue his corpse. While the verses sung by local people reveal some human sympathy for Harris, the sight of whom was "enough to make a heart of stone run cold," he was nonetheless the ultimate outsider in a rural, settled, Christian environment.

The gibbeting of John Breads may have been inspired by that of Jacob Harris eight years earlier. The treatment of Breads's body, like that of Harris, was intended to show the strongest possible mark of rejection, a public casting out of a man whose actions had made him into an example of all that was evil and unworthy. The court denied Breads the ultimate privilege of Christian burial, which was allowed even to the most heinous criminals. To take this away from a man who owned a local inn, and who had dealings with many of Rye's leading residents, was to risk being perceived as vindictive. Yet no sermons were delivered in abhorrence of Breads's crime, no songs composed to execrate his memory. Within a century, as will be seen, most of the details of his life were forgotten. This may reflect a lack of public support for the way in which his body was treated.

The inhabitants of the town may have not have applauded some other aspects of the trial. The historian J. A. Sharpe has pointed out that the people of eighteenth-century England demanded of the law "a system which was cheap, speedy in its operation, and local."[43] This was not what the citizens of Rye got in Breads's case. Although the coroner's jury reported on the day of the murder, it took two months to bring Breads into court. The relatively lengthy trial proceedings were followed by an expensive dinner and a whopping payment to counsellor Knowler. The costs of imprisonment, fetters, hangman, and gibbet were considerable. The forfeiture of the dead man's estate was probably intended to cover what the corporation had spent on him. The expense could have been avoided if the mayor had not claimed the ancient privilege of the Cinque Ports to try felons, and Breads had been sent to Lewes or Horsham Assizes instead. This had apparently been done in the past when capital offences had been committed at Rye, and no doubt many expected it to happen in Breads's case. The only other person sentenced to death at the Rye sessions after Breads was a horse thief named William Pilcher, in 1756; but his punishment was changed to transportation by royal warrant, probably because the government did not want a repetition of the Breads case. In 1764, when Ann Westmore was accused of infanticide, she was sent Horsham Assizes, at the expense of the Rye corporation. Finally, in 1780, two soldiers were convicted of theft at the Rye sessions, and sentenced to death; one died in gaol, while the other was transported.[44] That was the end of capital trials in the sessions court. There is no evidence that the ordinary citizens of eighteenth-century Rye wanted serious crimes to be tried in the town.

The trial of John Breads was obviously controversial—far more so than any of its later chroniclers have suggested. It bears a message about how the law operated in the eighteenth century. Some historians have seen it as a forum for social negotiation between defendants and judges. If so, then the Breads trial stands as an example of how authority might assert itself aggressively and unrestrainedly, so as to prevent any negotiation whatsoever.[45] Contemporary observers might criticize them privately, but the last word belonged to the judges. Negotiation could never be claimed or assumed; it was a kind of paternalism based on the social (and hence moral) inequality between defendant and judge, and it was only possible when allowed by the bench. Unless a jury chose to assert itself against them, it was the opinion of the magistrates that counted.

In the Breads case, that opinion was echoed to posterity by the murdered man's memorial, still to be seen in Rye church:

> Here Lyeth the Body of ALLEN GREBELL Esqr. Who after having served the Office of Mayor of this Town for Ten Years, with the Greatest Honour and Integrity, fell by the Cruel Stab of a Sanguinary Butcher on the 17th of March 1742 Aged 50. He left Issue one Son & one Daughter.

The memorial is a curious artefact. Unlike other sepulchral statements of worldly achievement, it makes no reference to Grebell's lineage, reduces his personal qualities to two bland epithets, almost ignores his descendants, and includes no religious sentiments whatsoever. On the other hand, it defends Grebell's political career and condemns his killer as "Cruel" and "Sanguinary"—in other words, as malicious, deliberate, and definitely sane. The term "sanguinary" had been used for over a century to mean "bloodthirsty," an appropriate epithet for a butcher, although it was more commonly applied to soldiers or to judges themselves. "Sanguinary" was more precise and learned than "bloody," a word that was not avoided here out of a sense of propriety, as it did not become a slang expression of invective until the nineteenth century.[46] The point of the inscription is that a bloodthirsty murderer must have acted by "malice aforethought." Surely, these damning words were written by or at the instigation of James Lamb. The memorial constitutes a direct rebuke to the mayor's critics, who accused him of denying a fair trial to a madman. Whether or not we find the memorial convincing depends on whether we value fairness more than the prerogative of vengeance.

Telling Tales

Although the full details of the Rye murder will never be known, the conventional version that appears in guidebooks and pamphlets is clearly inaccurate in many respects. Before we go any further in examining the social and political background to the case, we should consider how this inaccuracy came about. How were the red cloak, the unnoticed stab, the anxious ghost, or the unrepentant killer at his trial introduced into the story? The answers are not obvious. The contemporary sources, which tell such a different story, are not particularly hard to find or to interpret. Even Dodson's memorandum has been in print since 1866! Yet the sources were never essential to those who wrote about the murder, not even to writers who seem to have had ready access to them. The Rye murder was fashioned and refashioned over the years by a succession of local chroniclers, for purposes that remained remarkably consistent—namely, to cast a positive light on the distinctive character of traditional civic institutions.[47] By understanding why they wrote as they did, we can gain insight into what the story came to mean for its publicists over the past two centuries.

The refashioning of the Grebell murder was brought about mainly by three individuals, all of them respectable middle-class inhabitants of Rye: William Holloway, Leopold Amon Vidler, and Edward Frederic Benson. Holloway was a failed farmer and failed brewer who turned himself into a printer, writer, and sometime banker. He was born in Hampshire, but married into the prominent Meryon family of Rye. His marriage brought him into the thick of local factionalism. Of Huguenot descent, the Meryons were brewers who became opponents of the Lamb domination, which had continued for three generations after 1743. Holloway's brother-in-law, Charles Lewis Meryon, a medical doctor, had left Rye to take up a London practice. Between 1825 and 1832, he returned to lead a reform group whose members called themselves the "Men of Rye," which attempted to overthrow the Lambs and their allies by reviving ancient privileges, including the right of all inhabitant householders "paying scot and bearing lot" to vote in mayoral or Parliamentary elections. For a time, as the radical printer Henry Pocock Clark put it, the news of reform at Rye "resounded throughout the country; it became the all absorbing topic of the day."[48] As much as Birmingham or Manchester, tiny Rye set off the movement that led to the Great Reform Act of 1832.

Although they would later be dubbed "Liberals," the reformers in Rye were traditionalists in their constitutional approach. They revived long forgotten practices, dug up old records, and set out to retrieve the history of Rye in order to show that the customs of the Cinque Ports were quasi-democratic rather than oligarchical. The Reform Act was supposed to satisfy them, but it did not meet their desires in every respect, because it restricted the franchise to property owners and removed one of Rye's two members of Parliament. It was followed by the Municipal Corporations Act, which ended many of the privileges of the Cinque Ports. However disappointed they may have been, by the 1840s the reformers had taken control of the corporation. They succeeded in shifting town government towards a program of economic "modernization" that would bring in the railways along with some unexpected results, such as rampant municipal corruption and voting fraud.[49]

Dr. Meryon began writing a history of his native town in the late 1820s, before the reformers' dream had soured. His purpose was to vindicate the "Men of Rye," by determining "whether serious and dangerous encroachments have not been made on the rights of the inhabitants collectively by the abuses which have crept in, or have been clandestinely introduced." Meryon mentions the Breads case only once in his history, noting that in 1743, "the lands of John Breeds were escheated to the corporation . . . for felony." Another hand added the comment, "He murdered Mr. Gribble the mayor." It is interesting that the fate of Breads's property was the best-remembered aspect of the crime eighty years later. Yet Meryon says nothing about the extraordinary efforts made by the corporation to lay hands on it. Perhaps they had been forgotten, along with the fact that Grebell was not mayor at the time of his death.[50]

Meryon's unfinished manuscript was never published. His brother-in-law William Holloway used it as a scrapbook, and drew on parts of it in writing *The History and Antiquities of the Ancient Town and Port of Rye*, which appeared in 1847. The murder is described in a section of Holloway's work that deals with a provision in the charter of Edward IV that awarded the chattels of convicted felons to "the Barons and good men of the Ports," that is, to the corporation. Again, the forfeiture of Breads's estate was seen as its most important consequence. Holloway's account of the killing consists of an unascribed quotation, possibly derived from an elderly witness. It is slightly inaccurate — Breads's intended victim is wrongly named "Thomas Lamb," and the deed is said to have taken place on the night of March 17 rather than in the early morning of that day. On the other hand, some details are consistent with contemporary records. Breads is said to have "rushed on" his victim, and the blow that he strikes is not described as coming from behind. The motive for the crime is Breads's "diabolical passion" to kill Mr. Lamb. The parallel between this and the murderer's own testimony that he imagined himself among devils is interesting — by the mid-nineteenth century, the devil was no longer outside him but was part of his inner "passion."

The most important additions that Holloway (or rather, his unnamed source) made to the contemporary records are found in this sentence:

> [Grebell] had just strength enough to reach his house . . . to take his seat in a chair, out of which he very soon fell and died, to the no small alarm and astonishment of his servant, who was at first rather suspected to be the murderer; but all doubts on this head were soon cleared up by Breeds [sic] himself, who, in the paroxysm of his rage (being generally of an ungovernable temper), ran about the streets with scarcely any clothes, exclaiming, "butchers should kill lambs!" in allusion to his supposed victim.[51]

These additions have the air of local gossip, but that does not invalidate them. If Grebell was walking alone when he was stabbed, and was capable of going further in spite of his severe wounds, then he may well have traversed the short distance from the churchyard to his house before dying. As for the "butchers should kill lambs" comment, it sounds suspiciously like a later interpolation, as does Breads's state of undress when he reportedly said it. The nakedness of the mad was a conventional stereotype, a sign of their return to a primitive state of savagery, so by wearing "scarcely any clothes," Breads could be identified as a madman.[52] Of course, this implies that by 1847, Breads was acknowledged to have been insane, a point that was not accepted by the jury or magistrates at his trial.

What is most surprising about the narrative in Holloway's *History* is that it is not noticeably unfavourable to the Lambs, although its transcriber was a leading opponent of his family's political interest. Holloway's lack of criticism was understandable; after all, the story was told to illustrate the importance of ancient legal privileges, which he supported. He was completely silent about the judicial role of Mr. Lamb (who is never identified as the mayor), either because he was not aware of it, or because any critical commentary might have suggested that ancient rights were not always consistent with justice. In presenting Breads as a madman, however, Holloway unwittingly undermined the legal basis of his conviction for homicide—namely, that he was in his right mind when he killed Allen Grebell. Holloway's obliviousness to the implications of Breads's madness revealed how many educated people in the first half of the nineteenth century conceived mental illness—as a kind of savagery, a regression into the primitive that easily led to violence and could only be treated with severe measures.

The next major retelling of the Grebell story was made by Leopold Amon Vidler in 1934. His grandfather, John Vidler, had established a shipping firm at Rye around 1820, using the same warehouse in the Strand in which Breads's trial had been held. As cautious in politics as they were in business, the Vidlers were originally connected with the Lamb interest, then joined the reform or "Liberal" party when its rise became unstoppable. Leopold Amon was managing director of the family firm, and served as mayor of Rye in 1927 and 1928. He founded the charming town museum, which can still be visited in the Ypres Tower. Vidler himself lived in the "Friary of the Sack," an ancient stone building in the churchyard, later the home of his son Alec, a noted theologian and church historian.[53] Leopold Amon was acutely conscious of the contribution of his ancestors to the town, and he had no intention of stirring up their ghosts when in 1934 he published his *New History of Rye*, designed as a shorter and more readable update of Holloway. Trying hard to offend no one, as well as to preserve the dignity of the town's offices, Vidler characterized the most grasping and self-serving of Rye's corporate leaders as "honourable and public spirited men."[54]

Dignity, however, had nothing to do with Vidler's fantastic retelling of the Grebell killing. Almost every inaccuracy that has adhered to the conventional account of the murder is found in the *New History*, embellished with a plethora of imaginative details. According to Vidler, it happened in this dramatic fashion: James Lamb was preparing to attend a dinner for his son John, "who had entered the service of H.M. Customs," when he began to feel unwell, and asked his brother-in-law to go in his place. "To this Grebell agreed, and as it looked likely to rain, said he would fetch his cloak, but after persuasion agreed, to save time, to put on that belonging to Lamb." Returning "towards midnight," the unfortunate Grebell was hit from behind by Breads, but "staggered home, quite unaware of the seriousness of his injury." Vidler even cites direct quotes from the protagonists, among them the dying man's last words to his manservant, the warning sent by the ghost of Martha Lamb to her husband (she visited him no fewer than three times before he stirred!), and Breads's threat to the mayor at his sentencing. He makes no judgement on the fairness of the trial, although Henry Dodson's note had long been in print and must have been known to him. Most importantly, he does not describe Breads as mad. Instead, he maintains that he was motivated by "a bitter grudge" over the short-weights affair, and that he was found "shouting around the town in a drunken frenzy" on the morning after the murder.[55]

Why would a staid, respectable member of the Rye community, whose historical research was usually impeccable, have invented such an outrageous fiction? Of course, we cannot be sure that he did; there may be some further, hidden source that will come to light in the future. Yet Vidler was experienced enough as an historian to recognize the more absurd aspects of his version of the Grebell murder, whatever their origins. Almost certainly, the invented quotes were his, as were such macabre details as Martha Lamb's three ghostly visits. To understand why he would have thrown away scholarly integrity so wantonly, in an age when fictionalized history was not as acceptable as it is now, we should glance at Vidler's papers in the East Sussex Record Office. They include the draft of a horror story, the manuscript of a one-act play about smugglers, and a notebook containing "The Strange Story of Susanna Swapper," a tale of witchcraft that will figure in the next chapter.[56] Leopold Amon Vidler, small-town businessman and civic organizer, apparently aspired to being a fiction writer or dramatist. The Grebell murder story is his best creation, and the only one that made it into print. It has been replayed in various forms ever since. Vidler revived it himself after the Second World War in a brief article published in an antiquarian journal. He noted there with some pride that the famous murderer's skull had been sent to Brighton for the Police Exhibition of 1946.[57] In Vidler's exciting (and excited) retelling, John Breads, far from being a victim of dementia or of injustice, had become the archetype of a vicious killer.

The story as Vidler had reinvented it was presented to a much broader audience by his acquaintance and successor as mayor of Rye, the professional writer E. F. Benson. We have already met him as the tenant of Lamb House after Henry James's death. He was the son of a ruthlessly domineering clergyman who became Archbishop of Canterbury and apparently gave James the idea for *The Turn of the Screw*.[58] It may have been in reaction to his self-righteous Victorian father that E. F. Benson (or Fred, as he was known) became a fashionable, frivolous Edwardian writer, the author of scores of novels and short stories that gently laughed at social conventions without in any way undermining them. Among the best of his works are the "Mapp and Lucia" books, some of which are set in "Tilling," a fictional Rye. Benson's many ghost stories, one of which has already been described, are gripping and often frightening, although they lack psychological depth.[59] The same can be said of his vivid retelling of the Grebell murder, which appeared in 1940 in *Final Edition*, his last book.

Final Edition is a memoir that deals with the whole Benson clan as well as with Fred's life at Lamb House. The book is suffused with a deep sense of loss, and with hints of past torments. One of Benson's sisters, Maggie, suffered from severe mental illness. At one point, according to her brother, she "was in the grip of violent homicidal mania." Fred describes her condition with the precision of a skilled writer, but he clearly did not understand it any better than his mother, who wrote to him that "we are in very deep waters." Maggie was confined first to an insane asylum, then to a private home, where she died in 1916.[60]

Benson drew no parallel between his sister's "violent homicidal mania" and that of John Breads. On the contrary, like Vidler, he depicted Breads as a natural-born killer, motivated by a desire for revenge for the "heavy fine" supposedly levied on him by James Lamb in the short-weights affair. Benson was writing, of course, for an audience familiar with Jack the Ripper and other "psychotic" killers, and he did not fail to titillate them. He even added some quaint details to the story that were spun out of his own vibrant imagination. For example, George Lamb, the godson and namesake of King George I, is identified as the young man setting out for France, rather than his brother John. The captain of the ship is alleged to have ordered "some extra viand to do honour to his guest" from John Breads himself. The evening of March 17 is described as "raw . . . with driving sleet," and Grebell's hidden wound is compared to that of the Empress Elizabeth of Austria, who in 1898 was fatally stabbed in Switzerland but did not notice it until she collapsed some minutes later. The vengeful father-figure of James Lamb receives no criticism—just as in an earlier chapter, the awful Archbishop Benson is given no responsibility for his daughter Maggie's madness.

Building on a tentative remark by Vidler about old women looting Breads's skeleton, Benson states with grim assurance that the butcher's bones "were broken off by wayfarers, for any fragment of a man who had been hanged was held to be a sovereign cure for the crippling rheumatisms and agues that were prevalent among the dwellers in the marsh." Only at the end of the gnarly tale, after noting that Breads's skull "is of the most degenerate type," does Benson acknowledge "that today the sentence of law would never have been carried out but that, after observation by the prison doctor, Breads would have been placed in the asylum at Broadmoor for convicted lunatics." He moves away quickly from that astute and sympathetic observation, towards further ghostly enhancements. He notes that he now possesses Grebell's death-chair, and that a spiritualist medium saw a man in a cloak sitting in it during a séance ten years earlier. Later in the book, Benson recounts how he and the vicar of Rye witnessed a similar apparition, a man in a dark cape, in the garden of Lamb House, although he does not name his ghostly visitor as Allen Grebell.[61] The appearance of these spirits allows the author to put aside the deeper emotional issues connected with Breads's crime.

The Grebell murder had ended up as another of Benson's popular "spook stories." In that entertaining guise, it still amuses the Rye trippers today. The most important theme raised by the case, however, had been almost entirely lost: namely, the fairness of John Breads's treatment by James Lamb. It was forgotten because all the later writers who dealt with the case were admirers of the traditional (albeit defunct) privileges of the Rye corporation. They had no wish to cast a shadow over what Henry James called "the faint identity," Rye's history as a Cinque Port, with all the rights that it entailed. Holloway wanted to revive those rights, not to destroy them; Vidler sought to enshrine their memory; and Benson, in his jovial, unassuming way, simply saw them as part of the town's historic charm. That the corporate privileges of the past might have led to abuses of power was not an acceptable interpretation for any of them. Vidler and Benson, moreover, were champions of the middle-class values of Edwardian England, values that, in their view, Mayor Lamb had shared. They were not prepared to believe that a successful merchant and magistrate like Lamb, living in a polite age of "honourable and public spirited men," could have behaved at the Breads trial as anything other than an English gentleman.

There is a lesson here for modern academic historians, who may not share the prejudices of Victorian and Edwardian writers, but who have often overlooked the negative aspects of local affairs—injustice and oppression—in order to present a cheerfully bland picture of progress towards civility, commerce and consumerism. Charles Meryon's bitter complaints about greed and corruption, which his brother-in-law chose not to repeat, should remind us that the vices of oligarchy were not always such a matter of indifference.

There is more to the story than that. The theme of madness played a larger part than it has so far been given. We have seen that the retellings of the Grebell murder reflected nineteenth- and twentieth-century attitudes towards madness. Those attitudes were coming to prominence around the time of the Breads trial, and they may have affected its outcome. The butcher's own conception of insanity was wholly traditional, but he was judged according to newer interpretations that recognized "true" madness as a mental disease rather than a moral condition.

Before the eighteenth century, madness had been seen "as a mark of man's fallen state, vitiated by sin, folly and pride."[62] Although they bore the marks of human frailty and error, the mad were in the grip of a divinely determined destiny and were no longer responsible for their actions. They could be feared or pitied, but they could not be judged like other people. Such was the opinion of the seventeenth-century writer Robert Burton in his encyclopaedic *Anatomy of Melancholy*. In typically breathless prose, Burton depicted madness as a horrifying state of incapacity characterized by uncontrollable violence: "*Madnesse* is therefore defined to be a vehement *Dotage*, or raving without a feaver, farre more violent than *Melancholy*, full of anger and clamor, horrible looks, actions, gestures, . . . with such impetuous force and boldnesse, that sometimes three or four men cannot hold them." Burton argued that cases of suicide or murder "by stabbing, slashing, &c. are to be mitigated, as in such as are mad . . . they knowe not what they doe, deprived of reason, judgement, all, as a ship is void of a Pilot, must needs impinge upon the next rocke or sands, and suffer shipwracke." In this passage we can detect a compassion for the mad, based on the assumption that their actions meant social self-destruction, an overturning of order, submission, and neighbourliness. Even if it did not always culminate in violence against one's person, madness was a kind of suicide, tantamount to wiping out one's place in the community.[63]

In 1743, the traditional view of insanity still prevailed among most people in England, especially in small towns like Rye. Breads used a term to describe his state of mind, "Distraction," that had long been favoured as a description of mental illness. Reverend Richard Napier, a popular healer of the first half of the seventeenth century, had diagnosed hundreds of patients as "distracted." The murderer's claim that he had been tormented by devils was also one that Richard Napier would have taken seriously. While the legal authorities of the early eighteenth century were not likely to cite devils, they continued to see madness as a "visitation of God," to quote the judge in the "Mad Ned" Arnold case. From this perspective, madness was never far removed from the supernatural.[64]

What John Breads did not know was that he was standing on the cusp of an intellectual transition that would turn madness from "human frailty" into "mental degeneracy." At the root of this change was a debate between followers and critics of the philosopher John Locke. In 1689, Locke had proposed in his *Essay Concerning Human Understanding* that madness arose not from the inability to reason, but from a defect in the imagination that led to wrong conclusions. Madmen, "having joined together some ideas very wrongly, they mistake them for truths; and they err as men do that argue right from wrong principles. For by the violence of their imaginations, having taken their fancies for realities, they make right deductions from them." Like other writers of the time, Locke associated the imagination, or "fancy," with the summoning up of ideas from the memory. A violent imagination called up the wrong ideas. It followed that any opposition to reason might be called madness, "and there is scarce a man so free from it, but that if he should always, on all occasions, argue or do as in some cases he constantly does, would not be thought fitter for Bedlam, than civil conversation."[65] The madman was not the victim of an external, diabolical power, and he could be identified only by the consistency with which his imagination opposed reason.

Locke's ideas were adapted by Dr. William Battie, the inaptly named physician at St. Luke's Hospital and President of the Royal College of Physicians, in his *Treatise on Madness*. Battie defined madness as *"deluded Imagination,"* by which the mad-man "is fully and unalterably persuaded of the Existence or of the appearance of any thing, which either does not exist or does not actually appear to him, and who believes according to such erroneous persuasion." Realizing, as had Locke, that such a defi-nition might make everyone a little mad, Battie was very con-cerned to separate madness, a physical disorder of "the nervous or medullary substance," from anxiety, or "the perpetual tem-pests of love, hatred and other turbulent passions produced by nothing or at most by trifles." Anxiety often led to suicide, but Battie condemned the "good-natured" juries that ascribed such suicides to lunacy, opining that "they are no more entitled to the benefit of passing for pardonable acts of madness, than he who deliberately has killed the man he hated deserves to be acquitted as not knowing what he did."[66]

From the tone of this last remark, Battie does not sound as if he would have been very sympathetic to John Breads. On the other hand, Breads might not have been very sympathetic to Battie either. The butcher of Rye clearly did not subscribe to the Lockean concepts that inspired the great doctor. Breads claimed to be innocent, not because he had made an error in reason-ing, but because devils had made him unable to reason at all. As for Mayor Lamb and the other judges, they do not seem to have been Lockeans either. If they refused to believe that Breads was mad, it was surely because they interpreted his behaviour as in keeping with what they already knew about his character. This unscientific, anti-Lockean approach might have perturbed Dr. Battie, but it would have satisfied Dr. John Monro, the chief physician of Bedlam.

Monro's ideas were formally set down in an exasperated reply to William Battie, but they had been circulating for years before that, and probably reflect the views of many "mad-doctors." Monro argued that, if madness might be understood at all, which he doubted, it must be by its effects or consequences, which were characterized not by "deluded imagination" but by *"vitiated judgment."* The mad "see right, but judge wrong." Monro gave as an example the man who "from being abstemious, reserved, and modest, shall become quite the contrary; drink freely, talk boldly, obscenely, swear, sit up till midnight; sleep little, rise suddenly from bed, go out a hunting, return again immediately, set all his servants to work, and employ five times the number that is necessary. . . . Nobody can doubt that this is real Madness." By such a standard, any behaviour or action that was eccentric, impulsive or unconventional might be deemed mad. This was how Monro tried to explain Lord Ferrers's lunacy when he testified on the peer's behalf at his trial for murder.[67] On the other hand, if an action showed calculation or suited the character of the patient, then it was sane. Madness, in short, was nothing more than social abnormality, a lack of civility for which the mad themselves might be held more than a little responsible.

Monro presented his views as long-established common sense, so it is not anachronistic to see them reflected in the attitude of James Lamb at the Breads trial. Although we do not know exactly what he said, Lamb seems to have argued that the murder of Allen Grebell did not qualify as an action abnormal enough to be considered insane. Like the members of the jury, he knew the defendant well and was able to apply a personal assessment of Breads's personality and circumstances to the case. Whatever the killer may have imagined that he was doing, the mayor did not accept that his judgement had been impaired on the night that he killed Mr. Grebell. The savagery of his act did not in itself place him outside the rules of civil behaviour. By such standards, John Breads was not mad.

Mayor Lamb did not ask for any medical opinion on the matter of the defendant's madness. If he had, his desire to hang the murderer might have been thwarted, because strangely enough, the most celebrated doctor in Rye was an old foe of the Monro family. This extraordinary physician was Thomas Frewen, one of the earliest proponents of inoculation against smallpox. In 1739, Frewen had become involved in the case of Alexander Cruden, a Scottish tutor and bookseller who had been confined for madness because he imagined himself to be on a divine mission to reform Britain. With Frewen's support, Cruden sued Dr. James Monro, John's father, for unlawful confinement, but the suit was lost when the judge, Chief Justice Sir John Willes, instructed the jury to find for the defendants on the grounds that they had no bad intentions in committing the plaintiff.[68] Dr. Frewen was no admirer of the masters of Bedlam; nor was he a supporter of the ruling oligarchs of Rye. Frewen's family were committed Tories as well as prominent local landowners, and the good doctor shared their attitudes towards the "Mercenary Crew" of Whigs. "I cannot refrain from Tears to see our native Land in such bondage, and in so dangerous Hands," he wrote in 1741, a statement that would not have been appreciated by the Whig magistrates of Rye. Because of his proximity to the crime, Frewen may well have been one of the "Dockters" who conducted the autopsy on Allen Grebell's corpse, from which, as has been seen, no indictment ensued. Did he resist indicting Breads for wilful murder because he doubted that the perpetrator of the murder had been in control of his actions? Did he think the butcher was mad in a way that the harmless eccentric Alexander Cruden was not?[69]

Frewen's later writings provide some answers. His Lockean views on madness or mania were expressed in a major treatise on physiological medicine, published in 1780. He defined mania as an illness of the mind, "a most violent, and acute species of *delirium,* arising from a perturbation of the imagination and judgment." Mania was recognized, not by the eccentricity of the sufferer's behaviour, but by the potential for violent misperceptions: "If, then, the cause inducing a *delirium,* be of that nature, that it can excite ideas, or notions of a considerable impetus, without any regularity, or order; such a *delirium* will be attended with boldness and rage, and violent motions of the body; that is, a *mania* will be produced." He may have been thinking of John Breads when he wrote that "sometimes mad people have been known to murder others; and they have always so much strength, as to over-power almost any one person." Like William Battie, Frewen was careful to separate mania from anxiety, although he had no doubt that both were "passions of the mind," related to extreme sensations of pleasure and pain. "When the desire is very keen, and intense," he wrote, "we see what a prodigious force it will impress on the nerves, by the actions of *madmen,* and men in a fright. the organs of sensation, and imagination, in the brain, are brought into such violent vibrations, as to disturb the operations of reason."[70]

If Dr. Frewen had given testimony in the Breads trial that was consistent with his later writings, he would not have advised the court that the defendant was simply pretending to be mad. Breads gave all the signs of mania: notions without regularity or order, boldness and rage, violent motions of the body, strategic cunning, unstoppable strength. Why else had he been fettered for weeks in prison? Mayor Lamb's dismissal of the insanity defence would have seemed even more arbitrary. Happily for the mayor, Frewen does not appear to have been called upon to testify. After 1760, it is likely that he would have been. By then, madness was widely perceived not as a matter of judgement or character, but as an affliction of the mind that could be cured only by medical care and removal of the sufferer from contact with society. As a result, it became common for medical doctors to appear as expert witnesses in cases that involved an insanity defense.[71] Those found to be mad were sent directly to hospitals or mental asylums by the court, and they lived there for the rest of their lives. Just such an asylum, in fact, was founded in the 1790s at Ticehurst, about twenty miles from Rye. Although it catered for rich, paying patients rather than lower-class criminals, its benign methods would be imitated in the larger county asylums of nineteenth-century England.[72]

John Breads had the misfortune to be tried at just the point when older and more sympathetic concepts of madness were changing into modern ones. Fifty years earlier, he might have been pitied and spared from the gallows; fifty years later, he might have been diagnosed by doctors and sent to an asylum. Even by the shifting standards of his own time, however, Mayor Lamb's attitude towards madness was unenlightened. Aware of the leniency with which an insanity plea might be treated by the jury, he broke several legal precedents so as to ensure a murder conviction. Whereas the newspapers described Breads's crime as "barbarous," Lamb strove to prove that its incivility was intentional. Yet he failed to present any explanation of its motive.

Although it may be fair to vilify Lamb, it is pointless to try to vindicate Breads. An appearance at the Assizes before a different judge and jury might have produced exactly the same result. If he had been saved from death, Breads might have found a lifetime of angry confinement more intolerable than a quick passage into oblivion. If he had lived in a later period, his own views would have been dismissed as delusions. Would the modern labels of paranoid schizophrenic or sociopath have given him greater comfort than his self-diagnosis of distraction by devils? Would they have allowed him to die with so strong a hope of salvation? Historians can now read the case as an example of the abuses that could happen in a legal system that placed so much power in the hands of magistrates with very little accountability. We can regard the defendant with greater sympathy. In the end, however, we cannot give him any better justice than he received.

2

A Parcel of Devils

To obey is better than sacrifice, and to hearken than the
fat of rams. For rebellion is as the sin of witchcraft.

—I Samuel 15:22

How does the crime of John Breads connect with the wider context of social change in early modern Rye? We can begin where
the preceding chapter ended, with the meaning of his madness.
John Breads made only one comment about his own "Distraction." According to the newspaper report of his trial, he an-
nounced to the court that "the Night he met William Fowl in
a Lane, call'd the Dead-Man's Lane, just without the Town, he
thought he was then among a Parcel of Devils." In other words,
Breads likened madness to demonic possession. So did Robert
Burton in *The Anatomy of Melancholy:* "For *mens miseries, calamities & ruines, are the Divells banqueting Dishes.* By many temptations and severall engines, he seeks to captivate our soules."[1]
Breads's conception of madness was widespread among ordinary
people in the 1700s, but it looked back to the preceding century
and beyond. To understand it within a local context, we have to
look back that far as well. We will find that the fear of devils had
a particular resonance in the town of Rye.

We do not know whether Breads's judges or the members of
his jury believed in devils. A century earlier, they certainly would
have; in fact, many people thought sixteenth- and seventeenth-
century Rye was positively pullulating with the agents of Satan,
who were held responsible for every type of misfortune and may-

hem. A jury of 1543 or 1643 might well have considered Breads to be possessed, although it would not necessarily have saved him from death. This was less likely in 1743, seven years after an Act of Parliament had ended witchcraft prosecutions. Clearly, something had changed—an intellectual shift that has often been associated with modern scepticism and worldliness, and has been linked with a crisis in the values of good neighbourhood.

To feel a sense of how great that shift was, we can compare the Breads trial with the publicity that surrounded Rye's previous celebrated murder: the killing of Bridget Robinson by her husband Thomas in 1594. As in the Breads case, there are two versions of the Robinson story, the legal and the literary. To begin with the legal: Thomas Robinson or Robson, a sailor and fisherman, was languishing in Rye gaol, probably as a prisoner for debt. A fellow prisoner named Humphrey persuaded Robinson to poison his wife with ratsbane or arsenic, for with her dead Robinson could sell their meagre possessions—listed in an inventory as a cupboard, a table with bench and stools, two beds, three chests, two spinning wheels, and some lumber—in order to redeem himself from captivity. His method of murder was peculiarly horrible. On the morning of May 26, his wife visited him in prison, and the couple had sex. Robinson then "did conveye into the boddy at her secret partes certeyne broken glasse and poyson." As it seemed to have no effect, he asked his brother-in-law to purchase more ratsbane for him, claiming that he wanted to dissolve the prison locks with it. He had no need to administer the new poison, as his wife took ill and died on June 12. Under examination by the mayor and jurats, Robinson broke down and confessed everything. When arraigned in the Rye sessions court, he pleaded not guilty but was convicted and hanged. His body was buried under the gallows, a treatment similar to gibbeting.[2]

Four years later, a distorted version of the story appeared in a sensational pamphlet published at London. In the pamphlet, Robinson becomes "Henry Robson," and his confederate Humphrey is metamorphosed into a sinister character named Glasier, who obtains a pennyworth of ratsbane, wrapped in a mutton's skin. He assures the fisherman that "in the night when his wife should next come to lie with him, he should convey it into her privie parts, which hee would warrant without danger to him shuld kil her." After her next conjugal visit, described as "the dearest nights pleasure that ever woman had," Mrs. Robson falls ill with a swelling and dies in extreme pain. The physicians who examine her body are suspicious, however, and they question a local mercer about recent sales of poison. He informs them that he sold ratsbane to Glasier, who has since fled. Robson has to be tricked into a confession by the brilliant town clerk and recorder of the sessions court, Francis Boulton. Once found out, Robson is convicted and hanged.

The author of the pamphlet had no doubt at all about who was ultimately responsible for the crime: it was the devil. He claimed that he had written about this awful murder "that others may beware of being deceived by Sathan to doe the like." Robson was no more than a dupe, "for when *Lucifer* had found a meanes how to accomplish his will, he never left him, til by his devilish practices he had brought him to the gallowes." In other words, he was guilty of mental weakness, but he could not help his evil thoughts. The lustfulness of Robson's wife made her into Satan's tool as well, and the writer did not express much sympathy for "the poore sillie woman." Robson was undone at last when he tried to lie to the recorder, who responded by pointing out to him that "the Devill is the father of lyers, and I feare thou art his sonne." The pamphlet's conclusion takes the form of a prayer: "The Lord of his infinit grace graunt every one better to withstand Sathans temptations, and eschew his subtilties, that they be not led by his allurements, nor intrapped in his snares, who seeketh by all means to bring every one to confusion."[3]

This account of Robson's crime is an example of what the historian Stuart Clark has called "thinking with demons." From medieval times until the late seventeenth century, the reality and ubiquity of demonic power was defended by a formidable host of writers, who accepted that "Satan's temptations" could indeed account for worldly events. Devils made sense to them, as they did to the author of the Robson murder pamphlet, and they took it for granted that they were responsible for horrendous crimes.[4] Among the most active servants of the devil were witches and conjurors, to whom Robson's wicked amanuensis Glasier bears some resemblance. Witches and conjurors were surprisingly numerous in the little town of Rye between the 1550s and the 1660s, as this chapter will describe. Perhaps their numbers were not so surprising. Rye was, after all, a godly town, deeply influenced by Puritan ideals of religious reform, and godly magistracy was the reverse side of the demonic coin. Although ordinary individuals, acting without the assistance of higher powers, had little hope of defending themselves against the devil's attempts "to bring every one to confusion," righteous judges like Francis Boulton could help them defeat the great enemy, just as they did in Scripture. Godly magistracy was the Christian society's antidote to the disruptions of neighbourliness that arose from the workings of the devil.

By the mid-eighteenth century, when John Breads faced Mayor Lamb in the sessions court, godly magistracy was a thing of the past in Rye, as elsewhere. The goal of purging the town of all sorts of satanic influences, of making it into a "city on a hill," had largely been forgotten. As a result, the rhetoric of ascribing evil deeds to the devil had become less common, witchcraft accusations had sputtered to an end, and the goal of purifying the community seemed to have been lost beyond all hope of retrieval. By 1743, it was unlikely that any educated person in Rye would have accepted that the murder of Allen Grebell was the work of devils, any more than they would have seen the magistrates who tried him as agents of God. Justice itself had become human and fallible, which was how Henry Dodson represented it in the scathing commentary he wrote in his Bible. Earlier generations would have been horrified by this assessment. In his few recorded words, John Breads seemed to speak for those generations, in ascribing his misdeeds to evil forces, and in hoping for a justice that was more divine than human. How did Breads come to be so out of step with authority in the age in which he lived? We can answer that question by tracing how the devil and the devout interacted in early modern Rye.

Godly Rye

The long chronicle of the devil's works in Rye begins with the Reformation and ends in the 1660s, around the time Breads's parents were born. It is mostly a tale of witchcraft and sorcery, as prosecuted by the town's magistrates. It also speaks of deep social anxieties, aggravated by religious partisanship. From the 1530s onward, Rye was divided between groups of religiously motivated reformers and their moderate opponents, who struggled for control of the corporation. Both sides sought to purge the town of what were seen as the devil's works—drunkenness, blasphemy, Sabbath-breaking, fornication, and, of course, magic—by placing strict controls on social behaviour. Both sides recognized witches and saw magistracy as an instrument of divine grace; but it was the reformers who most fervently wanted tiny Rye to provide a model of godliness for the whole kingdom. When belief in that ideal began to fade, so, too, did witch accusations.[5]

The struggles between the godly and the moderates began while Rye was still a prosperous town, with a bustling population of 3,500 people, a fishing fleet of more than two dozen boats, and a thriving port.[6] The town's troubles were at first ideological, not economic. They began with Henry VIII's reformation of 1532–34, and worsened with the second Reformation of the late 1530s, which introduced justification by faith and altered the practices of the church.[7] Events at Rye reflected those at Westminster, and they illustrated how local squabbles could be magnified into serious confrontations by the intervention of outside authorities. The main fomenter of trouble was the traditionalist curate, William Inhold, whose fortunes were a bellwether of religious change. He was jailed by the lord warden of the Cinque Ports in 1533, because he had defended papal authority. Freed two years later, Inhold took the oath of supremacy, but he continued to observe holy days that had been abolished. By denouncing his critics as "heretics," Inhold succeeded in splitting the corporation into two bickering parties, one for and the other against him. He came to the attention of Lord Chancellor Cromwell himself after Inhold preached an allegedly seditious sermon before a large audience at Burwash in 1537. Seventy-five leading men of Rye, including the mayor and several jurats, supported Inhold in a petition to Cromwell; but he was opposed by John Yonge and others whom he had accused of making Lutheran remarks about every man's being a priest. The turbulent cleric was finally arrested on Cromwell's order, accused of dereliction of his duties and imprisoned. Two years later, however, Inhold returned in triumph when King Henry's great minister Cromwell fell from power.[8]

Inhold was a fractious man, but not a fantasist; he was right to believe that there were crypto-Lutherans in Rye. One of them, a capper named Randall Bell, shocked the town in 1539 when he strode to the altar and seized the host from the priest's hands during an Assumption Day mass, "callying the pryst false knave and sayd thow cannyst nott make God." Bell was tried by the town magistrates, although some were themselves leaning towards religious reform. After King Henry's death, these reformers were encouraged by a rector, Edmund Scambler, who was a convinced Protestant. He was appointed in the first year of Edward VI's reign, but was deprived under Queen Mary because he was married. Scambler went on to become an underground Protestant leader and eventually a bishop. He left behind a legacy of civic commitment to the new religion. From this point on, Rye was unwavering in its Protestantism, which was why the restoration of the Mass under Queen Mary caused a riot in Rye church. A series of investigations followed, carried out by the scandalized episcopal authorities as well as by the Privy Council.[9] Again, Rye was at the centre of a national religious storm.

Queen Mary's loss of Calais was a major setback to Rye's commerce and must have made her memory even more odious to the town's merchants. The accession of Elizabeth in 1558 seems to have restored unity in the corporation, under the auspices of godly Protestants like John Yonge, who was chosen mayor one month after the new queen's accession. Yonge and his friends carried reform further and faster than in most English towns, although they had counterparts in other parts of East Sussex. A delighted William Barlow, the bishop of Chichester, noted that Rye, Hastings, Lewes, and Brighton "ar governed with such officers as be faythfull favourers of goddess word and earnestly given to mainteyn godly orders." The town magistrates had accomplished this without much aid from the bishop, whose authority was weak in the eastern half of the county. They soon welcomed with open arms a flood of Huguenot refugees from Normandy, especially Rouen and Dieppe, who carried with them their own variety of Protestant zeal. According to the corporation, "1500 and odd" Huguenots were living in Rye by 1586.[10]

It was in the midst of the Protestant victory that the first identified witch appeared in the town. Just as the old Catholic nemesis seemed to be defeated, the satanic enemy raised his head. Between 1561 and 1668, the Rye magistrates would deal with eight women and one man who were accused of witchcraft or conjuring. This was a small number of cases, but their impact was far from insignificant. Every generation of Rye jurats from the reign of Elizabeth to that of Charles II judged at least one witch. Furthermore, there were twice as many witch accusations in Rye as in any other town or village in Sussex. Surviving records reveal only twenty individuals who were indicted or accused of witchcraft in the whole county of Sussex, excluding Rye, between 1572 and 1680. In addition, two men (one of them the bailiff of Lewes) were examined in 1578 by the Privy Council for "conjuration." This may be compared with ninety-two Assize cases of witchcraft in Kent and almost three hundred in witch-infested Essex.[11] Sussex as a whole was not by any standard a hotbed of witch accusations; but Rye came close to being one.

The incidence of witchcraft accusations in Rye reflects the enthusiasm of its reformed Protestantism, as well as its connections with the upland villages of the Weald, the rolling hill country that lies north of the town. Fourteen of the accused witches in Sussex, half of the county total, lived in the Weald. Three witch cases were recorded in tiny Dallington, a Wealden village about ten miles from Rye. By comparison, a mere six alleged witches or conjurors resided on the South Downs, in spite of their later reputation for magical practices, and only two were from the coast, other than Rye. These numbers show that witchcraft accusations were more common in the Weald than elsewhere, an impression that is strengthened by evidence from

Kent, where 22 percent of the total cases involved defendants from the Weald.[12] The population of the Weald was increasing throughout this period, but the level of Wealden witchcraft accusations was disproportionate to the area's share of the inhabitants of either Sussex or Kent.[13]

Why so many Wealden witches? The historian David Underdown has pointed to a cultural difference between upland wood-pasture areas like the Weald and the open-field, arable downlands. He has characterized the former as "more divided and less cohesive communities," where fears of disorder abounded and the ideals of neighbourliness were constantly under threat. The looser bonds of community in wood-pasture areas encouraged individualism. "Even the undisciplined poorer folk," Underdown argues, "shared some elements of the more individualistic outlook of their superiors." This helps to explain why the uplands were teeming with Puritans at all social levels.[14] Their presence can be observed in the use of biblical names for children in the Weald, which has been called "the heartland of puritan nomenclature." The same pattern of naming children for biblical figures has been noted in Rye.[15]

The fear in upland areas that neighbourliness was dissolving could also heighten anxiety about the dominance of men over women. A widespread perception held that patriarchy was under challenge from disorderly women, whether they were scolds, gossips, or witches.[16] It may be going too far to claim that witchcraft accusations were a method of social control over disorderly women, because not all accused witches were women, not all were particularly disorderly, and any semblance of control was very haphazard. Still, most witches were seen by their neighbours as falling outside the accepted pattern of demure and submissive female behaviour.[17]

Witches are often imagined as impoverished old women, marginal figures dependent on charity, who were judged to be nuisances by their more affluent neighbours.[18] This model fits many cases of witchcraft, but it does not apply to all. Witches were not always marginal figures, and their accusers were not necessarily better off than they were. Political and factional struggles were just as important to many witchcraft cases as were social conflicts; and we cannot grasp the meaning of witch beliefs without taking into account popular understandings of magic and the supernatural.[19] In Rye, witchcraft cannot be separated from the factionalism that plagued the corporation, or from the tension between godliness and popular mentalities. "Thinking with demons" often meant demonizing one's political opponents, representing them as enemies of good order and of neighbourliness—in short, as witches.

The first witch surfaced in 1561. The mayor that year was John Bredes, a merchant and probably a distant relative of the eighteenth-century murderer. He had been appointed to the magistracy shortly after the accession of Elizabeth, along with four other jurats who leaned strongly in a Protestant direction. Bredes would serve twice as mayor and sat in the 1563 Parliament as M.P. for Rye. During his first mayoralty in 1561, he had the mayor's pew moved from the choir to the main body of the town church, an emphatic assertion of the distinction between the sacred and the secular. He also installed the clock in the church tower, to make the townsfolk aware of the importance of time and perhaps to emphasize the approach of the world's final days. John Bredes was clearly an advocate of change.[20]

It was during Bredes's first mayoralty that a certain Mother Margery was turned out of the new almshouses that had been constructed just outside the Landgate. She was accused of practices "such as any Christian harte wold abhore to here spoken of much less to be used," including casting spells. The mayor ordered a search of the almshouses, and "a good quantitie of rawe beff" was found. Apparently, as the beef decayed, so would the bodies of persons whom Mother Margery had cursed. One of her victims, "being by her wytchcraft most cruelly tormented in his body," had hanged himself. The almshouses, built in Edward VI's reign, were showpieces for the Protestant reformers in Rye. The treatment of Mother Margery demonstrated that only the deserving poor were to be allowed to reside there. The incident also revealed how anxious Protestants were about the potential malice of the ungodly, whom they had so recently displaced. The accused witch's punishment was restrained, however, implying that the jurats were less interested in making an example out of her than in removing her bad influence from the town.[21]

As an elderly woman living on charity, Mother Margery was certainly marginal. Her case fits the social model of witchcraft, and her rough treatment might be used to illustrate the beginnings of the decline of neighbourliness in Rye. To a contemporary eye, however, it would have been Mother Margery, with her grudges and raw beef, who was breaking with neighbourly values. The concerns of the town's governors were with preserving social and religious harmony through a godly cleansing or purging; they saw themselves as the protectors of traditional order. For a while, they seemed successful. We know about Mother Margery only because the mayor and jurats declared in a certificate ten years later that their town had not been troubled with witches since her expulsion—in other words, moral cleansing was going smoothly.

In fact, this was not true. Sixteen months before the certificate was written, another witch, or more precisely a wizard, had turned up in the town. In June 1570, the magistrates had ordered the pillorying of John Page "for his Abuse in practicyng inchantiments." He also owned "wichcrafte books" that were publicly burned in the market place. To make matters worse for him, Page had been caught with Katherine Herste in a "Lewde act in whoredome," unlawful sex, for which both were carted through the town and ordered to leave it within ten days. Page was apparently a cunning man or conjuror. Wealthy enough to own books, he was not a marginal figure. Nor was he alone in his practice of enchantments, as other conjurors would appear soon after at Lewes and Hastings. Nothing is known about his books, but Page's collection might have been coveted by two more respectable men of seventeenth-century Rye who collected works on occult matters and practiced astrology—namely, Samuel Jeake the elder and his son, Samuel junior. Learned magi rather than cunning men, the Jeakes did not practice petty enchantments, and they were celebrated for their godliness. They would have approved of the actions of their pious predecessors in punishing Page's scandalous behaviour, although they might have spared his library. The conjuror was pilloried, and his books were burned. The mayor in that year of holy conflagration was again John Bredes.[22]

Rye's Protestant zeal burned hotly through the 1570s, but it became more and more divisive. The turning point came in 1574, when the magistrates asked the bishop of Chichester to expand the ecclesiastical jurisdiction of the town preacher, Richard Fletcher, "as we may the more stronglier subdue vice and advaunce virtue." Fletcher, a future bishop of London and father of the playwright John Fletcher, was unquestionably a reformer, but he turned out to be a defender of clerical privileges as well, and this began to irritate lay Protestants. By levying fines for Sabbath-breaking, he made enemies of the Bennetts, a family of butchers who were close allies of the reforming mayor, John Fagge. In 1579, the town was disturbed by an armed riot in which the mayor's friends assaulted Reverend Fletcher and a group of moderate jurats who supported him. Caused by a disputed will, the riot led to accusations of counterfeiting against one of Mayor Fagge's supporters, who was said to have been "trained in all sortes of develishe devises." Once again, the devil was held responsible for spreading mischief in Rye. Proceedings against the rioters were initiated in the court of Star Chamber. In the short term, the riot increased Mayor Fagge's popularity, but it also made the moderate Protestants in the corporation politically visible for the first time since Elizabeth's accession.[23]

The reformers tried to tighten their control by creating new freemen, among them Allen Grebell. Like Fagge and the Bennetts, Grebell was a butcher, who occupied the long, rambling building at the top of East Street that would later be called the Flushing Inn. It was not unusual for a tradesman to be elevated to the freedom in this period, although it would be unheard of in the eighteenth century. Apparently, the residents of the Flushing Inn had for some time been reform-minded, inasmuch as their front room contained a wall painting showing the coat of arms of Jane Seymour, mother of the Protestant hero Edward VI.[24]

The reformers soon initiated a new campaign for moral purification in Rye, whose most extraordinary result was a 1581 "Decree against whordom." This was adopted "ffor the better avoydinge of whoredom within the saide towne of Rye for which no Doubte god is highly Displeased." Prostitution was widespread in Rye, as in many other ports, but it is notable that the magistrates invoked divine displeasure as the justification for their initiative. For them, "whoredom" was a moral rather than a social crime. Unmarried pregnant women or suspected prostitutes were to wear a partlet of yellow and green cloth around their necks. If they were found without it, they were "to be sett in the Cage with gods yoke by the space of three houres."[25] The effects of such a measure in a small town, where everyone's private affairs were common knowledge, can be imagined. Underlying this decree were a deep distrust of female sexuality and a fierce desire to uphold godly order, no matter what the cost in human degradation. Both of these impulses would feed into witch accusations. The decree may also remind us of the special costume imposed on Jews during the Middle Ages, or of the scarlet letter worn by the colonial adulteress Hester Prynne in Nathaniel Hawthorne's famous story. The yellow and green partlet was designed to mark the wearer as an outsider, a threat to religious and neighbourly values. The Rye decree, however, was unenforceable from the start, and it was soon forgotten amidst the turmoil of war.

The struggle against Catholic Spain was hailed by reformers as a final confrontation with the Popish Antichrist, but it led to the temporary downfall of godly rule at Rye. War brought new military expenses and an outbreak of plague. It struck a heavy blow at the fishing fleet, which could no longer set out for the Channel in safety. The situation was aggravated by civil war in France. Trade at Rye harbour plummeted, as is shown by the figures for ship entries and clearances recorded in the Maltod Books. In 1585, 431 vessels passed in or out of the harbour; by 1592, this figure had sunk to 209, and seven years later it hit a dismal 127, from which it did not recover before the end of the war.[26] Economic decline heightened social tensions in the town, and it gradually undermined the influence of the reformers, whose enthusiasm for the conflict was probably greater than that of their moderate counterparts.

With economic crisis came new religious fears. By 1591, moderate jurats had become concerned about the appearance of "a smale secte of purytanes, more holy in shewe then in dede." Assisted by "one Browne, an informer," the Puritans had tried to remove the curate for non-residence. In spite of his similar surname, Browne was not Robert Browne, the famous separatist and founder of the so-called Brownists who later emigrated to Plymouth Colony. Unlike the Brownists, the "purytanes" of Rye, who included a surgeon, a shoemaker, a carpenter, and a gentleman's servant, did not seek to separate from the church. Moreover, they could count on friends within the corporation. When one of them was denounced for calling the Archbishop of Canterbury "the Pope of Inglande," and the Book of Common Prayer "but masse translated and dumdogs to reade it," it resulted in the accuser himself being committed to prison for making a false report. The furor over the "purytanes" soon disappeared, but this did not prevent further insults from flying, as in 1594 when the vicar denounced the reformist town preacher, who was appointed and paid by the corporation, as a "mutynous fellowe, a sower of sedycion and an enemye to the State." Six years later the vicar's successor was actually imprisoned by the mayor, Thomas Hamon, for enclosing a suspiciously Catholic silver crucifix in a letter to his wife's family.[27]

Like the jurats, many of Rye's less distinguished inhabitants dealt with the misfortunes of the 1590s by lodging angry accusations against their neighbours. Some worried souls even made appeals to the supernatural. In 1593, suspecting that her child was bewitched, Elizabeth Drynkwater of Rye consulted "a connynge man" or wizard, Zacharias of Hastings. He assured her that Mother Rogers had bewitched the child and advised her "to fetch blodd" from the old woman's buttock in order to break the spell. Getting blood from a witch was a common sympathetic cure. Flinching at the prospect of having to bleed a witch's backside involuntarily, Drynkwater "tooke another corse for she prycked her in the hande." Happily, the child recovered in spite of its mother's mistake.[28] It seems that no prosecution arose from this information, which is hardly surprising. Drynkwater's testimony reveals not a pious horror of witchcraft, but a willingness to resort to a wizard and to adopt counter-measures that would have appeared mere superstition to the godly. She was "thinking with demons" on a level that went well beyond conventional Christian precepts. Drynkwater or Rogers could easily have ended up in court, as John Page had twenty-three years before, charged with witchcraft. Zacharias's occult library was confiscated, as John Page's books had been. This time, however, the offending tomes were not burned; they were put in the custody of a clergyman. There is no evidence that any of the individuals involved in the case was indigent, but stabbing an old woman in the hand surely qualifies as the apogee of bad neighbourliness. It was a sign of wider troubles in Rye during the late sixteenth century.

The reformers had expelled Mother Marjorie and burned John Page's books, but they had not banished demons from Rye, as was evident both in the Drynkwater case and in the diabolical murder committed by Thomas Robinson in 1594. Robinson's imprisonment for debt further typified a situation that was becoming common at the end of Elizabeth's reign: personal financial ruin. The reformers had utterly failed to reverse the decay of Rye's trade or the decline of its population, which began to fall around 1590 and plummeted to less than two thousand in the first two decades of the seventeenth century.[29]

Although the port of Rye never fully recovered, the peace that began soon after James I's accession shored up the town's decline by bringing trade back into the harbour. It also seems to have entrenched the moderates in power. Some reformers, like Thomas Hamon, son of a Huguenot minister, joined the moderate faction, possibly in reaction to the disturbing rise of Presbyterianism. From this point until the 1630s, the godly were a minority faction in Rye. If we call them Puritans, as their enemies did, we should understand that they were more zealous Protestants, not sectarians. Very few of them were bent on overturning the Church of England. Their social values, like piety, self-discipline and good order, were shared by their moderate opponents, but Puritans promoted them further and faster. By the 1650s, they had pushed them to the point at which the bonds of neighbourliness themselves began to crack.

Fairies into Devils

With the moderates in power, it might be assumed that Rye's religious turbulence would abate, and that witchcraft accusations would disappear. Hitherto, it was the godly who had shown the most interest in detecting witches. Within a few years of cementing their dominance, however, the moderates launched into the most sensational witch case in Rye's history, proving that they matched their opponents in anxiety as well as in vindictiveness. It turned out to be a complex case, and it provides unusual insight into how the supernatural affected the lives of ordinary people in the seventeenth century.

It began on 26 September 1607, when Susanna Swapper, the wife of a sawyer, was questioned by the mayor, Thomas Higgons, and the jurats about her nocturnal visions of spirits or "Fayries." Swapper claimed that she had been visited by two men and two women, dressed in white and green, who had instructed her to dig for treasure with "young Anne Bennett." This person was Swapper's neighbour, the daughter of Robert Bennett, a godly butcher who had been deeply involved in the 1579 riot, and his wife Anne, a healer known for magical cures. "Young Anne" had married George Tayler, a minor gentleman, and the couple had recently experienced the loss of two small children. Perhaps this was why Mrs. Tayler assured Susanna that she too had seen spirits, to the number of eighty or a hundred, "and they were all Fayries." She offered to help Susanna in searching for the treasure, which Tayler regarded as rightfully hers. She even paid Roger Swapper a penny every night to sleep away from his wife, so that he wouldn't interrupt her conversations with her night-time visitors! Susanna became quite attached to one of the spirits, whose name was revealed as Richard, and she began to see him in public places. She espied him at the Strandgate when Sir Thomas Waller, Lieutenant of Dover Castle, came to Rye by ferry, and at the funeral of Mrs. Tayler's son, sitting among the congregation. Susanna began to leave small presents for the spirits—apples, nosegays, powdered beef, a piece of cloth—which seem to have been connected, either directly or symbolically, with pregnancy, childbirth, and the treatment of sick children.[30]

Susanna Swapper's initial revelations invite a psychological interpretation. Unlike the nerve-racking devils who spoke to John Breads 135 years later, leading him to commit murder, her spirits seem to have calmed her anxieties about money, children, and even her husband, who was said by her neighbour to be "a Lewde and wicked Lyver." They became a means for her to establish a sense of control over the domestic space to which, as a wife and mother, she was largely confined. Richard, her male spirit guide, helped her to confront an external, male-dominated world that was beyond her control. Anne Tayler, on the other hand, was more interested in prophecy and public power than in spiritual comfort. Her visions extended beyond the household sphere, and her narrative was less conventionally feminine. In her examination, she described her own revelation of "A man very leike unto Mr Hamon deceased" who had appeared in a glass window shortly after the death of her first child. She also claimed that Swapper had encouraged her to "lookeup into the Element," where she saw "two Angells," who told her they had come "to cutt off the wicked from the yearth." Her husband George had also seen macabre visions of death, reflected in a neighbour's window.

The magistrates began to suspect that these marvellous sights had something to do with the recent death of Thomas Hamon, the moderate mayor, and they subjected Susanna Swapper to two more examinations in order to prove it. Finally, on December 3, she confessed that Mrs. Tayler had foretold the death of the mayor and that "one of the Spirites befor his death should geve him A grype upon his members and that they should looke very blacke after his death." When he died, "she doubted that the divell had his soule alreddy for that he was an evil Lyver, for she said he had misused his other wife greatly . . . he did never any man good but such as was of his Religion."

This opened the floodgates of accusation against both women. Over the ensuing eighteen months, witnesses would appear to denounce Anne Tayler for bewitching her neighbour Robert Burdett (a barber and town gunner, killed by an exploding cannon), for poisoning a servant girl with deadly medicine and even for murdering her own children. Prisoners from the town gaol eagerly testified that they had overheard Susanna Swapper, who was confined throughout this period, making incriminating statements. Martha Higgons, widow of Thomas Hamon and newly wed to his successor in the mayoralty, Thomas Higgons, not only told the jurats that she believed Anne Tayler had bewitched her late husband, but hinted that a poor woman who had appeared at her door, to whom she had given one of Hamon's shirt sleeves along with threepence, was none other than the witch herself in a magical disguise. Seeking a satanic line of succession from the conjurors of the late 1500s, the magistrates asked one witness, the widow Elizabeth Byshopp, who may have been the Elizabeth Drynkwater of 1593, about another notorious conjuror, Zacharias of Hastings. They wanted to know whether any of the "conniving Bookes" owned by Zacharias, and kept in the custody of the late John Prescott, vicar of Rye, had somehow found their way into the possession of Anne Tayler or her mother Anne Bennett. Byshopp did not answer the question.[31]

The affair was getting out of hand. What had begun as the touching and somewhat pathetic story of a woman seeking consolation in occult dreams had become a horrifying and twisted labyrinth of malicious narratives, with political murder at their centre. The sceptical lord warden of the Cinque Ports attempted to suppress Martha Higgons's accusation of murder against Tayler and Swapper, claiming that it was based on "some pryvate displeasure" and was anyway beyond the jurisdiction of the town magistrates. His letter leaves a foretaste of 1743, when Lord Chancellor Hardwicke tried to dissuade James Lamb from trying John Breads in the sessions court. The lord warden was no more successful than Hardwicke would be, and in 1609 Anne Tayler was brought to trial for conjuring, as well as for bewitching to death Thomas Hamon. She was acquitted of both charges. Less well-connected and no doubt abandoned by her erstwhile friends the Taylers, Susanna Swapper spent two more years in prison before being released under a general pardon.[32]

Annabel Gregory has interpreted the Tayler-Swapper case in terms of factional rivalry between the godly, led by the town's butchers, and the moderates, headed by brewers like Thomas Hamon. Anne Tayler's apocalyptic vision, and her insistence that Hamon had a religion different from hers, tied her to the reformers. Clearly, belief in fairies and spirits was not incompatible with godliness; in fact, Mrs. Tayler often made God-fearing comments to her associate Susanna Swapper. Neither of the defendants was socially marginal; Anne Tayler was married to a gentleman and mingled with the elite of Rye, while Susanna Swapper was poor but not dependent on charity.[33] Only the poor old woman at Martha Higgons's door conforms to the stereotype of a witch.

The most fascinating aspect of the case, however, may be what it suggests about the reality of spirits and apparitions. Both women conversed freely with spiritual beings, not through an elaborate magical ritual but in the course of their daily (and nightly) lives. They were not so much "thinking with demons" as cohabiting with them. Under normal circumstances, this easy familiarity with the spirit world may have been widely accepted in Rye. Certainly, George Tayler did not hesitate to tell all his friends and associates about what he had seen in the glass window. His mother-in-law, Anne Bennett, had a reputation as a supernatural healer that seemed to do her no great harm, until she was dragged into the accusations against her daughter. Where the boundary lay between quasi-learned magic and superstition or witchcraft seems to have had more to do with the practitioner's social and political connections than with any clear intellectual demarcation.

The difficulty of separating witchcraft from other supernatural healing practices was again illustrated by a deposition made in 1610 by Joan Bayly. An octogenarian, Bayly had become convinced that the child of a local fisherman, Thomas Hart, was bewitched. She told the fisherman's wife to bring her a piece of red cloth, needles, and pins, "and by God's help she would cure the child." She stuck the needles and pins in the cloth, put it on the embers of the fire, and then thrust a dagger into it. The next person to enter the house would surely be the witch. Unfortunately, although the burning cloth "did seem to be like unto a toad," nobody came into the house. A teenager named Thomas Hart was a witness to the disputed will that caused the riot of 1579, so this accusation may have been another attempt to implicate friends of the reformers in withcraft.[34] As in the Drynkwater case, it was not clear who should be charged here, or with what offence. The magistrates, already embroiled in the Tayler-Swapper affair, seem to have indicted nobody. The incident, however, strengthens the impression that godly Rye still wallowed in popular superstition, especially among the poor.

The town of Rye in the mid-seventeenth century. The contemporary painting on which this nineteenth-century print is based can be seen in the Rye Castle Museum. St. Mary's Church is visible at the top of the hill. The harbour is on the right, and on the left the sea comes up to the bottom of the East Cliff.

The tower of St. Mary's Church, Rye, showing the clock installed during the mayoralty of John Bredes in 1559–60, and the Quarter-boys provided by Mayor Thomas Lamb around 1760.

Lamb House, the residence of Mayor James Lamb, Henry James, and E. F. Benson. A garden room stood to the left of the picture in the eighteenth century but was destroyed by a bomb in the Second World War.

The churchyard where the murder of Allen Grebell took place. The site of the crime was most probably at the right of the photograph, where the path leads up from the Ypres Tower and Gungarden.

The Ypres Tower. John Breads was imprisoned here, under constant
guard and in fetters, for more than two months while awaiting trial.

The warehouse in which the trial of John Breads took place. The property of Mayor James Lamb in 1743, it was later owned and renovated by the Vidler family.

The Flushing Inn, owned by John Breads and leased to John Igglesdon.

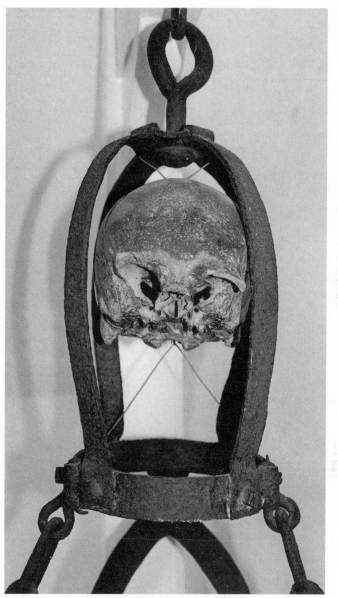

The skull of John Breads, still enclosed in the iron gibbet.

Samuel Jeake the younger's house in Middle Street, now Mermaid Street. It was later used by his widow, Elizabeth, for Baptist meetings.

Thomas Peacock's School, built in the early seventeenth century.

The Mermaid Inn. The inn belonged to the Cadmans in the seventeenth century and to William Rockett in 1743.

The water tower in the churchyard.

The Court Hall. Construction began in 1743, shortly before the murder of Allen Grebell.

Looking down from the tower of St. Mary's, with one of the Quarter-boys on the right.

The main political consequence of the Tayler-Swapper case was the entrenchment of the moderates in power. If they had proven nothing else, they had at least shown that they could assert themselves against outside authority, in the form of a disapproving lord warden. As always in early modern Rye, the defence of local autonomy created a sense of purpose among the ruling jurats. This helped them to dominate the Rye magistracy for the next thirty years. Their leaders were Richard Cockram, one of the examiners in the Tayler-Swapper affair, who served as mayor eight times between 1609 and 1650, and Mark Thomas senior, who wed the unmerry widow of Thomas Hamon and Thomas Higgons. Cockram and Thomas were both substantial merchants who dealt in canvas, draperies and wine. Cockram also invested in privateering, which in this period was equivalent to piracy. The more cautious Thomas put his earnings into property in Playden and East Guldeford as well as Rye.[35] Both men were socially distinct from, and probably richer than, the tradesmen (butchers, bakers, brewers) who had dominated the reform faction. Their politics focused on economic affairs rather than religion. The improvement of Rye harbour was their principal goal, and under their leadership, the corporation did not hesitate to instruct its parliamentary representatives as to how this might be achieved. In 1623, for example, the town lobbied for a lighthouse at Dungeness, the sandy point of land on the south edge of Romney Marsh where more than one thousand bodies from shipwrecks had washed ashore in one awful winter. A coal-fire light was finally installed there.[36]

The religious views of Cockram, Thomas, and their supporters were in the Protestant mainstream of early Stuart England; that is, they were cautious about reform rather than openly hostile to it. Cockram was actually called a Puritan in 1610 by a

Rye innkeeper, who told a traveling musician that the mayor would give him nothing for his playing. Whatever his views on music, Cockram was no reformer, but neither did he espouse the so-called Arminian doctrines promoted in the 1630s by Archbishop William Laud, doctrines that bolstered the authority of the clergy and the sanctity of the altar. Their distaste for Laudianism put the magistrates of Rye at odds with the vicar, the Oxford antiquary Brian Twyne, who happened to be the editor of Laud's university statutes. Luckily, Twyne was nonresident, but his curate continued to object to the appointment of a town preacher or lecturer by the corporation, and in 1623–25 there was a confrontation over the issue that resulted in the resignations of both curate and lecturer. However moderate they may have seemed in comparison to reformers in the town, the jurats nonetheless gained a reputation for Puritanism simply by defending established civic privileges against the rising tide of Laudianism.[37]

If there was a lay advocate of the Laudian position in Rye, it was the brewer and churchwarden Anthony Norton, who in a letter to the bishop of Chichester denounced the "many abuses committed by divers persons in our toun against God's service, honor, and reverence due to holy and consecrated places, against the lawe statutes and canons of the Church." Norton also accused the new curate, Christopher Blackwood, of preaching two hours instead of reading the service, a common complaint against Puritan clergy. Mark Thomas, the moderate mayor, stood up for the curate, which must have fed the spreading perception among outsiders that everyone in Rye was a Puritan. Norton's enemies included some stronger minded anti-Arminians, like Joseph Benbrigge, mayor of Rye in 1629, who denounced the disgruntled churchwardens as "drunkards, adulterers and fornicators."[38]

The threat from these mischievous Laudians revitalized the

reforming spirit of the Rye corporation and elevated Allen Grebell to the mayoralty in 1631. Like his father, Grebell was a
butcher (although he would later be described as a merchant and
a gentleman) as well as a zealous Protestant. Not everyone, however, was prepared to wait for him to restore Zion. Around the
time of Grebell's mayoralty, a group of townsfolk left ungodly
England to settle in the newfound Connecticut colony. Some of
them moved to Rye, a border town that was eventually claimed
by New York. How many of them left the town, and for what
reasons, is unclear, but it is likely that they were seeking economic opportunity as well as a different religious climate. The
lord warden of the Cinque Ports was trying hard to discourage
further emigration, so by allowing the departure of the settlers,
the corporation was again asserting itself against external authority.[39] Hostility to such interference was found among both
moderates and reformers, which may explain why the ideological
gap was narrowing in the years before the Civil War.

This gradual convergence of views was far from complete
when the elections to the Long Parliament were held in October 1640. It was a complicated four-way contest in which both
Puritans and moderates were faced with a number of voting
options. The candidates for Rye's two parliamentary seats included a courtier, Sir John Jacob; a mild Puritan, John White;
the more strident Puritan gentleman William Hay; and a jurat,
John Fagge, who was descended from the reforming Elizabethan mayor of the same name. Hay and White were chosen on
an initial tally, but the town clerk forced those who had voted
only once to declare for a second candidate, a tactic that returned White and Jacob. Petitioning Parliament about the result, a furious William Hay accused the town clerk of falsifying
the return by including absentees for Jacob. His charge was hotly
denied by Richard Cockram. The poll split both freemen and
jurats, but there were signs of division *between* the two groups

as well. Seven freemen (but no jurats) voted for both Hay and Fagge; Allen Grebell voted for White alone; and John Fagge voted only once, for himself! The moderate mayor and the Laudian Anthony Norton supported Jacob and Hay, while the town clerk and three jurats supported Jacob and White. The election created a sorry mess; the corporation was in obvious disarray, and in danger of losing touch with the wishes of the freemen.[40]

Facing a potentially crippling resurgence of factionalism, the moderates gave way to the Puritans. At the outbreak of the Civil War, Richard Cockram joined hands with Allen Grebell in supporting Parliament against the king. In the course of the war, the corporation provided money and materials for the Parliamentary cause, especially for the navy, and welcomed the presence of a military garrison in the town. With Irish and Flemish privateers roaming the Channel, the war was never far away.[41] Any royalists who may have lived in Rye were careful to keep their silence during these years.

Allen Grebell was mayor again from 1644 to 1646, and he presided over two more witchcraft cases in Rye. They centred on Anne Hownsell, a widow who was accused of making nocturnal visits to the home of William and Frances Royall. The howling of a dog had awakened Mrs. Royall at midnight. Anne Hownsell then appeared in her bedroom without opening the door, and commanded Goody Royall to come "Home" with her. When she refused, Hownsell vanished. On another occasion, when Mrs. Royall was sick in bed, Hownsell arrived through a pane of glass. Upon examination, Hownsell was found to have a red mark on her body, commonly thought to be the sign of a witch. The mark or "teat" was supposedly the place from which a witch's satanic familiar—in this case, her dog—sucked the blood that sustained it. In 1645, Mayor Grebell ordered Hownsell and another woman, Martha Bruff, the wife of shoemaker Stephen Bruff, "to be tried by putting them into the water." If they floated, then they were witches. Contrary to what is often believed, the absurd water trial was not widely used by early modern magistrates, although it had popular approval. It reflects some desperation on Grebell's part as to how the witches were to be judged. Did they come up to the surface or sink? The corporation records do not tell us; but in November 1645 both Anne Hownsell and Martha Bruff were found guilty of an unnamed felony by the Rye sessions court, presided over by Allen Grebell, and sentenced to be hanged.[42] If the sentences were carried out, as seems likely, then they were the only witches to be put to death in Rye. Clearly, the great-grandfather of the murdered Allen Grebell was as harsh a judge as James Lamb proved to be.

The accused witch Anne Hownsell cannot be called a marginal figure. The Hownsell or Howsell family were fishermen and bricklayers living in the Strandgate. Several of them were substantial enough to appear in a 1660 estate tax roll.[43] Once again, the witchcraft charge against Anne Hownsell seems to reflect personal animosities among people who were roughly social equals. Yet it also demonstrates a subtle change in local thinking about witches. Previously, they had been accused of acts of magical malevolence, or even of talking to spirits, but not of having direct physical contact with the devil. However wicked their intentions, the witchcraft of Mother Margery, Mother Rogers, Anne Tayler, and Susanna Swapper was not seen as an alternative to Christianity, and was not far removed from common beliefs or practices. Anne Hownsell, however, was suspected of direct physical contact with Satan through her familiar. Her acts threatened not Frances Royall's physical health, but her soul. While the bedside apparition was reminiscent of Susanna Swapper's case, it also suggests a sexual threat that is entirely absent from previous witch accusations. For Swapper, the male fairies were sexually seductive. For Frances Royall, the devil was a sexual predator who entered her bedroom in the shape of a woman. In keeping with this reconfiguration of local witchcraft, the town magistrates dealt with the accused witches in a novel and aggressive way, without regard to local precedent, by testing them in water and ordering them to the gallows. In the midst of godly revolution, the devil was to be purged for good.

The impact of a more focused and confident Puritanism on the Hownsell episode was palpable. Many Puritans had become convinced of an absolute separation between the elect and the unregenerate. This explains why Anne Hownsell was seen not just as a foolish dabbler in forbidden arts, but as the incarnation of the devil himself. In that important respect, her case was reminiscent of other personal accusations that were flying around Rye in this period, accusations that singled out certain members of the community as the carriers of demonic influence. Many of these accusations came from the mouth of a young attorney, Samuel Jeake.

Jeake was the son of a baker of Huguenot extraction, Henry Jeake. His mother, Anne, came from a pious Puritan family of Peasmarsh. Before her marriage, she had been warned by a Puritan friend, John Wilmshurst, that Rye was "given to much prophaneness as I have been certified: Swearinge Curseinge whoredom scolding and many such sinnes they say do there abound." On another occasion, Wilmshurst assured her that "wee that feare the Lorde being amonge the people of this worlde are in greate daunger therefore we must continually pray unto God to keepe us from evill."[44] Anne Jeake seems to have taken to heart these messages, with their underlying vision of a complete separation between the godly and the wicked world. Her son was brought up to believe them too. From a very young age, he was "thinking with demons," and he saw their handiwork all around him. It was shortly after the death of his mother, "my dearest friend under God" as he called her, that Samuel Jeake, aged seventeen, embarked on a mission to impose his way of thinking on others.[45]

Samuel Jeake's principal demon in the early 1640s was the curate of Rye, John Beaton, a Puritan to be sure, but one who was less inclined to make absolute distinctions between the saints and the reprobate. Jeake was particularly disgusted that Beaton should have used the term "dear sister" at the burial of a Roman Catholic gentlewoman, and that he should have prayed for the recovery of a female "fornicator" who had borne an illegitimate child, "before she had beene soundly reproved." As he wistfully noted later in life, "at the doing of either my tender yeares & apprehensions tooke offense." He may have been tender in years, but the young Jeake was unrestrained in his disgust for such behaviour: "What Concord hath Christ with Belial? And what part hath a believer with an Infidel?" In 1642, Jeake and some of his friends walked out of a baptism service because Beaton had dared to bless "the children of visible unbelievers." In a letter to the curate, they argued that to allow the wicked into the church would create "a synagogue of Sattan nay Babylon, an habitation of devills and a cage of all foule spirits."[46] The division Jeake and his friends made between "visible saints" and the agents of Satan was not far removed from the accusation made by Frances Royall against Anne Hownsell. Like her, they were prepared to disrupt the peace of the community, on which neighbourly values rested, in order to impose a conception of purity that was founded on individual conscience.

It is significant that Jeake was so deeply offended by the unregenerate sinfulness of two women. Whether as witches or recusants or fornicators, women stood for worldliness and were more likely to fall from grace than men. Yet women came in two distinct varieties, good and bad, and Jeake "readily granted" the right to "libertie of conscience" demanded by Frances Hartredge, to whom he had proposed marriage. Frances was sister-in-law to Christopher Blackwood, the former curate of Rye, who was close to Jeake. Before she would agree to marry him, she wisely presented her unorthodox suitor with an extraordinary set of written proposals concerning her jointure, his father's property, and her own freedom of religion, "because I know not the manner of yor worship nor whether there will be any thing that will offend my Conscience therein." He agreed to all; they were married in 1650; and according to her husband, "she never tooke offence that I ever learned."[47]

By this time, Samuel Jeake's friends were moving towards Anabaptism, the belief that church membership should be conferred by adult baptism. Whether or not Jeake himself became a Baptist is a moot point, but many of his associates did, including Christopher Blackwood. The jurats, both Puritans and moderates, were not willing to go so far, and in 1647 they imprisoned a Baptist who had led prayers in a private house at Rye.[48] Remarkably, this incident did not lead to a further breakdown of political unity. The town remained staunchly anti-royalist during the second Civil War, when a rising of royalists and moderates broke out in Kent. Not far from Rye, at Sandwich and Deal, sailors mutinied against Parliament. At the successful conclusion of this tense campaign, Jeake and his friends wrote an enthusiastic letter to the Parliamentary general Sir Thomas Fairfax, urging him to find out "the Actors & Fomentors of the late warre & bringing in of the Scots," and to mete out "condigne punishment" to them. Whether out of fear or conviction, his fellow townsmen followed in Jeake's anti-royalist footsteps. In 1650 all of the leading men of Rye—Richard Cockram, Mark Thomas junior, Allen Grebell, Samuel Jeake, even Anthony Norton—subscribed to the Engagement in support of the new republican government.[49] Nobody now wanted to be perceived as a royalist.

As moderates in Westminster had foreseen, the republic

brought the sweet taste of victory, however fleeting it may have been, to the new sectarians. Samuel Jeake became a freeman and town clerk in 1651, and two years later a radical religious reformer, Reverend John Allin, was appointed as rector. Allin was a Harvard graduate who espoused Independency, the right of each congregation to decide on the form of service. Parliament remained wary of full freedom of conscience, but this did not worry Frances Hartredge Jeake, who could write with confidence that "it is but a littel while and he that shall come will come and not tary and then what will these things profit." She meant that the second coming of Christ was surely at hand—and that event would solve everything for the sectarians. For a short time, it must have seemed to the town reformers as if the devils of division had been driven out for good, that true godly neighbourliness had at last been restored, and that Rye had finally accepted what Samuel Jeake called "the manifesta-con of the sonnes of God," the rule of the saints that would be the glorious preamble to the end of the world.[50]

World Weariness

It was a heady time for the godly of Rye. "You are as a city set on a hill," wrote Christopher Blackwood to Frances Jeake in 1652. Not everyone was impressed, however. The diarist John Evelyn, who visited the town in 1652, was disgusted with the alteration in religious services there. Evelyn recorded how on Whit Sunday he "went to Church (which is a very faire one) [heard] one of their Canters, who dismiss'd the Assembly rudely, and without any blessing: I was displeased when I came home, that I was present at it, having hitherto kept my Eares incontaminate from their new fangled service." In the following year, Rye was visited by John Taylor the water-poet, who penned some irreverent lines about the local sectarians, making a scatological pun on "Jeake" and "Jakes," meaning a privy or toilet: "In all the Town you'll scarce find a Privy / For as our Sectaries, In Tubs preach here / They make (Sir Reverence) Reverend Jakeses there, / Of Pulpits of Profanity, and these / When they are full, are empti'd in the Seas."[51]

Jeake, who had little sense of humour, would have dismissed Taylor's lines as blasphemous filth, typical of the unregenerate. Godly rule meant the exclusion of blasphemers and other moral offenders, who were harassed at Rye with petty prosecutions. Thirty-five moral offences were presented to the sessions court in 1652 alone, including many fines for profane swearing. Not surprisingly, the most committed verbal opponent of the new regime turned out to be the old Laudian Anthony Norton, who in 1651 was censured by the assembly for disaffection against the state. Three years later, he was fined six shillings for saying that "none but rogues fought against the King and that Cromwell and all that followed him were rogues."[52] The city on the hill was not prepared to tolerate such back-sliders.

In 1655–56, the total number of moral offences prosecuted at Rye began to drop. This may indicate that godly rule was failing, or it may show that it was working. In many respects, reformation was only warming up. Presentments for Sabbath-breaking, for example, began with an order by the mayor in 1656, pursuant to an Act of Parliament, and continued down to the end of the republic. Six violators of the Sabbath were presented in 1660, including the grandson of the moderate mayor, Mark Thomas. Offenders were fined ten shillings, with the additional provision that "upon nonpayment they are to be set in the Stockes six houres." Was this divisive fanaticism or the height of neighbourly control? In fact, it was both. It represented a turning point in the town's social relations. From now on, the values of neighbourliness and godliness themselves would bear in some minds the taint of sectarianism and republicanism.[53]

The corporation's devotion to republican government certainly did not diminish throughout this period. In August 1659, the mayor, jurats, and "commonalty" (a select group of godly freemen who now attended assembly meetings) assured the Council of State at Whitehall that "the inhabitants of this place in generall ever since the beginning of the late warres have beene and still remaine cordially affected unto the Parliament," adding that 120 men had recently enlisted "for the cause and service of the comon wealth." Allen Grebell, son of the Puritan mayor, became a freeman that year, to continue the republican legacy.[54]

The anti-royalism of the Rye magistrates persisted amidst the collapse of the English republic, an event that clearly surprised them. As late as March 1660, a local mariner's wife was prosecuted for hanging an apple tree branch on the Strandgate "saying it was the Kings' Collours." The apple blossom, evoking the renewal of spring, had become a symbol of the return of Charles II, but it was very unwelcome to the town governors. The woman was ordered to stand in a collar at the Butchery on market day, "with a paper before her breast written declaring her said offence." The first sign of change, however, came in the same month, when Richard Norton, son of the royalist Anthony, was made a freeman. By mid-April 1660, the political situation must have been confusing even to Samuel Jeake. As town clerk, he recorded a bond made "in full Court of the Keeper of the liberty of England by authority of Parliamt." That title, first used in the town records in December 1649, might now refer to Charles II, General Monck, Lord Protector Richard Cromwell, or perhaps Major General John Lambert, who had just escaped from prison and was trying to raise a republican insurrection. Three weeks later, on 12 May 1660, godly rule came to a crashing halt in Rye. The restoration of King Charles II was proclaimed; but it was done by the mayor and jurats only after the "commoners" were dismissed. The "commonalty" would not meet again as a body until 1680, and then only briefly. Facing the end of his political dreams, Jeake immediately offered his resignation as town clerk, although he attended a Cinque Ports meeting in July and continued to write the assembly minutes until August 25.[55]

The aftermath of the Restoration made a great divide in the early modern history of Rye. Throughout the late sixteenth and early seventeenth centuries, although the population was falling and trade declining, the town's leading men retained a strong sense of the religious importance of their town. With its zealous magistrates, its godly laws and its town preacher, Rye was at the forefront of reformation, a beacon not only to the other Cinque Ports but to all of England, which they saw as the new Israel. The mayor and jurats could pride themselves, as they wrote in 1575, on "endevoringe ourselves (as dutie byndeth) to the uttermost of our powers to bringe the people . . . to suche a civill and vertuous order of lyvinge as the worde of God dayly taught unto us doth require."[56] After 1660, the town's rulers began to lose that spiritual confidence. For the next five decades, the moral order that the magistrates had sought to impose on the inhabitants of Rye decayed, as the corporation went into periodic political convulsions. Concurrently, while belief in the impact of the supernatural on everyday life did not disappear, it became less acceptable among Rye's more worldly rulers. After the Restoration, it was harder to "think with demons," just as it was harder to imagine the triumph of godly rule.

Samuel Jeake was bitterly aware of these changes, although he hoped they could be reversed. As a religious Dissenter, a Protestant outside the Church of England, the Restoration settlements barred him from holding office and from worshiping freely. He greeted this situation bravely. His correspondence is full of resignation and a desperate longing for signs of the second coming of Christ. Hope mingled with despair in a letter Jeake wrote in 1663, as he considered

> the Atheisticall Scoffers on the one Side, that say, where is the promise of his coming: the raging Oppressors on the other hand, that upbraide us, with where is our God, &c.: our infirmities within us, the divisions amongst us, the darkness of the present night, and sealed up prophecies amongst us, when none can tell us how long: it cannot but quicken our cries to heaven, that God would arise, & plead his owne cause, & decide the great Controversie, who are on his side, & discriminate between them that feare him & feare him not.[57]

How long would it be before deliverance? Jeake clung to reports of supernatural occurrences that might presage the final days: a unicorn seen fighting a lion at Ely; a six-month-old child who spoke to its nurse, saying "it was a woefull world"; a gentleman who dreamed vainly of the Restoration while another dreamed of salvation.[58] Jeake's son Samuel later traced his own religious conversion to "a Prodigy (whether true or false I know not) related at my Father's house" in 1663: "A Throne appeared in the heavens, & one like a King sitting theron, over whose head were the 2 letters C.R. After which another Throne, & another person in royal Letters I.R. which my childish apprehensions interpreted, That after the present King C[harles] 2 Jesus Christ should come to reign."[59]

As this vision reveals, the political radicalism of the Jeake family was undiminished. The elder Jeake did not hesitate to criticize monarchy in the sermons he delivered to his friends. "All Kings and Monarchs," he preached in 1665, "wch. spend most of their time in conquering & Getting countries are full of vexation & trouble in the best." Recalling the events of the 1640s, he added that kings were "sometimes turn'd out of their kingdomes whereby they see wt. vanity it is to trust in them."[60] The conventicles of Jeake and his associates, held surreptitiously in private houses, provided republicanism and radical reform with their last bastion. Jeake might have had little impact on a bigger town, or one with a more royalist past, but his activities would severely polarize the corporation of Rye, as the next chapter will show.

At first, the Restoration had brought about very limited change in the town, because the moderates did not yet care to test their own strength. Reverend John Allin, a close friend of Samuel Jeake, remained the vicar.[61] The moderate Mark Thomas junior was already mayor. Jeake resigned as town clerk and did not have to be forced out. The magistrates elected as one of their members of Parliament Sir Richard Spencer, who was nominated by the Duke of York, the new warden of the Cinque Ports, although Spencer was "a stranger to us." The other M.P., however, was a Presbyterian and former republican, Herbert Morley of Glynde.[62] If Spencer had lived, the peace of the corporation might have been preserved longer; but he died within six months of the election. The Duke's nominee as his replacement, Sir John Robinson, was opposed by a Puritan lawyer, Samuel Gott of Hastings. Gott's old friend Samuel Jeake appears to have managed the candidacy—"I wholy depend upon your advice," Gott wrote to him from London, where he remained until the election was over. Robinson was chosen by twelve votes to nine for Gott—a very narrow margin. The defeated candidate declared himself to be "well satisfied with Gods Providence in the late proceedings," but warned Jeake that as "there are severall persons secured in many places I shall advise all my ffriends to be wise as Serpents & innocent as doves."[63]

The commissioners for regulating corporations did not think

Jeake and his friends were innocent as doves, and they now purged at least seven of them from the ranks of freemen. The Privy Council then initiated *quo warranto* proceedings against the corporation, noting its alleged "disaffection to his Majesty and his government." Meanwhile, John Allin was ejected for refusing to accept the Act of Uniformity imposed on all ministers of the Church of England. The assembly books, less neatly kept than in Jeake's day, reveal a growing anxiety among the magistrates about dissension and disorder. Fines were levied for interrupting speakers during assemblies, and disenfranchisement was threatened against any who "shall devulge or declare any Speech Spoken in the corte hall." The corporation records were finally removed from Jeake's care in August 1663. He and other purged members were compelled to pay town dues "as if they were never freemen." To prevent them from holding "Seditious meetings," the town watchmen were ordered in 1665 "to take an accompt of the severall Carriages & transactions of all such as shall meete at unseasonable times & places."[64]

In this atmosphere of fear and suspicion, the magistrates considered the last witch case in Rye's history. The only extant reference to the case is in an 1894 article by F. A. Inderwick, who mentioned that in 1668 "Alice, wife of John Huelstone of Rye, Ferryman, was bound over to prosecute Alice, wife of Henry Marten of Rye, Brazier, for witchcraft." Inderwick probably derived his information from the sessions records, which have since disappeared. Henry Marten and his wife Alice lived in the impoverished Strandgate ward. He was described as a labourer in a 1660 tax list. He and his wife paid only sixpence each, the lowest rate, on their estate. His progeny, however, lived in the affluent Landgate ward, and several of them practiced the profitable trade of fellmonger or skinner. John Huelstone or Hurlstone, fisherman, lived in 1660 with his daughter Elizabeth in Baddings ward, a very poor area below the south cliff on which the church stands. Father and daughter were each taxed at one shilling, suggesting that they were slightly better off than the Martens, although less well connected. Alice must have been John Huelstone's second wife, as he was apparently a widower in 1660.[65]

The witchcraft accusation resulted from the strange death of Henry Marten. The parish register for September 1668 reveals that "att the Election of the Majore," Marten "fell downe dead in the Courtt Hall." No doubt his wife was accused by Alice Huelstone of bewitching him. Reminiscent of the Tayler-Swapper case of 1609, which also involved the strange death of a mayor, the charge against Mrs. Marten was politically motivated. The 1668 mayoral election, during which Henry Marten suddenly died, had returned James Welsh, a moderate who was strongly disliked by the religious radicals in Rye. One of them, Thomas Palmer, recently purged by the commissioners for corporations, fumed at Welsh in 1663: "you are Maior and you would be Minister too, Church warden, Survaier, & overseer for the poore, wee will make you Constable too and you shall be all."[66] The accusation foreshadows what Henry Dodson would later say about James Lamb. The Marten family were supporters of the radical faction in the 1670s, so it is plausible that the accusation against Alice Marten in 1668 was devised by the adherents of Mayor Welsh in order to embarrass their enemies. A magistrate must have encouraged the case for it to have reached the stage of a presentment at the sessions court, but whether it was tried, and what verdict was given, are not known.

Witchcraft accusations ended in Rye after 1668. In fact, they were dwindling everywhere in England. The final witch trial in Sussex took place in 1680, when Alice Nash of Battle, a Wealden town not far from Rye, was accused of killing two little girls by supernatural means. The grand jury found the indictment to be a true bill, but the outcome of the trial is unknown. Eighteen years later, Mary Clerke of Ashford was the last witch indicted at the Kent Assizes, for bewitching a thirteen-year-old boy, "who was wasted, consumed, etc." Again, the fate of the accused witch is a blank.[67]

Was the disappearance of witch accusations a result of growing scepticism among the magistrates? Sceptics had plenty of ammunition to use before the 1660s. In particular, they could turn to *The Discoverie of Witchcraft* by the Kentish justice Reginald Scot, published as long ago as 1584, which denounced as "popish" the notion "that certeine old women heere on earth, called witches, must needs be the contrivers of all mens calamities." Scot maintained that modern miracles were "cheeflie done by deceipt, legierdemaine, or confederacie," and condemned the "arrogancie and cousenage" of self-styled prophets.[68] His words may have had more resonance eighty years later than they did when he published them. The moderate magistrates of Restoration Rye had certainly tired of prophets, and they may have become weary of other supernatural claims as well. Both moderates and radicals must have recognized from past experience that witchcraft lent itself to malicious and contentious prosecutions. Assuming that the sentences of Anne Hownsell and Martha Bruff were carried out, only two witches were ever hanged in Rye. This was because allegations of witchcraft generally fell apart in the sessions court, as they did in the Tayler-Swapper case and almost certainly in the Marten case. As for the ordinary inhabitants of Rye, they had seldom brought accusations of witchcraft before the magistrates, and had never prosecuted them without the active encouragement of members of the corporation.

The last half of the seventeenth century saw a general alteration in attitudes towards the supernatural throughout England, especially among the educated, for whom magic and astrology, prophecy and divination, became less convincing or at least less important.[69] Some among the learned had begun to think without devils. The sudden disappearance of witches from Rye, however, was probably due more to changing social circumstances than to intellectual factors. In a recent study of the final phase of witch prosecutions in England, Ian Bostridge has argued that belief in witchcraft was based on a desire for religious and political consensus. "The continuing relevance of witchcraft," he has written, "indicates a continuing commitment to a vision in which religious identity and civic identity merged, the product of a society scandalized by the idea of schism and still harking back to a vision of a unified Christendom." The possibility of consensus faded in the late seventeenth century, for two main reasons: first, the Christian polity became hopelessly divided by religious pluralism, and second, witchcraft became a matter of intellectual dispute.[70] The second factor is hard to observe in a local context, but the first is highly evident at Rye. Fear of witchcraft, which had thrived on the hope of an ideal unity, began to die away as unity began to seem impossible and division, both confessional and political, became embedded in the system of governance. What would then become of neighbourliness? Already weakened by the abuses of the godly, it further succumbed with the removal of its demonic nemesis. After 1660, it became little more than an instrument for partisan control and social police.

Looking forward seventy-five years, from the last witch accusation in Rye to the trial of John Breads, we can see that nobody other than the accused was willing to "think with demons," at least publicly. This does not mean that the people of Rye had ceased to believe in the devil. As late as the mid-nineteenth century, they continued to hang horseshoes outside their doors "to prevent being bewitched."[71] Demonic beliefs also persisted among the educated. Only six years before Breads's crime, the vicar of Battersea, Thomas Church, wrote a pamphlet defending the literal truth of biblical possession by demons. Arguing against the notion that demoniacs were simply madmen, he proposed that madness was "one Attendant, or Sign, or Effect of such *Possession;* but it will not therefore follow, that it was the *whole* of it." Church followed the pamphlet up with two more instalments on the same theme. Notably, however, the learned clergyman limited his discussion to the New Testament; he did not allow that demons could be recognized, or cast out, in the present day, as the wrong-headed Methodists sought to do.[72]

Similarly, the jurors of the Rye sessions court may have believed in the reality of devils, but they did not permit such considerations to interfere with the course of justice. After all, their forebears had been involved in the witch trials of the sixteenth and seventeenth centuries, which had brought such divisiveness to Rye. John Breads was surely aware of that history as well, but he did not hesitate to use the language of an earlier age in describing his state of mind. Was he trying to appeal to a memory of Satan's works that was deeply buried in the consciousness of his audience? When he said that he had thought himself to be among "a Parcel of Devils," Breads may simply have wished to impress on the jury the severity of his delusions. In light of Rye's history of witch trials, however, he may have meant something more.

3

The Valley of Humiliation

But, I say, my Neighbours were amazed at this my great
Conversion, from prodigious prophaneness, to something
like a moral life; And truly so they well might, for this my
Conversion was as great, as for *Tom* of *Bedlam* to become
a sober man.

—John Bunyan, *Grace Abounding to
the Chief of Sinners* (1666)

Religion was the catalyst of social and political change in early
modern Rye. Its absence from the John Breads case therefore
seems all the more conspicuous. The murderer was not attended
by a clergyman in prison or on the scaffold. What were his religious sentiments? We can judge them only from his reported
final words, which amount to a last-ditch attempt to expiate his
guilt. Breads said of himself that he was "a very wicked Liver,
and deserv'd the Punishment he was subjected to by Law. He
desir'd all People to take Warning by his unhappy End."[1] More
interesting is what he did *not* say. Insisting to the end that he
had been suffering from "Distraction," Breads never admitted
that he had meant to kill Allen Grebell, or anyone else, for that
matter. He acknowledged the providential nature of his punishment, but he did not affirm that it was appropriate to his deed.
He never expressed submission to his earthly judges, and he died
"praying to the Lord to receive his Soul."

A century earlier, John Breads's last words might have been

regarded as indicative of his spiritual state. Seventeenth-century observers made much of what criminals said, or failed to say, on the scaffold. They were shocked by the grim silence of another homicidal madman, Enoch ap Evan, who was hanged and gibbeted at Shrewsbury in 1633 for the murder and decapitation of his brother and mother. A yeoman farmer, ap Evan refused to repent and offered no explanation of his horrendous crime, other than that he objected to kneeling at communion, a practice his butchered relatives had apparently defended. Astonishingly, ap Evan's violence was interpreted as religiously motivated. On the basis of his reluctance to kneel, he was accused in print by a local vicar of having imbibed all the false tenets of Puritanism.[2] This was seen as a complement to his madness. Fervent godliness was often paired with insanity by its critics, such as Richard Burton, who described religious "Precisians" as "certainly farre gone with melancholy, if not quite mad." By the eighteenth century, the identification of religious sectarians as "the carriers of mental disease" had become "a ruling class shibboleth."[3]

Nobody branded John Breads as a religious zealot, which would of course have strengthened his claim of madness. However, as it happened, sectarianism was rooted in Breads's family background, a point to which we will return later. The magistrates who tried him would have known this. Indeed, their own relationship to Rye's religious past was as complicated as his. Several of the jurats were descended from seventeenth-century sectarians, but they had long since abandoned the religion of their ancestors. Turning their backs on the ideal of godly rule, which had become associated with factional strife, they now wanted social peace, not purity. Breads's last words could be interpreted as an indirect reproach to them, a call to heed his example and reject worldly desires. The newspaper correspondent who reported it may have heard it in this way. There is a hint of irony in the writer's remark that Breads's fate would be "a proper Spectacle to deter the Practicers of Wickedness, and (if possible) reclaim every Evil-doer in this Corporation." Was he implying that there might be evil-doers serving *within* the corporation?

Breads apparently thought so, for the devils he claimed to see were standing very close to real or imagined jurats. Like everyone else in Rye, he was aware that the once-godly corporation had changed dramatically between the late seventeenth and mid-eighteenth centuries. He also knew that the change had been resisted, and that members of his own family had been involved in opposing it. Contrary to what many had hoped, the restoration of Charles II had not been the last word in the history of Puritan Rye. The religious radicals had not simply surrendered to the new regime. Instead, between 1679 and 1683, they had surged back to take control of the corporation, through a combination of physical violence and legal manoeuvre. It turned out to be the last outburst of the beliefs associated with godly rule, and it came as close to a minor revolution as anything that happened in England during those turbulent years. The bitterness and recriminations to which it gave rise would not have been forgotten by the 1740s.

The radical revival of 1679–83 deserves close attention, because it was the last point at which Rye attempted to lead the nation towards a government by the saints. It provides a key to understanding the separation of the magistrates from the dangerous mentalities of the common people, which led to the emergence of an ironclad oligarchy in the eighteenth century. It also helps to explain the loss of confidence in local autonomy and the attractiveness of a national political culture. The so-called Exclusion Crisis is key to understanding the history of eighteenth-century Rye, as it is in the case of many other English towns. The consequences of that final godly gambit were still felt in 1743, when John Breads turned his back on worldly justice and called so hopefully on his God in the moments before he dropped to an ignominious death.

Rich and Poor

The radical revival of the late seventeenth century seems at first glance to have flown in the face of economic realities. The wealth of Rye was disappearing, its population sinking; yet its leading families appeared to be fixated on religious conflict rather than on addressing the problems of a decaying port and a dwindling fishery. On closer inspection, however, there was a clear relationship between Rye's economic plight and the re-emergence of ideological conflict.

The main reason for the harbour's loss of trade was silt, carried down to the shore by the town's three little rivers, the Tillingham, Brede, and Rother. The inhabitants of Rye were well aware of the problem, and called for something to be done about it. The first printed pamphlet to argue for national aid to the harbour appeared in 1677. It was aimed at members of Parliament, as well as at courtiers, merchants, and other influential people who might put pressure on Parliament to pass a harbour bill. The pamphlet argued that an improved port "could receive a great Fleet of Ships of considerable burden," which was unrealistic, but which may have impressed the naval commissioners. More important, the writer put blame for damage to the harbour on the "inning" of the marshes by local landowners, which had altered the drainage system and dumped masses of silt into the rivers.[4] Of course, those same enterprising landowners were the leaders of county society after the Restoration. Thus, economic recovery pitted the town elite against prominent representatives of the gentry and aristocracy, including well-known royalists like the Frewens of Northiam.

The initial attempt to lobby Parliament in favour of a harbour bill was a failure. It would be repeated several times over the next century, but it met with no success until 1724. Meanwhile, Rye seemed to be falling further and further into ruin, with its population tumbling from 1,300 in 1660 to about 1,000 (600 adults) in 1676.⁵ This was less than one third of the number of inhabitants in 1570. The fishing fleet had dwindled to a few vessels, and in a tax list of 1660 only sixteen fishermen and the widows of two others were wealthy enough to be included. In the same year, the corporation exerted itself to protect its right to send a bailiff to the autumn "free fair" for fishing vessels at Great Yarmouth; but this was the last time that the ancient privilege of Rye fishermen was exercised. By the late 1670s, the magistrates had become alarmed by the encroachments of French fishing vessels. One of them was seized near Rye by their orders and its master wounded, which brought an angry protest from the French ambassador and a rebuke from Whitehall. It was an empty gesture; French ships from Dieppe dominated the herring and mackerel fisheries, and the Rye fleet had become insignificant.⁶

The result was increasing poverty among the lowest social classes. The level of poverty in Rye is impossible to measure with certainty, but it has been estimated that two-thirds to three-quarters of the people of the town were either very poor or of the "poorer sort" in the 1660s. That decade saw a flurry of activity by the town magistrates to control vagrancy, in response to the 1662 settlement legislation that allowed those applying for relief to be transported back to the parish where they had been born. The settlement law led to nasty games of kick-ball between parishes, played with the bodies of the poor. In March 1670, for example, when a young woman who had been a servant at Rye was sent back to the town from Battle, the magistrates indignantly asserted that she was not a resident and would be dispatched to Brede. The overseers' accounts of poor relief in 1679–80, the only accounts to survive for this period, list 108 beggars and vagrants who resided in or passed through the town, including fifty-three men, twenty-two women, and at least thirty-three children. The majority of these men, but only a few of the women and children, had passes, meaning that they were soldiers or sailors or vagrants lawfully returning to their parish of birth. Because they usually had small dependents and no passes, being poor was probably a harder state for women. Most vagrants at Rye were given twopence or threepence each to hasten them on their journey home, but a group of maimed soldiers, presumably more "deserving" than the others, was treated to 14s.11d worth of beer, bread, mutton, and tobacco by the overseers.[7]

On a more productive note, attempts were made to improve the lot of the resident poor by putting them into apprenticeships. In March 1662, six girls and three boys were apprenticed by order of the corporation, probably as wool spinners. The sessions court also developed a keen interest in the unlawful reproduction of the poor, because any child born outside wedlock was "likely to be chargeable to the parish of Rye." In 1683, Sarah Corke of Rye, an unmarried servant, testified to the court that she had gone into a field in Playden with another servant, Daniell Tharpe, where after "being very urgent and pressing in discourse," he "Did then & there carnally lye with, and had carnall knowledge of the body of her this Depon[t]." Tharpe was bailed in the considerable amount of £100, which shows how worried the magistrates were that he would abscond. If he were found guilty, he would have been required to pay a small fine to support his child.[8]

A different type of local response to poverty was the growth of smuggling. The opportunities for profit offered by the contraband trade expanded dramatically after 1679 on account of the increase of duties on French goods. Smugglers known as "owlers" carried wool from Romney Marsh to the coast of France, where it was exchanged for wine and brandy. It was an attractive commercial alternative for an unemployed fisherman or seaman. Because the town had no effective police force, the Rye sessions court limited its involvement in the suppression of smuggling to relatively insignificant cases of evasion of duties by shipowners and masters. It left alone the larger groups of smugglers that operated along the coasts. These malefactors were pursued, at his own expense, by the zealous clothier and self-appointed coastal defender William Carter. Carter was an effective lobbyist against any relaxation of the restrictions on trade in raw wool, which he saw as essential to local prosperity. In 1671, he asked his friend Samuel Jeake to forward to the mayor of Rye a copy of a book written by him "which comprehends not only the business of wooll but trade in generall & in pticular aboute ffishing." In the 1680s, Carter's deputies executed government warrants against the smugglers of Romney Marsh. They had a close escape in December 1688, when fifty angry owlers from Lydd, mounted on horseback and firing guns, chased them along Camber Sands towards Rye. Luckily, the beleaguered lawmen were rescued by a passing boat.[9]

It would be a simplification to assume, as William Carter did, that the growth of smuggling spelled the ruin of legitimate trade at Rye. The story of Rye's overseas and coastal commerce was more complicated than that, and in telling it we can gain some insight into how at least part of the town's erstwhile prosperity was preserved. The fluctuations of Rye's maritime trade can be traced through the port books, which recorded vessels and cargoes that entered or left the port for the purpose of either foreign or coastal trade. Rye's port books for the late seventeenth century are not complete, and in any case they record only what interested the customs officers: that is, goods in foreign trade on which duties might be imposed, and goods in coastal trade that might be re-exported to a foreign country. We cannot measure with any precision the total amount or value of goods that entered the port of Rye in the period, but we can derive a general idea of overall trends.[10]

How many ships were entering and leaving the harbour? In providing an answer, we should remember that ships were of various sizes and tonnages and were filled to different capacities with cargoes that had different values, so that counting them will provide only a rough impression of the dimensions of trade. At five-year intervals (or thereabouts, inasmuch as so many of the books are missing or damaged beyond readability), here is the number of ships entering and leaving the port of Rye during the Restoration period, recorded for twelve months from December 25:[11]

	OUT	IN
1661–62: Overseas	50	37
1662–63: Coastal	37	14
1664–65: Overseas	32 (3 prizes)	13
1666–67: Coastal	27	2
1671–72: Overseas	31	17
Coastal	25	13
1674–75: Overseas	36	24
Coastal	35	22
1680–81: Overseas	20	15
Coastal	29	24
1684–85: Overseas	12	19
Coastal	32	13

Unsophisticated as they may be, these figures show that Rye was sending out fewer vessels on foreign voyages, but was more or less holding its own in receiving foreign cargoes and in the coasting trade.

Most of Rye's foreign trade was with the ports of northern France, especially Dieppe. The ships that took part in this cross-

Channel commerce were small, typically three- to four-tonne "shalloops." The chief cargoes going outward from Rye to Dieppe were worsted stockings, calfskins, hops, and horses or geldings. The profitable trade in horses became legal only in 1657, at which point English breeders, many of them aristocrats, began supplying French dealers through the small ports of the southeast.[12] Occasionally, cargoes of textiles are listed, especially in the years between the Dutch wars, when shipping across the Channel was more secure. In the summer of 1667, for example, three substantial shipments of northern cottons, Yorkshire kerseys, serges, and bays were despatched to Dieppe. There was even trade with the Dutch in peacetime, as in March 1671 when the *James* of Hastings carried three hundred quarters of barley from Rye to Amsterdam. These were exceptional voyages, however. The town's main imports from France were Normandy canvas, wrought silk, and silk gloves. The customer's overseas port book for 1664–65 records the entry of 19 1/2 gross of French gloves, 5,625 ells of Normandy canvas, and 1,000 pounds of wrought silk, along with hats, paper fans, buckrams, salt, and, of course, wine. Unfortunately, after 1669 new duties began to pile up on French wines, which clearly hampered the merchants of Rye.[13] They turned to Dutch prize ships and wrecks, from which wine or brandy could be taken without duty. A small amount of Portuguese wine was imported in the 1680s, carefully marked in the port books as "not of the growth of ffrance." By then, duties on Normandy canvas had effectively killed off that lucrative trade as well. In sum, while Rye never lacked overseas commerce, it was badly hurt by national policies and, like many southeastern ports, failed to keep pace with the three- to fourfold increase in tonnage experienced by British shipping as a whole in the fifty years before 1688.[14]

The most striking development in Rye's overseas trade in the Restoration period was the growing presence of local merchants.

In a study of Rye in the first half of the seventeenth century, Stephen Hipkin found that few townsmen took part in overseas trade, except for brief periods of time.[15] After the Restoration, the names of Rye residents became very common among overseas merchants. Foremost among them were Lewis Gillart senior, Thomas Miller, and William Key, who were the major importers of Normandy canvas in the 1660s. Gillart had a hand in all areas of commerce with France. In 1664–65, for example, he brought in two tonnes of French wine, 40 gallons of brandy, 44 dozen buckrams, 147 pounds of silk, 682 yards of camlets, 17 gross of gloves, plus salt, vinegar, haberdashery, and "small toys." He also took wine out of prize ships. Over to France he sent calf-skins and horses. The elder Gillart, Miller, and Key were all religious Dissenters and associates of Samuel Jeake the elder. They dealt with like-minded Protestant merchants in Normandy, where more than forty thousand members of the reformed church still lived before the Revocation of the Edict of Nantes.[16]

The number of ships engaged in the coastal trade at Rye remained steady, but the value of their cargoes declined. This was due partly to changes in the town's industrial hinterland. The trading wealth of medieval and Tudor Rye had been built on iron from the Weald and wool from Romney Marsh. Production at Wealden iron furnaces and gun foundries peaked in the first half of the seventeenth century. Under the Protectorate, thirty-five furnaces and forty-five forges were operating in the Weald, and 1,500 or more people were employed in them. The iron and guns that they made were sent down the Rother to Rye. In 1632–33, the harbour shipped 523 tons of iron, of which 394 tons were sent to London, along with 50 tons of ordnance, most of it probably cannons. Over the next fifty years, however, the strength of Wealden iron-making was gradually sapped by Swedish competition. The situation was not helped by the poor quality of local roads and a possible timber shortage. In 1680–

81, Rye sent to London only 55 tons of pig-iron, 41 tons of cast iron, and 107 tons of "Iron Guns" with 3,465 pieces of "shott." Two years later, a meagre 15 tons of Wealden pig-iron left the port of Rye, 80 percent of it bound for Newcastle. To be sure, guns continued to be cast in the Weald, and 180 tons of ordnance were sent out in 1682–83; but the armaments industry enjoyed only a fitful prosperity, marked by wartime growth and peacetime retrenchment.[17] William Key, the Rye merchant who was most involved in the iron trade, died in 1666, and his fellow Dissenters seem to have withdrawn from this area of business over the next twenty years.

The wool trade fared better. It was nourished on the ryegrass of Romney Marsh, which provided large flocks of sheep with particularly fine coats. Falling wool prices hit the graziers of the Marsh hard in the late seventeenth century, and an invasion of clover reduced the value of grassland. The level of production was sustained, however, as landowners ejected small tenants and engaged "lookers" who could oversee large holdings. Although the cloth-making industry of the Weald disappeared after 1630, there was still heavy demand for Romney Marsh wool from clothiers in London and the West Country. As a result, exports of wool through the port of Rye were three times in 1700 what they had been in 1640.[18] The trade was subject, however, to dramatic fits and starts. To illustrate the point: 55,440 pounds of wool left the harbour in 1632–33, all of it bound for London. Only 34,586 pounds of wool sailed from Rye to the capital in 1674–75, but an additional 26,144 pounds was sent to Exeter, 9,000 pounds to Topsham and 1,537 pounds to Southampton. In the early 1680s, wool exports to London and the West Country suddenly sank to virtually nothing, probably because of the rumours of war with France. The graziers were not so badly hurt, because they could send flocks overland to Smithfield market in London; but local merchants who dealt in wool, among them

Lewis Gillart, Thomas Crouch, and Benjamin Marten, must have suffered heavy losses.

The merchants of Rye showed considerable ingenuity in adapting to the changes of the Restoration period. They started shipping wool to Colchester in 1681, as the London trade faltered. Nicholas Skinner and others began to replace wool with hops on ships sent to London and the West Country. The commerce in coals from Newcastle was also expanded, so that by 1682–83, 113 shipments of coal were reaching Rye from the northeast, more than were sent to Hastings or Chichester. A portion of these coal shipments was exported, legally or illegally, to France.[19]

The remarkable adaptability of the Rye merchants can be appreciated in the surviving general ledger book of Samuel Jeake the younger, which covers the period 1680–88. Using double entries, careful sub-headings, and cross-references, Jeake calculated his yearly "stock" or capital, his excess of income over expenditure, and the balance placed to his next account. As a merchant, Jeake dealt in wool, hops, malt, horses, Normandy canvas, lockrams, and timber. His local business associates included Thomas Miller, who by 1688 was running a company in London, Nicholas Skinner, Lewis Gillart, and Samuel Gillart. Jeake recorded no wool sales at all in 1685, but the following year he sold £722.17.8 of it. He borrowed money from his father and his friends; he loaned money to Martha Grebell, Thomas Grebell, and the innkeeper Michael Cadman. He showed a profit to stock, and a steady increase in the balance carried forward to account, for every year except 1684. By 1688 his capital had increased almost threefold, from £762.15.6 1/4 to £2009.14.10 1/2 — and this in a decade of persecution and exile.[20]

The economic patterns that have been outlined so far provide some insight into the social and political situation of the Restoration period at Rye. An energetic mercantile elite kept up a modest level of commercial prosperity that helped to support the small tradesmen and artisans of the town. Most of the merchants, however, were religious Dissenters, who were prevented from holding office in the corporation. Supported by trading connections with each other, as well as with associates in London and other small ports, the Dissenting merchants formed a tight, protective economic nexus that was able to withstand the pressure to conform. At the bottom of Rye's social scale were impoverished fishermen resentful of French encroachments, tradesmen who might turn to smuggling because they could not be sure of their livelihood, and the dependent poor, whose lives were under the constant scrutiny of parish officers and town magistrates. Comprising the vast majority of the town's residents, the poor and "poorer sort" were not likely to rally behind the defence of a town government that seemed to have failed in defending their interests. Nor did they have much attachment to a national regime that had burdened them with settlement laws, allowed foreigners to invade the fisheries, and levied new taxes on French goods. They would provide the radicals with the popular support they needed to overturn the moderates and seize control of Rye.

RADICAL CULTURE

The Compton Census of 1676 found about three hundred adult Protestant Dissenters in Rye, the same as the number attending Anglican services. The figure gives a sharply defined picture of how polarized the town was. By comparison, about one-quarter of the inhabitants of Rye's member port of Tenterden, about one-quarter of Old Romney, and one-third of Lewes were Dissenters. Most rural areas were overwhelmingly Anglican. No Dissenters resided in Playden, and only two were reported among the 215 adult inhabitants of Brede. The village of Smarden near Tenterden, however, contained 110 adult Anglicans and 100 Dissenters, including Baptists, Brownists, and three or four followers of the radical prophet Lodowick Muggleton! Towns did not always harbour sectarians; in fact, the Dissenting population of St. Clement's Hastings was less than 3 percent of the total.[21] Evidently, religious Dissent in East Sussex was mostly confined to towns with a strong Puritan tradition, like Rye.

It would be wrong, however, to simplify party conflict at Rye into an outright confrontation between Dissenters and Anglicans. The town corporation was dominated between 1661 and 1679 by men who had not entirely abandoned the Puritan ideal of godly order, and who were often no more than half-hearted Anglicans. They were less concerned than their Puritan predecessors with moral offences such as swearing, but they took Sabbath-breaking just as seriously. Violators of the Sabbath continued to be presented to the sessions court: nine of them in 1663, nine more in 1666, three in 1670 (all women accused of fetching water), a record sixteen in 1678, and two in 1679. Many of the miscreants were brewers and innkeepers, selling beer. The fines were sixpence or a shilling, far less than under the Commonwealth and probably less resented. Concern for Sunday observance also motivated an ordinance of 1673, which lamented that "the Saboth hath often been violated to the Greate dishonor of Allmighty God" by unruly corporate procession to the church on holy days. The proposed solution (probably not very effective) was to make the procession leave the mayor's house precisely at nine o'clock, to avoid the crowds entering the church.[22]

If strict observance of the Sabbath was a mark of Puritanism, then the royalist magistrates of Rye were still in some sense Puritans. Several of them were also fined or excommunicated by the Lewes archdeaconry court for failing to attend the Anglican parish church. (Excommunication has an awful ring to it, but was reversible by payment of a small fine.) The archdeaconry court records for 1660–79 include many names that we might expect to see cited for not coming to church: Samuel Jeake, Thomas Miller, and Nicholas Skinner, as well as Thomas and Martha Grebell, children of the Puritan mayor. More surprisingly, they include men who were political enemies of Jeake, especially Lewis Gillart junior and the butcher John Crouch the elder, who "never received the Sacramant but when made jurats or for other advantages." As late as 1682, the moderate mayor Thomas Crouch was accused, apparently by one of the Breads family, of absenting himself from church for a full twelve months. When Crouch died later the same year, the words "a lover of his King and the Church of England" were inscribed on his memorial in a belated attempt to refute the charge against him. Church taxes or rates were another source of friction with the archdeaconry court. The town clerk Thomas Tournay, leader of the radical party, was excommunicated in 1675 for refusing to pay church tax; but a similar charge was made against the moderate jurat James Welsh, who served as a churchwarden.[23] Apparently, strict submission to the Church of England was not the rule even among those who were known as Anglicans.

In short, religious differences between the reformers and the moderates were a matter of degree. The same can be said about wealth: the two sides were different, but not in entirely separate categories. Leaving out of consideration the plutocrat Dissenter Lewis Gillart senior, by far the richest man in Rye, whose family switched political sides after his death, we can conclude that the moderates were generally richer than the Dissenters, but not by much. An estate tax list of 1660 evaluated both their real estate (property) and personal estate (money, possessions). The moderate jurats James Welsh and Thomas Crouch junior were two of the wealthiest men in Rye, with personal estates totalling more than £300 each. Mayor Mark Thomas junior, owner of £50 of real estate, was one of the town's largest property holders. Apart from Samuel Jeake, none of the Dissenters owned as much real estate as the leading moderates. The personal estates of the Dissenting merchants Nicholas Skinner and William Key were valued at £250 and £200 respectively, slightly behind Welsh and Crouch. The hearth tax records of 1663 suggest that the moderate and radical leaders lived in similar sized houses (innkeepers like the Cadmans have to be excluded from consideration). Mark Thomas junior's house had nine hearths, James Welsh's five, and Richard Norton's eight plus five more in a second house. On the radical side, the Grebell home had four hearths and Jeake the elder only two, but his friends Skinner, Key, and Thomas Miller had five apiece, and the expelled freeman Thomas Palmer, whom we met in the last chapter as a furious critic of Mayor Welsh, had seven. Geography divided the two groups more strongly. All of the moderates lived at the foot of the hill in the Landgate, the richest town ward. The radicals were more spread out. Among the Dissenting freemen who were expelled from the corporation in 1662, three lived in the Landgate ward, while three others, including Samuel Jeake, resided in the less affluent Middlestreet ward, around the present Mermaid Street.[24]

The sources of wealth may provide the best key to political affiliations. The moderates Thomas, Crouch, and Welsh were less active in mercantile trade than their opponents, and seem to have invested more heavily in property. The most active merchants, such as Palmer, Jeake, Miller, Skinner, and Key, tended to support the radicals, whereas the town's brewers and butchers were divided between the two sides. No brewer or butcher was a member of Jeake's inner religious circle, but several of them hovered on its edges, among them the prominent brewer-innkeeper Michael Cadman, owner of the Mermaid Inn.

How do the Dissenters of Rye compare with those in other places? In London during the Restoration period, independent mercantile capitalism was often associated with religious dissent. All of the Dissenting merchants of Rye, in fact, had close connections with London, and Thomas Miller's business was run from there after 1680. At Bristol, on the other hand, Dissent drew its main strength from artisans and tradesmen rather than merchants. Dissent in Bristol, however, also appealed to small-scale free traders who challenged the privileges of the company of Merchant Venturers.[25] The independent Dissenting merchants of Rye were cast in the same free-trading mould. As inhabitants of the Cinque Ports, they were relatively unhampered by external controls and were able to do business with men of similar religious and political opinions. For them, economic individualism and religious sectarianism went hand in hand.

Dissent at Rye was preserved by marriage alliances. Samuel Jeake the elder's sister Anne took William Key as her second husband, and Jeake's sister-in-law Mary Hartridge married the Baptist preacher Christopher Blackwood. In the next generation, John Mackley, who became the younger Jeake's main business contact in London, married William Key's daughter Elizabeth; and Lewis Gillart's daughter became the wife of John Byndlos, one of Jeake the elder's closest friends. "Cozen" is a term that appears with great frequency in the Jeake correspondence. Apprenticeship, which involved living in a master's household, provided another significant tie among co-religionists. The woollen draper Thomas Markwicke, for example served as an apprentice in the household of Thomas Miller. In the mid-1660s, Jeake the elder and the Reverend John Allin spent a good deal of time and trouble helping John Osmonton of Rye to find a suitable apprenticeship with an "honest man" in London. He ended up as a schoolteacher in Ashford.[26]

Like friendships, personal animosities had a role to play in determining religious alliances, as is shown by the example of the Gillarts, who shifted from radicals to moderates in one generation. Judging by the amount he was assessed on the 1660 tax list, Lewis Gillart senior had wealth beyond anyone else in Rye, with an estate of about £10,000, or thirty times what any other inhabitant of the town was worth. Shunning the Church-going high society of the Landgate, he continued to live in the impoverished Strandgate, in a big house with seven hearths. According to his will, written in 1673 and witnessed by "my Loving ffreind Samuel Jeake senior," Gillart depended "on the meritts of Jesus Christ to receive remission of my sinns," which implies that he was a strict Calvinist. His eldest son Lewis, however, was to inherit only his "Mansion house" and a small bequest for a remembrance ring. He appointed his Dissenting son-in-law John Byndlos as executor of the estate, giving him the authority to divide Gillart's personal estate among the heirs. This caused deep bitterness among his offspring. In a letter to Jeake, Byndlos worried that being executor "will be troublesome to me," but he noted of his father-in-law that "I value his reputation equall with my owne & had hee not such ill children I woulde take his words for more then I am worth."[27] Within two years of his father's death in 1678, one of those "ill children," Lewis Gillart junior, had become a leader of the moderate faction and a violent enemy to Samuel Jeake and his friends. Surely, resentment at the terms of his father's will pushed him in that direction.

The Dissenting radicals may have been set apart from the moderates in more subtle, cultural ways as well, at least in the early years of the Restoration. They tended to live abstemiously, without engaging in much conspicuous consumption. If William Key was typical, the Rye Dissenters did not fill their homes with luxury goods. An inventory of his estate drawn up by his brother-in-law Samuel Jeake the elder after his death in 1666 reveals that in his house, besides furniture and household linens,

Key had eleven "paper pictures" or prints, seven rings, a watch, "a Bible with some other small bookes, a sea Booke & two sea chartes in paper." His warehouse, by contrast, was crammed with Normandy canvas, cambric, flaxen sheets, Holland sheets, tablecloths, and napkins.[28] Whereas ownership of books and pictures was a sign of expanding household consumption, Key's luxury possessions—his Bible, nautical books, prints, and watch—served practical or didactic purposes.[29] His jewellery included such sentimental keepsakes as a wedding ring and a mourning ring, probably in memory of his wife who had died in 1655. He had nothing that was primarily a token of wealth. The correspondence of the elder Jeake gives a similar impression of restrained habits of consumption. He purchased many books, often from estate sales, and on one occasion bought some globes, but he seldom gave or received gifts and never mentioned the purchase of a luxury item other than those that were to be included in his library. The Dissenters of Rye do not seem to have invested in gold or silver plate; neither did they buy expensive types of furniture.[30] It is notable that not a single painted portrait of any of them is known to have existed.

We should not exaggerate the cultural divide between radicals and moderates. During the Restoration period, very little is known about the local distribution of the perishable goods on which consumer demand in early modern England was founded, namely tobacco, sugar products, and caffeine drinks. That tobacco was smoked at Rye is certain—John Byndlos once gave Samuel Jeake the elder "a small token of my Love which is a tobacco stopper," and later sent him "a paper worth your reading" wrapped up in "a Paper of Tobacco." The addictive weed must have been locally available in shops, and a shilling's worth of it was distributed to the group of maimed soldiers who passed through the town in 1680. Rye did not trade directly with the sugar colonies of the West Indies, and unlike Deal or other small ports, it did not participate in the slave trade. Tea is not mentioned until it became a major smuggled commodity in the early eighteenth century. As for durable goods, lighter-weight fabrics and books were certainly available at Rye, but they were mostly sent down from London, which made them expensive. The local glass and pottery industries had largely vanished, and port records do not often mention these goods.[31]

What set the elder Jeake and his friends firmly apart from the other inhabitants of Rye was something less concrete than possessions: namely, their desire to introduce godliness into every aspect of their lives. They were not always sure what this should mean in a practical sense. For example, Jeake wondered whether vegetarianism was demanded of Christians, and after considering the question, he became "very sparing & [had] seldome eaten either blood or things strangled sometimes doubting lest through my ignorance I might breake one of God's least commandments."[32] He and his friends agonized over such behavioural questions, as well as over more explicit doctrinal issues such as the lawfulness of infant baptism.

A similar note of anxiety about what was godly could appear when Rye Dissenters thought about human love. They did not hesitate to enlist religion in the service of courtship, but it blended strangely with more profane themes. When Richard Hartshorne, master of the Peacock School, wrote in 1663 to his paramour, the recently widowed Barbara Harding, he began with the sighs of an unrequited suitor: "Ah my Dear (but unkind) Heart. Hath not all my Love merited a line from thee to be satisfied of thy welfare? I have not forgotten since I was promised letters full of kisses, and that often." His amorous discontent was quick to enter a more erotic vein: "oh that I might enjoy thee one night instead of every nights dreames on thee."

A few lines later, however, we find the godly lover's entreaties unexpectedly merging with thoughts of the final days and divine judgement:

> the God of Heaven mollify thy hard heart, and make it more naturall and not so stony to me. I know thou expetest [*sic*] mercy at gods hands (which I pray God Grant in the hour of Death & day of Judgement) but how canst thou looke for any & exercise so much cruelty & falseness? Indeed if there were not another world it would not at all matter what our acions were, but My Love there will be a time of searching all the secrets of our hearts, no covers nor pretences can cloake us from the seeing eye of God.[33]

What was Mrs. Harding's response to the eschatological onslaught of her godly lover? Reader, she married him.

Love was not a common theme in the writings of the Rye Dissenters, although judgement certainly was. Given this rhetorical emphasis, did godliness make the Dissenters more loving than their neighbours with regard to the less fortunate? The historian Paul Slack has argued that "godly cities" in the Tudor and early Stuart period were keen to address social problems like poverty and indigence, but most of the efforts of the Rye Puritans before 1660 had to do with discipline rather than relief.[34] A hint of greater compassion, however, may be detected in a letter written in 1662 to the corporation by the Dissenting lawyer Samuel Gott. In his opinion, "one settled in a Parish & begging there is not a vagrant who may be sent to the place of birth for a Vagrant is one that doth Vagari or goe begging a roguing from place to place." Gott at least acknowledged that the poor could not be disposed of by conveying them elsewhere. On a personal

level, some Rye Dissenters of the Restoration era were generous in assisting the poor. Samuel Jeake the younger's ledger reveals that he regularly gave one-tenth of his "clear profit" in alms
every year. In 1680 he noted £15.15.02 "distributed to necessitous
persons," with an additional £1.15.08 in goods given to Elizabeth Steed. Whether the moderates of Rye were less giving than
Jeake is impossible to say, but under their guidance the corporation was not known for its generosity. We have already noted the
tight-fistedness of the overseers of the poor, who were Anglicans
rather than Dissenters. The local poor rate was actually lowered
in 1665, at a time of distress during the second Dutch war.[35] The
perception that Dissenters were more charitable than Anglicans
to the lowest classes of Rye had some substance, and it may have
helped them gather political support from "the poorer sort" in
1679–82.

The economic, social, and cultural divisions of Rye relate to a
debate among historians about how the emergence of party politics in 1679–83 should be interpreted. Some have argued that national events gave rise to the Whig and Tory parties; others have
emphasized the polarizing effects of local conflicts.[36] Among the
latter is Paul Halliday, who has paid special attention to Rye.
The version of events offered here owes a lot to Halliday's account, but it differs in some respects from his conclusions.[37] I will
argue that factionalism between radicals and moderates, rather
than Whigs and Tories, remained the basis of politics in Rye
until after the Glorious Revolution. Whig and Tory designa-
tions were sometimes used, but they neither fully replaced nor
precisely duplicated older distinctions. The language of the Civil
War period persisted. One of the elder Jeake's friends, for example, referred to the radical faction as "the despised Interest
of our Dear Lord Jesus in Rye." Harkening back to 1642, the
customs collector Robert Hall wrote of Rye that "they have

two parties, one for the King, the other for the country."[38] The newer party ideologies, which dealt with a broad range of religious, constitutional, and socio-economic issues, took a decade to establish themselves in the town.

Rye was different from larger English towns, like London, Bristol, Exeter, Norwich, or Newcastle, where Whig and Tory party structures emerged quickly in 1679–80, and politicians won popular support through party-based publicity campaigns. Rye was not big enough to sustain a partisan press, and although it had many connections with London, it was too remote to be affected directly by the frenzied publicity of London politics. The radicals of Rye knew what was going on in the capital, but they do not seem to have purchased contemporary political pamphlets, broadsides, or illustrated prints. None of the voluminous pamphlet literature associated with the Exclusion Crisis appears in the comprehensive list of Samuel Jeake the elder's library, although he possessed many radical political works of the 1640s and 1650s, including Leveller and republican writings.[39]

Rye was also distinct from nearby towns like Lewes, where the Tory party was constructed on Anglican religious identity and was bolstered by the local gentry.[40] The Church of England was weak in Rye, and the Sussex gentry had very little influence. As a result, there were as few Tories in the town as there had been Arminians or Civil War royalists. Yet Rye was not unique; it resembled not only the other Cinque Ports but also small boroughs like Sudbury or Coventry, where Puritanism had once burned very brightly. Most of these small towns were located in or on the edge of the upland zones that David Underdown has identified with political and religious individualism. After 1688, the majority of them became safe Whig strongholds and eventually turned into "rotten boroughs." They provided the Whigs with their majorities in Parliament, and for that reason alone they are worth studying. Their political history in the late Stuart period is characterized less by struggles over party principles than by the slow, difficult birth of a Whig oligarchy that absorbed both the radicals and the moderates of the Restoration period.

RADICAL RESURGENCE

Before the late 1670s, parliamentary elections gave the radicals only a feeble spark of life in Rye. In 1667, a minor Kentish land-owner, Sir John Austen, was chosen by the freemen to represent the town over a court candidate, "to the great dissatisfaction of his Majesty's friends," according to James Welsh. Unlike Samuel Gott, however, Austen was not a Dissenter, and he had no re-forming ambitions. Here, then, was the archetypical court Whig of the future—which is exactly what Sir John Austen became under William and Mary.[41] More radical sentiments abruptly resurfaced eleven years later, when Titus Oates revealed the fab-ricated details of the Popish Plot. "Whereas by the providence of Allmighty God a Horrid Plott hath been lately discovered," declared the assembly book in December 1678, "wherein was de-signed not onely the Murder of his Sacred Ma.tie but the sub-version of the Protestant Religion and introduceing Popery into the Nation," special measures of defence had become necessary. An armed watch was appointed to keep guard at night against murderous Catholics.[42] No Rye magistrate could find fault with the ordinance, but it was infused with a Protestant zeal that must have energized the radical faction.

Within nine months, the radicals had managed to elect a new mayor, the illiterate fellmonger Benjamin Marten, possibly the son of Alice Marten, the last witch accused in Rye. Marten was said to be controlled by the town clerk, Thomas Tournay, a law-yer from Dover who was also town clerk of Hythe. A consum-mate politician, Tournay persuaded Marten to allow the seven Dissenting freemen who had been excluded in 1662 to vote in the parliamentary election of fall 1679, so as to insure the return of Sir John Darrell, a Kentish gentleman who wanted to exclude the Catholic James, Duke of York, from the succession. The moderates, led by Thomas Crouch, Lewis Gillart junior, and Robert Hall, now had an issue. In letters to the secretary of state, they howled about the readmitted freemen, fumed that the town was governed by Dissenters, and accused Darrell of being recommended by "the fanatics of Canterbury." In the spring of 1680, the Privy Council made inquiries about whether members of the corporation had recently taken the Anglican sacrament and sworn the necessary oaths. Embarrassingly for the moderates, the only one who clearly had not was the king's supposed friend, Lewis Gillart junior.[43]

Having satisfied the Privy Council, Tournay and his supporters seemed secure. In the mayoral elections of August 1680, "the fanatics" successfully put forward a suspended customs officer turned schoolmaster, Thomas Burdett. To offset his evident lack of occupational status, he was described as "Armigerous" (bearing a coat-of-arms) in the assembly book! True to Puritan tradition, Burdett immediately reinstated presentments "ffor prophane Swearing & Cursing." Among the foul-mouthed miscreants were the innkeeper Aaron Peadle, a leading moderate, and the jurat Lewis Gillart junior, each of whom was fined a shilling for swearing at two successive sessions.[44]

Even more galling to the moderates was the parliamentary election of March 1681, when the radicals nominated John Tedman, who was said to be a Fifth Monarchy man. Tedman came over from France at the start of the Exclusion Crisis, and was immediately jailed for refusing the oaths of allegiance to Charles II. After he had "ingratiated himself with the factious people here," he was set at liberty by Mayor Burdett. Francis Lightfoot, the collector of customs at Rye, in a letter to the secretary of state, described Tedman as having "a very voluble and fluent tongue," and accused him of treasonable expressions in an address to the freemen of Rye. According to Lightfoot, Tedman implicated King Charles in the Popish Plot and vilified the House of Lords, which had thrown out the first Exclusion Bill, by asking rhetorically, "what lords were they? The very footmen of the others [the Exclusionists] were better men than those lords were." Highly offended by such anti-aristocratic talk, Sir John Darrell refused to support the fiery radical. In the end, Tedman's "ragged regiment" failed to unseat Thomas Frewen, an anti-Exclusionist or Tory. Yet to Frewen's fifteen votes Tedman won eleven, six of them from the ejected freemen. After losing the election by this narrow margin, Tedman went up to London with the younger Jeake's brother-in-law, Nathaniel Hartshorne, whom he helped to place in an apprenticeship.[45]

The Tedman candidacy seemed to confirm that Rye's new governors were not simply Exclusionists or Whigs, but the old saints of the Commonwealth, now supported by "the rabble." Their electoral failure, however, emboldened the moderates, who staged a coup at the mayoral elections in August 1681. With the support of nine freemen, Thomas Crouch was declared mayor before their opponents were allowed to vote. When Lewis Gillart junior tried to administer the oaths of supremacy and allegiance to Crouch, a radical named John Spaine crossed the bar dividing the jurats from the freemen and "tore the said Mr. Gillart by the haire of the head and tooke from him the Booke wherein the said Oathes were contayned." The six ejected freemen, including the elder Jeake, then refused to take the oaths. Instead, they joined with five other freemen to elect Thomas Tournay as mayor. A petition to the king and Privy Council accused the six of "Confederating" with "divers other persons knowne Phanaticks, to disturbe yor. Ma.ties peace and the quietnesse of us yor. Subjects here." [46]

The situation at Rye was now of national concern. In September, the elder Jeake and his friends were summoned before Charles II and his Privy Council. The confrontation between the old Dissenter and the king was tense and memorable. According to his son, Jeake gave a tart reply to the king when asked "why he transgressed the Laws in preaching in a Conventicle," responding "that if he did transgress the Laws, his Majesties Courts were open." Dryly, King Charles "told him that if he were so much for Law, he should have it." Jeake's meeting house was shut down, and Crouch was confirmed as mayor. In a gesture of fairness, however, the Privy Council informed Tournay that "he may pursue the due Course of Law for his Releife."[47]

He did so. Tournay took his complaint to the court of King's Bench at Westminster, hoping to obtain a writ of mandamus, which was an order to a corporation to carry out a designated responsibility. In spite of efforts to stop him by Crouch and the attorney general, Tournay obtained his writ, with an additional order from the Lord Chief Justice to swear him as mayor. In a confusing twist, however, a suit by Tournay against Crouch for denying him the staff and "ensigns of mayoralty" was denied, and Tournay had to make a further motion to the court "that he might be quietly possessed of the mayoralty." The judges "told him he might quiet himself as well he could, but they did not see any title he had to it."

This equivocal answer was followed by unequivocal action. Tournay appeared at the Rye marketplace with three hundred supporters—an incredible number in a town with only six hundred adult inhabitants. They "would have gone into court to take possession," but were stopped by Lewis Gillart junior and some constables. Mayor Crouch made a complaint of the riot to King's Bench. The court repeated its initial opinion, that Tournay was the rightful mayor. Buoyed by the favourable decision, Tournay, Burdett, Marten, and Cadman, "with a rabble of near 300," marched again on the town hall and broke open its doors.

They chose a day when Crouch and his allies were in Hastings, where they had gone to oppose "the Fanaticks" there in a dispute over the election of parish officers. After seating himself and swearing in his jurats, Tournay ordered new locks to be put on the doors so that his enemies could not enter. The new mayor's success has been credited to King's Bench, and to judicial adherence "to a strict reading of legal propriety." At the time, however, his opponents ascribed it to the influence of Tournay's friend, Sir John Fagge of Wiston, on the chief justice. The threat of violence also played a part. As surely as a writ of mandamus, and more forcefully, popular acclaim had restored Thomas Tournay as mayor of Rye.[48]

The three months of his mayoralty, from June to September 1682, were marked by frenetic activity. Twelve new freemen who had been created by Mayor Crouch were disenfranchised, and Tournay nominated thirteen of his own, including John Breads and Joseph Breads. Many of Tournay's freemen belonged to families whose names had not appeared in recent town records. Presumably, they were less affluent than Crouch's freemen, or were perhaps more recent arrivals in the town. The rights of the freemen deprived in 1662 were recognized, and enemies of the radicals were targeted for retribution. The town clerk and Lewis Gillart junior were both thrown in jail. Even the vicar, William Williams, was summoned before the sessions, accused of "being the author and promoter of the differences in the town." In revenge, Williams complained to the bishop of Chichester that Tournay's ally Thomas Burdett had been speaking in favour of the Covenanting rebels in Scotland. "The spirit of anarchy and sedition," Williams moaned, "has prevailed amongst the generality of our people." He had no doubt about who had caused all the trouble: it was that "amphibious creature between an attorney and a scrivener," Samuel Jeake the elder.[49]

Tournay's mayoralty was what Jeake had been waiting for

since 1660. It was a radical revolution in miniature, and it enjoyed broad popular approval. Had it begun two years earlier, it might have moved further towards instituting godly rule; but it came too late, because by the summer of 1682 the Whigs were almost everywhere in retreat before a resurgent royalist party. In London, one of their last strongholds, they lost the mayoralty in 1681 and were defeated in a crucial contest over the election of the city sheriffs in July 1682.[50] Throughout England, the royalists or Tories were regaining power, with the assistance of the crown and of local landowners.

Tournay's re-election as mayor of Rye in August 1682 was a last hurrah for the local radicals. The election was attended by several apprehensive gentlemen of East Sussex who were also freemen of the town, among them Sir Denny Ashburnham and Thomas Frewen. Tournay's rival Thomas Crouch had died suddenly three weeks before. Lewis Gillart junior was prepared to stand against the mayor in a grudge match, but Ashburnham proposed a compromise candidate, the illiterate butcher Joseph Radford, "a quiet, peaceable and indifferent person." The radicals, "would hear of no accommodation, being animated thereto by Sir John Fagg and Sir John Dorrell," according to Reverend Williams. Tournay was then chosen by a majority of freemen, including those ejected in 1662. Their qualifications were not recognized by Radford's supporters, who proclaimed their own man to be elected. Some of the local gentlemen who were justices of the peace had to be recruited to give the mayoral oaths to the hapless Radford. At this, his indignant rival left the hall with his friends, among them all but one of the jurats. Carrying a white wand and with the mayoral mace before him, Tournay "was saluted as Mayor by a factious rabble prepared for that purpose." Radford went to law, challenging Tournay's victory through a suit at the court of Chancery, and petitioning the Privy Council. After losing the court case, Tournay locked Radford out of the town hall, denying him access to the corporation records. When the moderates finally got into the building, Tournay declared the assembly dissolved and withdrew, accompanied this time by two other jurats. In November, the Privy Council recognized Radford as mayor, ordering Tournay to "forbeare to intermeddle in the administration of the said Office."[51] The revolution was over.

Persecution

What followed was a series of purges and persecutions instigated by the agents of central government. In the end, local control was curtailed along with "fanaticism." The moderates began with the disenfranchisement of Tournay's freemen and a vendetta against his radical supporters.[52] It is notable that such extreme action had not previously been taken against the radicals. Reverend Williams had tried to present Jeake and his friends to the archdeaconry court in 1681 for absenting themselves from church, but he was unable to find witnesses, presumably because it looked at that point as if the sectarians might win.[53]

Within twelve months, the situation had changed. The number of presentments to the archdeaconry court for year-long absences from church doubled. Jeake the elder, Thomas Grebell, and Thomas Miller were excommunicated. Religious prosecutions shifted from ecclesiastical to civil courts, where the penalties were more severe. Lewis Gillart junior informed at the Crown Office in October 1682 against the elder Jeake and six others for Nonconformity, "against wch they to thier great cost & troble defended till the death of King Charles terminated the Sute." A more direct purge ensued. At midnight on Sunday, 18 March 1683, Radford, Gillart, and the newly appointed customs collector, Robert Hall, broke into the house of Thomas Miller, where Thomas Markwicke was preaching to an illegal

religious conventicle. Goods belonging to Miller and Markwicke were confiscated and sold. Members of the congregation
were fined. According to Samuel Jeake the younger, "we were
afterwards forced to meet in several parcells in our own families with 3 or 4 besides." During the summer of 1683, as rumours
about a Whig plot to kill the king proliferated, the house of
Jeake the younger was searched twice. The result was an exodus
from Rye to London of religious Dissenters, including both
Jeakes and Thomas Miller. The younger Jeake returned in 1684,
to face further harassment from Gillart and from the vicar, who
had been named a jurat.[54]

The new mayor and jurats initiated a spate of prosecutions
for scandalous and seditious words at the 1683 sessions. Thomas
Daniel was informed against for saying that Joseph Radford
"was as much Mayor as his Arse." Henry Duck was alleged to
have responded to the suppression of Miller's conventicle by
asking about the corporation, "Why don't the Towne rise & kill
'em all." When told that the king had power to replace a mayor,
Thomas Sargent reportedly answered with the remark, "Then
he is King absolute." Cornelius Gilliam of Brighton was accused
by a customs officer of saying, in a conversation at the victualling
house of Bartholomew Breads, that "he would goe a hundred
Miles to save" the king's illegitimate son, the Duke of Mon-
mouth.[55] All of these men were seamen, and none was a person of much social consequence in the town. Their prosecutions
revealed the nervousness of the magistrates about the political
sentiments of the common people. Still, this did not amount to
a political witch-hunt. The only radical leader who was prosecuted for seditious words was Thomas Tournay; but this happened at the Kent Assizes, not at Rye. Convicted in December
1685, Tournay was pardoned on the petition of Robert Hall, then
mayor of Rye, who thought the former radical was "now willing

to agree to such points as may be of use to the town and for the encouragement of the loyal men there."[56]

In many respects, Rye experienced a Tory reaction after 1682, such as happened elsewhere in the kingdom. The corporation attempted to turn its back on "the late Troubles" and bury "a Juncture of time when ffaction and Sedition were paramount."[57] In other respects, however, it was hardly Tory and not much of a reaction. For a start, apart from Reverend Williams and the churchwarden Joseph Radford, few of the leaders of Rye in this period can be identified as loyal Churchmen. As has been seen, Lewis Gillart junior was no church-goer and probably remained a Dissenter at heart. The vicar did not hesitate to report Henry Darrington, the new town clerk and Thomas Crouch's son-in-law, to the archdeaconry court for not paying church rates, although he was excused because he had no property in the town.[58] The degree of reaction, moreover, was limited. The Dissenting radicals of Jeake's conventicle were harshly persecuted, but those who did not worship with them, such as the innkeeper Michael Cadman or the ex-Mayor Thomas Burdett, were left alone. Finally, the corporation did not simply become a tool of the Tory government at Whitehall. The mayor and jurats continued to defend their own privileges against outside intrusions. In fact, they at first denied the traditional right of the lord warden to nominate one of the two members of Parliament, although they changed their minds when the elections for the Parliament of 1685 approached.[59]

The decision to accept a new charter from James II in 1685 has been seen as a craven abdication by the magistrates of the town's interests. Although it became one of the most notorious incidents in Rye's history, it was not simply a sell-out to Stuart "absolutism." The appeal for a new charter was unanimously voiced by an assembly that included several radical freemen. The jurats wanted broad acceptance for this bold move, so freemen who absented themselves from the ensuing discussions (which many did) were fined. Rye had never had a separate charter; rather, it had been included in those of the Cinque Ports, the latest version of which had been granted in 1668. Those charters made little reference to town governance.[60] It was far from clear, therefore, exactly what the corporation was giving up when it decreed in September 1685 that all its existing charters were "forthwith humbly yeilded up Surrendred and Granted unto our Sovereigne Lord James the second." The new charter, issued in March 1686, was far more specific about governance than those of the Cinque Ports had been. The number of jurats was fixed at twelve (most mayors had named between five and eight), and the common council of twenty-four freemen was restored. Only the jurats and common councillors, not the full body of freemen, could vote for members of Parliament. In practice this did not mean a smaller electorate, as there had rarely been more than thirty active freemen. The most important provision of the new charter allowed the corporation to levy an annual property tax on all inhabitants of the town. The revenues of Rye, based on fines and land rentals, were steadily decreasing, so this was a welcome innovation.[61]

For all that, it would be a mistake to represent the new charter as nothing more than a consensual effort at administrative rationalization. It was obviously intended to assert royal power over Rye, by revoking traditional rights and practices. Many other towns were subjected to the same type of drastic remodelling under James II.[62] The surrender was managed by Mayor Robert Hall, who as a customs officer was a representative of central authority. By naming them as jurats, moreover, the new charter entrenched the authority of Anglican royalists such as Hall and Reverend Williams. This must have irked local Dissenters, who were still excluded from government.

Yet the granting of the new charter was followed by an end to the persecution of Dissenters. In April 1686, Samuel Jeake the younger was named by the county sessions as overseer of the poor for Rye foreign, the part of the parish lying outside the town.[63] A more dramatic political change was the rapid rise of John Spaine, who in 1682 had torn Lewis Gillart junior's hair in the town hall. Spaine suddenly reappeared in the assembly book in February 1687, when he accompanied the mayor, Charles Crouch, to a meeting at Romney to discuss the renewal of the Cinque Ports charter. By the fall of that year, Samuel Jeake the younger was rejoicing at the "news about the alteration of Magistrates at Rye, & the putting in of Whigs & dissenters," although he later noted that this was based on "vain reports." Nevertheless, in August 1688, Spaine was named a jurat by Mayor Crouch, and within a week he had been elected as mayor. Spaine was a "Whig collaborator" with James II, who wanted the support of Whigs and Dissenters for his policy of religious toleration. His advancement was engineered by Mayor Crouch, who was following the well-established policy of re-integrating defeated opponents. The moderates still comprised the majority of jurats and continued to hold the upper hand in the corporation.[64]

Yet some of them seem to have been rethinking their allegiances. As early as February 1688, an insulting reference to the king was recorded in the assembly book, where he was titled "King *over* [rather than of] England." The author of this jibe was the town clerk Henry Darrington, once an ardent royalist. If he was hoping for another upheaval in local and national government, he was about to have his wish. By the time John Spaine became mayor, a Dutch invasion was imminent, as the insistent reports of Captain Robert Hall made clear. The king needed reliable supporters as magistrates of the Cinque Ports, and his attitude towards "Whig collaborators" became very confused. At the end of September 1688, Hall obtained an order in council to depose John Spaine and have himself named mayor. Henry Darrington was also removed by order, but he refused to hand over the town records. Whether Captain Hall was ever sworn in is unclear. In any case, the orders were undermined in early November by an unexpected writ of mandamus from the court of King's Bench, restoring seven freemen named by Thomas Tournay, including John Breads. The writ had been granted in connection with a desperate last-minute proclamation by the beleaguered James, reversing earlier proceedings against borough charters. It was too late; William of Orange had already landed, and in late December, King James fled to France.[65] Would the radicals now have another chance to make Rye into the biblical city on a hill?

The End of Radical Rye

The Glorious Revolution of 1688 passed in Rye with only one violent incident. Just before William's arrival, thirty armed French sailors from a Dieppe privateer landed at the town and engaged some Rye mariners in a brisk fight. The French government supported James II and wanted to forestall a Dutch invasion, so this could have turned into a serious confrontation. Pistols were shot off, swords were waved about, insults were exchanged ("Bougre je vous turay [*sic*]!" was the fiercest), but nobody was badly injured. The master of the privateer paid a £12 fine to the corporation. The intervention of the *corsaires* of Dieppe did nothing to help James II, who seems to have made himself extremely unpopular in the port of Rye.

Samuel Jeake the younger wrote of the king that "destruction came upon him like a Whirlwind," and he was right. In early December, some fishermen from Faversham in Kent abused both the fleeing James, whom they mistook for a Jesuit, and Sir Edward Hales, the lord warden of the Cinque Ports. The mariners of Rye probably had similar views about the Catholic monarch and his minions as their counterparts at Faversham, but they were not given an opportunity to act on them.[66]

The immediate effect of the Revolution at Rye was to restore the radicals, who tried to erase the past seven years of political history. The younger Jeake exulted: "now through the mercifull Providence of God, we were freed from the fears of Popery & Persecution."[67] At the first assembly meeting after the Revolution, most of Thomas Tournay's freemen were in attendance, along with the three survivors of the 1662 purge: Thomas Tutty, Nicholas Skinner, and Samuel Jeake the elder. Their opponents Lewis Gillart junior, Joseph Radford, and Robert Hall did not appear. A long ordinance was passed, reciting the struggles between Tournay and Crouch, who "in an insolent and Violent manner seised the Ensignes of the Mairalty." Joseph Radford was said to have "usurped" the mayor's office from Tournay. The freemen created by Crouch and Radford were disenfranchised. To perpetuate the radical heritage, the younger Thomas Grebell was made a freeman, along with Samuel Jeake the younger. Jeake's brother-in-law Nathaniel Hartshorne, a ne'er-do-well who as a troubled London apprentice had been jailed for burglary and had become an informer against radical plotters, was named as the town clerk. Jeake the elder, again a man of honour, was asked to draw up leases and rentals for the town. He was considered for the office of town clerk by some of the freemen, but "their Courage failing them to chuse a Dissenter slurr'd it." John Breads, the town sergeant under Tournay, was ordered to be paid his arrears of salary for the last seven years.[68]

The radical millennium, however, had not arrived. In the elections for the convention that would settle the crown, the radical Peter Gott, son of Jeake the elder's godly friend, came bottom of the poll at Rye, behind the moderate Whigs Sir John Darrell and Sir John Austen and the country Tory Thomas Frewen.[69] It was a major defeat for the radicals. In the following months, the Revolution settlement was decided by moderates from both the Whig and Tory parties. The subsequent Toleration Act granted most Protestant Dissenters the freedom to worship, but an attempt by the Whigs to repeal the Corporations Act and allow Dissenters to serve in town government failed.[70] This meant that the Jeakes and their friends could not legally hold offices in Rye. A further blow to the radicals was the defeat of a bill to restore corporations by excluding from office those who had surrendered charters. Although the 1686 Rye charter became ineffective and was declared illegal at a 1691 Brotherhood and Guestling of the Cinque Ports, its supporters were not ostracised. In fact, two of those who were most despised by the radicals, Lewis Gillart junior and Joseph Radford, returned as jurats in 1690.[71]

For their part, the radicals seem to have been drifting. It is doubtful whether they would have known what to do if the millennium had begun. Their conviction that godly rule was imminent seems to have weakened, as they had become increasingly concerned with the twists and turns of Providence that governed their daily lives. Their sights were fixed more on this world than on the next. The change can be observed in the writings and correspondence of the two Jeakes between the 1660s and the 1680s. After the Restoration, the elder Samuel met persecution with defiant separatism, counselling his friends in 1665 that "The Prophet [Isaiah] intends the Saints must remove their Stations from the Tents of ungodly men." In the same year, he preached on "Reasons why the Saints should hope." He concluded that "the end is not yet," a phrase that implied it might be soon.[72] Unfortunately, Christ did not come to reign in the 1660s, and by the end of the decade, Jeake may have agreed with his Baptist friend Christopher Blackwood that "Sion is in travell [i.e. travail] but I think by the Scriptures as I suppose shee is not near the time of her deliverance." The best response to defeat was not political action, but a Job-like patience. "I have many times proved the benefit of afflictions," Jeake wrote in 1668, "& with the Psalmist can truly say it is good for me that I have been afflicted."[73]

Jeake's few surviving letters from the 1670s and 1680s register no optimism, even in fleeting moments of political victory, and make no mention of the final days. Realizing that Rye might not prove to be the microcosm of a broader revolution, Jeake grew disillusioned with a national situation that he could not change. By the end of 1682, after being harried out of his native town, he wrote to his son from London with the prediction that "things will go bad here as well as in the Countrey with those that feare the Lord." When threatened with imprisonment for his religious beliefs in the spring of 1683, he assured the younger Samuel that "I yet am resolved to rest on providence & Let the Lord do with me as seemeth good in his sight." When he died in October 1690, his son recorded that "he never had the least murmuring expression against the Conduct of Providence towards him."[74]

The younger Jeake was more obsessed with astrology than with politics. He made horoscope charts or "nativities" for his relations and friends, including the Millers, the Grebells, and even members of the Crouch family. He composed an astrological diary of his life, and for the year 1687–88 kept an even more minute daily record, an "Astrological Experiment" in which he tried to connect his health and activities with minutely observed celestial configurations. The extensive library that Jeake inherited from his father, and whose volumes he carefully listed, included an extraordinary range of astrological and hermetic works, from Arthur Dee, Robert Fludd, and Paracelsus to his contemporaries William Lilly and J. B. Morin. As an astrologer, Jeake was not concerned with making "elections," that is, with predicting events, a practice that was considered suspect by some of the godly because it seemed to be an attempt to subvert Providence. Rather, he sought to explain the course of natural phenomena by relating them retrospectively to the movements of the heavens. His approach has been described as "rationalistic" and has even been called a kind of "secular providentialism." The younger Jeake saw it as experimental science. He regretted that the "Prognostiques" of astrology, "this most sublime & aethereal Science," did not "have equal Certitude with those of other Arts," and recommended to practitioners a year of experiment on an adult subject, so as to deduce "Astrological Theoremes" that would give meaning to daily events.[75]

By giving certainty to astrology, Jeake sought to rescue it from political as well as religious criticism. In the wake of the Restoration, the experimental scientists of the Royal Society had turned their eyes away from reading the stars, which they felt had inspired too many radical prophecies during the Interregnum. For his part, after one intense visionary experience in his childhood, the younger Jeake never again claimed to see revolution in the heavens, except in retrospect, as in 1688. He was more concerned with his own medical complaints, or with the fluctuations in his commercial fortunes, than with the course of national events. His efforts did not succeed in rehabilitating astrology, which was losing its appeal to the educated. For Jeake, however, the experimental reading of the night skies led to a focus on the mundane course of worldly existence rather than on the promise of an impending rule by the saints.[76]

This does not mean that he entirely forgot prophecy. At two important points in his diary, during the persecutions of 1683 and after his father's death in 1690, Jeake mentions that he lectured to his friends on the "Doctrine and Use" of the ninth chapter of the Book of Revelations, which deals with the attack of locusts with human faces "on those men which have not the seal of God in their foreheads." The locusts are led by a king named Apollyon, "the angel of the bottomless pit." Readers of John Bunyan's *Pilgrim's Progress* will recognize Apollyon as the wicked monster over whom the pilgrim Christian triumphs in the Valley of Humiliation. "I perceive thou art one of my Subjects," Bunyan's Apollyon tells Christian, "for all that Countrey is mine; and I am the Prince and God of it." The words of Apollyon resemble those of another Prince or false God, feared and detested by Dissenters like Bunyan: Charles II. In the younger Jeake's mind too, Apollyon undoubtedly stood for the persecuting king, while the locusts surely represented the royalists and their allies in Rye. We do not know how Jeake applied the prophecies of Revelations to the period after 1689, or what he made of the tenth chapter of that book, where the angel with a face like the sun announces the end of time. If he believed that rule by the saints was about to begin, he did not make his opinion public.[77]

The political ideas of the younger Jeake are elusive. His voluminous writings do not provide much insight into them. As has been mentioned, his father's library contained a number of republican works written during the Civil War and Commonwealth periods. If Jeake junior drew his conceptions of politics from them, then he must have longed for an irrecoverable republican past. Perhaps this explains why he did not play a very active role in politics after 1689. He welcomed the Glorious Revolution as providential, mainly because "God had restored the Liberty of the Gospel," but he did not place a prophetic value on it. Within a few years, he had given up politics entirely. In 1694, he made a gift of £60 to the corporation in order to be "excused from all manner of offices . . . and from comeing to all manner of Assemblyes." In a letter to the magistrates, he maintained that "a retired life & disengagmt. from the excesses of public business" were his "highest ambition." His astrological diary makes few references to local politics after 1690. The shorthand diary he kept in 1699, the year of his death, contains notes only on international affairs, showing his concern with events that might cause a fall in his Bank of England or East India Company stocks. The angel with the face of the sun seems far removed from his thoughts.[78]

Had the abstemious, God-centred culture of the Dissenters become more worldly by the end of the seventeenth century? Had commercial interests won out over godliness? As early as the 1670s, there were signs of a change in habits of consumption among Dissenters, for which women were primarily responsible. A surprising letter from Elizabeth Bonnick to her kinsman Samuel Jeake the elder, dated April 1672, encloses bills from her cousins for new clothes. She notes that "my Cozen Betty is not well pleased that I have not bought cloths for her & her Mirs. [i.e. Mistress] is ashamed to see her goe out of doors she wants cloaths. if my Cozens doe excel in ther cloaths they must have the less in ther portions for I know not how to help it." Other than the slight note of disapproval in the final comment, Bonnick issued no strong condemnation of her cousin Betty's vanity. The younger Jeake himself was not immune to conspicuous consumption; in 1674, for example, he recorded the extravagant gift of an engraved silver tobacco box. In an undated letter to Jeake's wife Elizabeth, probably sent shortly after her husband's death in 1699, Elisa Miller describes a cap for their infant son as "the newest fashon the Change affords." She continues in this fashion-conscious vein: "I hope your undercoat will please tis very moadish for This fashon has not bein seen before this winter."[79] The attitudes of Dissenters towards consumption may have softened after 1670 as they ceased to regard the end of the world as imminent. In a cultural sense, their political upsurge in 1679–82 may have represented a last effort to reassert on a civic level the godly values that they were gradually abandoning in their personal lives.

The spread of consumer culture emanating from London, the failure of godly rule, and the decline in acceptability of supernatural beliefs such as astrology set the stage for the rise of a politically moderate and religiously conformist Whig oligarchy at Rye, one that was as much attuned to national as to local interests. The oligarchs would construct a new kind of social stability and good neighbourhood, based on policing and punishment rather than communal surveillance. Theirs was a busy, self-interested regime that spent little time contemplating the recent past, although they could not erase the troubled history that had shaped them.

If the murderer John Breads gave any thought to history, he might have reflected on how his own family fell as the oligarchs rose. The reconstruction of his ancestry is conjectural, because the records are fragmentary and can be interpreted in more than one way. However, several members of the Breads family served in town government from the 1670s to the early 1690s, most of them ardent supporters of the radical cause. One of the freemen nominated by Thomas Tournay in 1682 was named John Breads. He became a jurat after the Glorious Revolution, served as town chamberlain, and died in 1694. The Breads family later became connected with the Dissenting congregation that was set up in 1703 at the house of Samuel Jeake the younger's widow, Elizabeth. The congregation practiced adult baptism, and the parish records show that daughters of Bartholomew Breads and Joseph Breads were among those "not Baptised according to the Rites and cerimonies of the Church of England." Dislike for the established Church ran high in the Breads family, as in 1715 a certain John Breads was presented to the episcopal court for profaning the Church of St. Clement's Hastings "by Shitting in it, to the great Offence of Sev. Psons who Saw him do it." It is tempting to believe that this impious defecator was related to the future murderer, but there is no direct evidence for it.

The murderer's father, like the other Breads, seems to have been raised as a Dissenter. In February 1705, the vicar of Rye baptized "John Breaths a man grown," along with his infant son John. By accepting baptism in the church, the older man was converting from Anabaptism to Anglicanism, possibly in order to qualify as a voter in the hotly contested parliamentary election of that year. As for the infant, he died before his second birthday. On 2 June 1710, however, another baby named John, son of John and Mary Breads, was baptized at Rye, according to the parish register. As no other John Breads appears to have been living in Rye at the time, we can assume that the father mentioned in this entry was the same man who had accepted adult baptism in 1705. Naming a child after its deceased sibling was a common practice. The infant named in the register had six brother and sisters, and there is no reason to doubt the claim of local historians, that he grew up to be the murderer in the gibbet, the sanguinary butcher who killed Allen Grebell.[80] He would later baptize his own two sons in St. Mary's, but neither he nor any other member of his family held a parish office. His dying words, as we have seen, were devoid of any declaration of allegiance to the Church of England.

Breads's relations had been deeply involved in Rye's radical religious past. By the time he was an adult, however, his family did not even enjoy the freedom of the town. This may have contributed to the resentment that drove him to murder. Perhaps the old promises of religious redemption fed into his state of mind. When he envisioned himself struggling with his butcher's knife against "a Parcel of Devils," did John Breads imagine that he was John Bunyan's Christian, meeting "a company of Fiends" in the Valley of Humiliation?[81] It may seem a fanciful image until we recall that Breads's father, like Bunyan, was a Baptist, so that his son may well have been familiar with this famous episode from the *Pilgrim's Progress*. It was based on the same passage from Revelations on which Samuel Jeake the younger had preached in 1690, to a congregation that may have included the elder Breads, then a boy. If the murderer had indeed inherited some of the radical views of his family, it would help to explain why he had negative attitudes towards Mayor Lamb and the other Whig oligarchs of Rye. This, however, is a story that will have to be told more fully in the following chapters.

4

Oligarchs

The reason why one private man must not kill another in society, even when he does that which deserves death, is, that in society no man must be his own judge, or take his own revenge. . . . But if the offender set himself above the law and the judges, he leaves a right to the person injured to seek redress his own way, and as he can get it . . . violence is a proper remedy for violence, when no other is left.

—John Trenchard and Thomas Gordon,
Cato's Letters, no. 55 (2 December 1721)

Political assassination was rare in eighteenth-century England. The previous century had been marked by famous attempts against kings and ministers, starting with the Gunpowder Plot. A few were successful, like the stabbing of the Duke of Buckingham in 1628. In the second half of the 1600s, numerous plots were hatched by disgruntled royalists or republicans to murder Oliver Cromwell and Charles II, although with these failed conspiracies it is difficult to sort out which were real and which invented by the authorities. The Assassination Plot of 1696 was the last politically motivated plan that posed a serious threat to the life of a British monarch until the Cato Street Conspiracy of 1820 (if the latter was not fabricated by informers). Between those two dates, in spite of many rumours of Jacobite or Jacobin attempts, only the mad struck out at kings. Margaret Nicholson, a thirty-six-year-old London needlewoman, stabbed at George

III in 1786 during a levee at St. James's Palace. "The poor creature is mad!" the king cried to the crowd, "Do not hurt her! She has not hurt me!" Nicholson saw King George as a father-figure and protector and was disappointed that he had not answered the twenty petitions she had addressed to him. In her case, assassination was a means of expressing her sense of rejection, and of gaining proximity to a ruler whom she had venerated. It was an act of spurned love rather than hatred. She was committed to Bedlam. John Frith, an ex-soldier, hurled a rock at the king's coach in 1790. He, too, was judged insane. In 1800, a third madman, James Hadfield, shot a bullet into the king's box at Drury Lane Theatre, but missed his royal target. His attempt led to an Act of Parliament declaring that treason could not be the result of lunacy.[1]

The safety of monarchs throughout this period extended to politicians also. Between the attack on Robert Harley by a secretary in 1711, and the murder of Spencer Perceval in the lobby of the House of Commons in 1809, no Prime Minister came close to losing his life by personal violence, except in duels. William Pitt the younger suffered threats of "publick execution" from radicals, but like Walpole and Newcastle, Bute and Rockingham, Lord North and Lord Liverpool, he died in his bed. Assassination attempts became more common again after 1815, however. An attack on Sir Robert Peel in 1843, which claimed the life of his secretary, resulted in the famous McNaughten Rules, equating insanity with not knowing that a crime is wrong. The rules are still in effect.[2]

No study has been made of political assaults and assassinations at the local level, but it seems likely that they became just as uncommon as those against national figures. The murder of the London justice Sir Edmund Berry Godfrey in 1678, allegedly by Papist thugs, horrified good Protestants throughout the kingdom, but its latest historian has judged it a suicide.[3] The attempt of "Mad Ned" Arnold to shoot the fox-hunting Lord Onslow in 1723 was in part political. Arnold blamed Onslow for "all the confusions, tumults, and noise, and wicked devices" that had accompanied the previous county elections. The would-be assassin was clearly eccentric; he slept in barns, lived by fishing and shooting, was tortured at night by dancing "imps," and thought Lord Onslow had "bewitched" him. He may have been mad. His brother, who had "observed him to burst out into a foolish laughter, and grin like any madman," was sure of it. Nevertheless, the jury took Arnold's blustering threats as proof of malice, and he was convicted under the recent Black Act, which made a capital felony of attempted murder while in disguise (although Arnold had not been wearing a disguise).[4] Similar threats of bloody murder against local magistrates abounded in the eighteenth century, particularly through the medium of anonymous letters, but I know no other instance in which the threat was carried into action.[5] Justices were sometimes manhandled by rioters during political or economic disturbances, but none seems to have died on account of the treatment. Although the provincial agents of English law and governance must occasionally have expired by other than natural causes in this period, no case attracted national attention.

Examining the general social picture, the historian Lawrence Stone argues that personal violence in England, measured through Assize indictments for assault and homicide, rose in the early seventeenth century but declined thereafter. A great deal of heated debate has ensued over Stone's hypothesis. Without doubt, he relies on incomplete statistics, ignores short-term fluctuations, and turns a blind eye to types of violence that were not usually pursued by the courts, such as wife-beating or the abuse of children and apprentices. If his central point is overstated, however, it is not misguided, at least for the southeastern counties of England. Whether we compare ten-year averages or rates per 100,000 of population, it is clear that fewer people in both Kent and Sussex were prosecuted for stabbing, strangling, hitting, kicking, burning, drowning, or poisoning their neighbours in the 1700s than in the 1600s. The high point of early modern homicide took place between 1580 and 1680, followed by a rapid decline to about 1720 and a levelling-off thereafter. Shooting deaths rose in the eighteenth century, because guns were more widely available (the prosecutors professed amazement at how easily "Mad Ned" had obtained one), but this exception did not reverse the overall pattern.[6] Statistics from the Rye sessions court are too fragmentary to provide a reliable picture, but at least twenty-seven homicides were prosecuted or reported by the town coroners between 1580 and 1660, and none at all from 1660 to 1743. Some were no doubt sent to Assizes, but it is unlikely that there can have been many, inasmuch as they have left no mark at all in town records.[7] If politicians were less apt to become the victims of murder in England during the 1700s, so perhaps was everybody else.

Against this backdrop of declining political and personal assassination, the murder of Allen Grebell by John Breads seems quite exceptional. Like "Mad Jack" Arnold, Margaret Nicholson, and James Hadfield, John Breads explicitly denied at his trial that the crime of which he accused was a premeditated act, or that he had any grudge against the victim. Yet he also confessed that he had believed at the time that the man he had killed in the churchyard was Mayor James Lamb, and that he had mistaken William Fowl, whom he attacked earlier in Deadman's Lane, for the jurat Ralph Norton. That both his intended victims were town magistrates suggests that some degree of political awareness informed Breads's crimes. Lamb and Norton were members of the merchant oligarchy that governed Rye from the 1690s until the 1830s. It was a privileged group from which John Breads was excluded by his wealth and occupation, in spite of his family's past connections with local affairs. Because town governance was vital to trade, commerce, justice, and social contact in Rye, as it was in all small towns, the magistracy had a constant impact on the life of John Breads. Viewed in this light, the oligarchs were obvious targets for his rage.

What did oligarchy mean at Rye? It signified government by a narrow, more or less self-perpetuating elite of men whose power was based more on wealth and economic influence than on inherited status. Oligarchy was typical of the political life of English towns in the early modern period. Growing administrative and fiscal demands, the decline of the guild system, and the disappearance of medieval civic ceremonies that emphasized community served to strengthen oligarchical control. Once established, oligarchy might sustain itself by methods that by contemporary standards could be seen as corrupt—manipulation, bribery, nepotism, profiteering, appropriation of public moneys. Perceived corruption could stir up opposition from excluded groups, whose representatives might have to be absorbed into the oligarchy in order to appease them.[8]

On a national level, the long-running Whig administration of 1714–62 has often been described as an oligarchy—and not always by its critics. The late J. H. Plumb expressed glowing admiration for what he called the "Venetian oligarchy" of the Whig party, a term he adopted from Benjamin Disraeli. He saw them as the creators of an "adamantine stability," based on public acceptance of their administration. On the other hand, E. P. Thompson depicted Whig oligarchy as typical of "a predatory phase of agrarian and commercial capitalism," when "the State was itself among the prime objects of prey." Thompson was convinced that beneath the appearance of stability, discontent was simmering among those who were victimized or marginalized by the rapacity of Whig rule.[9] Did Rye after the Glorious Revolution fit this pattern?

The question can be answered only by considering how oligarchy worked there. To accomplish that, we will begin by following up the story of economic decline and commercial consolidation that was begun in Chapter Three. Increasingly, economic power came to rest in the hands of a very few men: the Whig oligarchs. They came to define themselves in the twenty years after the Glorious Revolution as neither radicals nor Tories. The process of their self-definition was accelerated in the early 1700s by an unexpected series of efforts by Tory landowners, assisted by Churchmen within the town, to control parliamentary elections. This backfired, encouraging the Whigs to tighten their control over the corporation. The third part of the chapter will discuss the construction of a stable Whig political system by the Grebells and the Lambs in the years after the Hanoverian succession, through the monopolization of public offices and the exclusion or neutralization of opponents. John Breads struck a brutal blow against that system in 1743, and it punished him with a gruesome death. That he consciously wanted to undermine it seems unlikely, but he certainly knew that he was hurting more than just another human being when he thrust his knife into Allen Grebell in Rye churchyard.

The Sinews of Oligarchy

Oligarchy in eighteenth-century Rye was built on two broad economic factors: at the bottom of society, a lessening of the scale of dislocation and hardship; at the top, a concentration of commercial power in the hands of a few individuals who faced no effective rivals. This marked a clear shift from the misery, anxiety, and bitter competition of most of the seventeenth century. By 1740, the disgruntled fishermen and their families who had once populated the narrow streets and small houses of the Strandgate, Baddings, or Watchbell and Wish wards were mostly gone. Their descendants who continued to live in Rye were most likely able to make a better living from maritime trade, whether legally or through smuggling. Gone, too, were the Dissenting merchants of the Market and Middlestreet wards, whose radicalism had kept up the temperature of town politics under the Restoration. They had been replaced by a tiny mercantile elite that lived at the top of the hill, near the church. If the town was not prosperous, its modest commerce was at least capable of supporting its remaining inhabitants, and of making its leading citizens into rich men.

The causes of these economic changes were several and complex, but foremost among them was the town's reduced population. In the episcopal visitation of 1724, the vicar of Rye estimated the number of inhabitants in the parish at "about 200 Families."[10] This represents no more than nine hundred people, a loss of 10 percent or more since the Compton census of 1676. Moreover, it includes those who lived in Rye Foreign, the parish area outside the town boundaries. It is the lowest estimate ever given of Rye's population in the early modern period. From one point of view, it represented economic failure for a once-burgeoning port. From another perspective, however, it meant that those who continued to live in the town were less likely to become the victims of economic decline.

The fishing industry was almost defunct by 1740, despite concerted efforts to rescue it by regulation. In January 1700, during a year of peace between wars with France, the Rye corporation tried to end the over-harvesting of "Plaise, Soles or other flatt fish," by requiring the use of larger mesh nets and restricting the season and time of day when they might be caught. Plaice or sole brought higher prices than herring or mackerel and were particularly prized by French fishermen, who used nets with small mesh to harvest them. The corporation's early attempt at conservation was apparently unsuccessful in resurrecting the fishing fleet. When the duties on the fish and fruit markets were farmed out in 1733, they were worth only £7, as compared to £20 in 1689. The low value of the duties meant that their tenant was unsure of making a profit for himself, signalling a lack of confidence that the fishing industry could be revived. In 1759, in order to keep the fish market clean, the corporation was obliged to levy an additional shilling duty on every fishing boat coming to the harbour from outside Rye.[11] Most of the fishermen in the town by this time were probably "foreigners."

The virtual end of commercial fishing at Rye had at least one positive outcome: it made the problem of local poverty more manageable. By 1700, many of the very poor had either migrated or had failed to reproduce themselves. The wars with France accelerated the process by drawing young men away into the navy. Forced naval impressment was common at Rye as at other ports, and became an issue in the Parliamentary election of 1701, as will be seen. Up to 13 percent of the adult male population of England was drawn into the army or navy during the Nine Years' War, and the percentage was probably higher in Rye. It was not until forty years later, when only a handful of herring fishermen were left, that the Admiralty began regularly to issue protections from impressment for them.[12] Even when peace returned at the end of the Nine Years' War and the demobilization of soldiers and sailors plunged many young men into unemployment, no evidence can be found at Rye of a sudden increase in local poverty. The accounts of the overseers of the poor in 1698–99 have survived, and they reveal that most of the disbursements consisted of regular monthly payments to nine widows and elderly women with names like Goody Bishop, Short Moll, Widow Hounsell, and Mother Odiarne. Their surnames are familiar; these were the female relicts of families that had lived in Rye for generations, but now had no husbands or working children in the town to support them. Most of the women were employed by the corporation as spinners or weavers. The purchase of shoes for the "Paris Childern" is also mentioned, but how many children were dependent on the parish is nowhere stipulated. What about the vagabonds who were so numerous in the parish accounts of 1679–80? The main traces they have left on the later records are the small amounts paid to transport them back to their parish of settlement—for example, 4s. was needed "for a Horce to Cary a Maid to Tenterden."[13]

Poverty may not have been improving, but at least it was not worsening before the 1740s. In light of this situation, the astonishing growth of smuggling on the south coasts after 1689, and the emergence of organized gangs of smugglers after 1714, cannot be regarded as a desperate response to increasing misery. Rather, smuggling has to be seen as a viable commercial alternative for local folk who by 1713 had passed through the worst economic times and were eager to pick up on any opportunity of seeing better ones.[14] The prohibition of wool exports and the high tariffs on French wine offered the fishermen, seamen, and farm labourers of the south coasts an irresistible invitation to go "free-trading" across the Channel.

Undoubtedly, many of Rye's inhabitants were involved in this lucrative business. Still, with a customs sloop now stationed in the harbour, a full complement of officers attached to the customs house, and a magistracy that was known to be hostile to smugglers, Rye never became a major landing place or storage centre for the contraband gangs, as did the nearby port of Lydd, where as early as the 1680s the local authorities were mixed up in contraband. Lydd became an open town for the contraband gangs. It was from the George Inn there that two local smugglers, captured by the customs men after a furious fight with staves and broadswords, were rescued by armed comrades on a March night in 1721. "The several Gangs on this Coast are very great in Number," observed one of the officers, adding that a hundred men of Romney Marsh had been "bound in Oath to Rescue the Prisoners or Die."[15] The officers sometimes had to chase their opponents far inland. A dramatic confrontation between the Rye customs officers and thirty armed smugglers, probably from the gang known as the Transports, occurred near Lamberhurst in 1735. It resulted in three customs men and two dragoons being taken prisoner. A few months later, the notorious Gabriel Tompkins, a leader of the Transports, was captured at Rye on a warrant from the mayor, Allen Grebell.[16] The most serious incidents of smuggling at Rye belong to the 1740s, however, and they will be discussed in the next chapter.

In spite of the growth in illicit commerce, the decline of legal trade in the port of Rye was not as steady or as irreversible as might be imagined. The harbour continued to offer employment to shipmasters and seamen. The worst shocks to the maritime economy generally came during wartime, and the conflicts with France in 1689–97 and 1702–13 were no exceptions. Overseas trade virtually ceased, and coastal trade fell. Unlike the aftermath of the wars against Spain or the Dutch, however, the French wars were followed by a partial commercial recovery, part of a national expansion of trade, especially into the Baltic and Mediterranean.

The devastating initial effects of the French wars can be seen in the numbers of ships entering the harbour, as recorded in the port books of Rye. Unfortunately, the port books become sparse after 1714, and those that survive were sloppily kept. The coastal books stop in 1714, the overseas books in 1728. It should be remembered that the following figures do not reflect the size or value of cargoes. Nonetheless, they give a striking impression of sharp wartime downturns and sudden peacetime upturns in trade:[17]

	OUT	IN
1690–91: Overseas	1	3
Coastal	33	15
1694–95: Overseas	1	1 (plus 5 prizes)
Coastal	9	9
1699–1700: Overseas	15	5
Coastal	27	7
1704–5: Overseas	0	0
Coastal	4	3
1709–10: Overseas	1	1
Coastal	9	5
1713–14: Overseas	33	11
Coastal	18	?
1723–24: Overseas	16	17
1724–25: Overseas	6	17
1725–26: Overseas	9	9
1726–27: Overseas	6	17
1727–28: Overseas	8	20

These figures hint at the frightening exposure to enemy attack of ships using Rye harbour during the wars of 1689–1713. Vessels entering or leaving the southeastern ports were particularly vulnerable to seizure by French privateers from St.-Malo, Dieppe, Dunkirk, and other ports. The Malouins alone captured two hundred prize or ransom ships in 1692 and 194 in 1704. Privateers from Dieppe, the French port to which Rye was most closely linked, took seventy-four Allied ships during the War of the Spanish Succession. The convoy system was adopted by the British navy in the 1690s, but was not noticeably successful at preventing attacks by privateers during the Nine Years' War or until the last years of the War of the Spanish Succession. Worse still for Rye and other southeastern ports, the French fleet gained control of the Channel in the summer of 1707.[18] Very few south coast shipowners can have been willing to venture their fortunes on overseas voyages under these conditions.

The figures for Rye's overseas trade bolster the hypothesis that the wars of 1689–1713 were potentially disastrous for the English economy, because markets were lost overseas while consumption was lessened at home. The nation was saved from a crisis in its balance of payments only by an export boom after 1708, especially to northeastern Europe and Iberia.[19] At Rye, the boom came after 1713, and it was limited by geography, which made Norway and Portugal less accessible than they were from other English ports. Moreover, in spite of this recovery, the damaging effects of the French wars were felt for some time, on both a regional and a national level. For example, they contributed to a long-term decline in the percentage of English tonnage owned by southeastern ports, from 16.2 percent in 1582 to 8.4 percent in 1702 and only 5.3 percent in 1788. Nationally, English overseas trade doubled in value and tonnage between 1700 and 1750; but this compares with a tripling or quadrupling in 1633–88 and a further quadrupling in 1748–1815. The rate of increase in combined imports and exports was only .8 percent annually between 1700 and 1740; it then rose to 1.7 percent in 1740–70 and soared to 2.6 percent in 1770–1800. Thus, the early eighteenth century can be regarded as a period of slower growth between two half-centuries of tremendous expansion in trade.[20] Nevertheless, from Rye's vantage point, slower national growth may not have been a bad thing. It gave smaller ports a breathing space that they could use to improve their competitiveness. Rye took advantage of its modest revival of prosperity to begin the reconstruction of the harbour in 1724.

War also affected Rye's main trading partner across the Channel, Dieppe. The English fleet bombarded the Norman town for ten days in 1694, destroying 1,850 houses and causing massive damage to the harbour.[21] After the Peace of Ryswick in 1697, the high duties on French goods were maintained. The port of Dieppe did not recover until the tobacco boom of the 1770s. When Rye's own overseas trade began to revive in 1699–1700, its ships set sail for Boulogne as often as they did for Dieppe. They carried tanned leather and textiles, and brought back French wine. After the War of the Spanish Succession, the merchants of Rye again looked beyond the Norman or Breton coasts for trade. In 1713–14, of thirty-three vessels leaving the harbour, only seven went to Dieppe, one to Rouen, one to St. Valéry, and two to St.-Malo. The rest went further north or much further south. Five went to Boulogne, two to Dunkirk, eleven to Ostend, one to Norway, one to Cadiz, and one to Seville. To Boulogne and Ostend were shipped woollen goods, stockings, and barley, while to Spain the Rye merchants sent butter, herrings, pilchards, and some goat's hair that had been washed up on a wreck at Eastbourne. The fish, certified as "English Caught," probably came from Hastings rather than Rye. Into the harbour that year sailed four ships from Dieppe, two from Boulogne, two from Norway, and one each from Calais, St. Valéry, and Cadiz. The French ships now carried more mackerel and herrings than Norman canvas, reflecting both the growing French domination of the fisheries and the heavy duties on French textiles. From Calais came twenty bushels of "damaged Apples," proving that the Common Market did not initiate the dumping of inferior agricultural produce. Norway supplied wood, particularly deals and barrel staves. The Spanish ports sent raisins, oranges, lemons, and olives.

By the 1720s, Rye's overseas trade had completely altered and was changing almost every year in response to new markets and suppliers. For example, the year 1723–24 was a high point for the exportation of wheat from Rye to Portugal, the Canaries, Bordeaux, and Dieppe. Back into Rye flowed wine and vinegar from Lisbon, Oporto, the Canaries, Bordeaux, and even Rotterdam.

In the following year, however, the main exports were iron, sent to Livorno and Amsterdam; wheat, peas, and oats for Dieppe; coals for St. Valéry; and herrings for Ostend. Spanish iron came to Rye from San Sebastian, and Norway deals from Fredericks-hall. By the late 1720s French wine was again flowing into the port, in spite of high tariffs. The overseas trade of Rye was more notable for its diversity than for its scale, but the concentration on specialized cargoes gives the impression that it may have been more profitable than it had been for those who were engaged in it. No canny merchant would import small quantities of Spanish iron or export peas without knowing that there was a particular buyer for his goods, and that the selling price was high enough to warrant the shipping expenses.

Coastal trade was more consistent in terms of goods than overseas trade, although both fluctuated in scale with wartime conditions. Wool was carried from Rye to Exeter and Topsham; iron was taken up to London. Back came coals from Newcastle, often shipped via London, along with Iberian wine and various supplies from the capital. In the peaceful year 1699–1700, the port of Rye shipped 220 tons of bar iron and guns, along with a record 98,398 pounds of wool. War stimulated the production of armaments in the Weald, where a new forge was started at Lamberhurst in 1695; but it also limited the coastal trade, so that in 1704–5, Rye shipped only 61 tons of cast iron and guns, along with 40 tons of shot. No wool at all left the port.[22] Five years later, with an Allied army menacing the French Channel ports, 165 tons of iron was sent up to London, but again no wool. Peace was beneficial to internal as well as foreign trade. The last coastal port book, for 1713–14, is badly damaged, but it shows at least five shipments of iron, including one to Bristol, along with wool shipments to London and Exeter.

Of considerable interest in the years of peace are some of the smaller cargoes carried into Rye from other English ports, which speak of changing tastes and fashions as well as new sources of supply. In addition to Portuguese and Spanish wines shipped down from London, these include barrels of tobacco, tobacco pipe-staves, salt, raisins, cheese, gingerbread, earthenware, glassware, and household furniture. Rye clearly participated in the exchange of luxury consumer goods, both comestibles and durables, which was centred mainly on London. Now at last we can find concrete evidence of the spread of those products that have been identified with a "consumer revolution." In fact, the decade 1705–15 has been seen as a national watershed in terms of the level of ownership of consumer items. The rise in consumption was almost certainly fuelled by the export boom at the end of the War of the Spanish Succession. Exports revitalized London, which in turn began to spread luxury consumer goods throughout the kingdom.[23] Perhaps the old pattern of Puritan frugality endured a bit longer in Rye, however. It was still alive in 1716, when Francis Jeake, brother of Samuel III, wrote to his mother from London about his purchases of gold thread for her and a book of poems by Edmund Waller for his sister. He was mostly concerned about how cheaply he had obtained them. Still, buying the poetry of a turncoat to the Parliamentarian cause may have marked a watershed in patterns of consumption for an old Puritan family![24]

Although Rye harbour was under construction after 1724, it did not close down. We cannot know how busy it was in the 1730s and 1740s, inasmuch as no port books survive. The only sector of coastal trade that can be estimated is coal, because the shipping records were kept at Newcastle; and here the figures show an improvement. In 1682–83, Rye received 113 coal shipments, about half of one percent of the total number of shipments from Newcastle. In 1730–31, 244 coal barges entered Rye, or about nine-tenths of one percent of the total number of shipments from Newcastle.[25] One other set of figures provides a glimpse of what was going on in Rye harbour after 1730. The government gathered statistics on the total tonnage of coastwise shipping after 1709. They show the maintenance of a steady trade at Rye throughout the period of peace from 1716 to 1739, and a sudden fall thereafter:

1709	30
1716	280
1723	276
1730	266
1737	297
1744	210
1751	183

These tonnage statistics are not very accurate, but they do give an interesting picture of the relative prosperity of southeastern ports. Rye's share of coastal trade remained far behind that of Dover, Sandwich, Faversham, or Rochester and fell seriously behind Hastings in the 1720s and 1730s. By mid-century, even Newhaven was catching up; but there were still enough ships in Rye harbour to enrich a few families and support many others.[26]

This leads us to perhaps the most striking development in both the overseas and the coastal trade of Rye after 1690: its consolidation in the hands of fewer and fewer merchants. During the first decade after the Glorious Revolution, the names of merchants trading at Rye included Samuel Jeake the younger, Samuel Gillart, Francis Young, the Wealden gunfounders Thomas and Maximilian Western, and Peter Gott of Hastings, the radical parliamentary candidate who later became a court Whig. By the time peace returned in 1713, nobody with these surnames was trading at Rye, demonstrating a point made about merchant capitalism in the late seventeenth century, that it "had great influence, but no staying power."[27] The man who *would* show staying power, Thomas Grebell, first became prominent in 1699–1700, as a dealer in French wine and an expediter of horses and textiles to Dieppe. By 1710, he was also shipping iron to London. The end of the War of the Spanish Succession saw a boom in Grebell's business. He sent fish to Cadiz, wheat to St.-Malo, textiles and stockings to Ostend, and horsehair and oxen to Dieppe. He was named as the chief merchant on eleven of thirty-three overseas voyages from Rye in 1713–14. Ten years later, he was merchant on eight out of sixteen outward voyages, and his son-in-law James Lamb was merchant on six others. Grebell died in 1724, but James Lamb and Company remained the dominant overseas merchant house at Rye, and was involved in twenty-two of thirty-one outward voyages in 1724–25. Every year, Lamb imported shipments of Norway deals for his thriving timber business. The Norway lumber trade depended on bills of exchange, a kind of bank cheque that allowed merchants to make payments after cargoes had arrived. Remittances from Norway were usually made to Hamburg banks.[28] Lamb must have used bills of exchange, which shows what an up-to-date businessman he was. Allen Grebell and Company also appear in the port books for the mid-1720s, as the importers of hair from Dieppe, but the commercial interests of the younger Grebell never matched those of his father or brother-in-law.

James Lamb was not just an overseas merchant. He was also involved in the coastal trade, particularly in coal and timber. He did not leave behind any ledger books that chronicle his business, but we can reconstruct some of his local activities from the letters of the ironmaster and landowner, John Fuller of Brightling, written in the 1730s and early 1740s. Lamb apparently owned a coal barge and supplied Fuller with coal for his forges. He also furnished the ironmaster with old ship's masts for use as furnace tackle. He acted as an agent for Fuller in purchasing Norway deals from John Slade, who was the other leading timber merchant in Rye and can be considered a collaborator with rather than a rival of James Lamb and Company. Some of Lamb's profits were invested in the rental of marshlands from the Fullers.[29]

What emerges from the commercial history of Rye in the half-century after 1689 is a somewhat happier picture than was given of the Restoration period. The awful spiral of human misery that had been set in motion by the decline of the fisheries seems to have wound to an end, and many of the social anxieties that it had produced began to evaporate. Dealing with the indigent poor was no longer such a pressing concern. If oligarchy was accepted by those at the bottom of the social scale, it was because their economic condition was now stable rather than worsening. On the other end of society, there was also change. As it became harder and harder to make a profit through the old networks of maritime trade, the local Dissenting commercial community gradually disintegrated. By the end of the War of the Spanish Succession, it had been replaced by a family compact of Grebells and Lambs. They dealt with a multitude of smaller cargoes from different parts of Europe, and with domestic cargoes that supplied their own businesses on land. The catalyst for the emergence of a commercial oligarchy was two and a half decades of war against France after 1689, a conflict ardently supported by the national Whig party. The Grebells and Lambs were Whigs, not radicals of Jeake's stripe. They had closer ties to national government, and they were more concerned with rebuilding the port than with transforming Rye into a godly bastion. The new century would be dominated by these moderate, pliable Whigs who were adept at piloting the narrow economic channels still open to them. In short, the future belonged to James Lamb and Company.

The Whig oligarchy of Rye was the chief heir to the old radical faction, but it also inherited from the moderates. In the aftermath of the Glorious Revolution, it became clear that neither group could govern effectively without support from a national government dominated by the landed elite. The moderates turned for leadership to the local Tory gentry, but this aroused furious opposition from the Dissenters and their friends. After years of party conflict, centred on parliamentary elections, a new moderate faction arose out of the old radicals. Grafting itself to the national Whig party, it brought about a stability based largely on economic self-interest and the preservation of familial power. It was a stability that was not entirely consensual and remained far from adamantine, but it worked.

Two individuals were more responsible than anyone else in Rye for causing these developments. The first was Thomas Grebell, whom we have already met. The second was Nicholas Mannooch, who was elected mayor of Rye seven times between 1690 and 1704. Mannooch was the master of Peacock's School, a free school founded in 1638 through a testamentary bequest by a jurat of Rye, Thomas Peacock. The handsome brick school building, built in a flamboyant Dutch Baroque style, still stands on the High Street. Mannooch's position there put him in the thick of Rye politics. The schoolmaster was appointed by the mayor and jurats, with the advice of a "learned counsel" from Hastings. From the start, Puritan jurats such as Thomas Grebell's grandfather Allen were active in directing the school's affairs. The first master was Richard Hartshorne, whose love letters were discussed in Chapter Two, and whose daughter Elizabeth married Samuel Jeake the younger. Thomas Burdett, the radical mayor of 1680–81, served as schoolmaster after the Restoration. In contrast to his predecessors, however, Nicholas Mannooch was neither a Dissenter nor a radical. He had been ordained as a deacon of the Church of England, which made him acceptable to the moderates in the corporation. Nevertheless, Mannooch had Dissenting connections. His wife, Mercy Francis of Lamberhurst, was sister-in-law to Thomas Markwicke, a prominent member of Jeake the elder's conventicle.[30] Mannooch began his political career with the help of John Spaine, who made him a freeman in the confusing days at the end of James II's reign. Not surprisingly, Mannooch was a supporter of the Glorious Revolution, and publicly signed the Test Act, a declaration of allegiance to the crown and against transubstantiation.[31]

Nicholas Mannooch was first elected mayor in August 1690. By that time, Rye had experienced two divisive parliamentary elections within the space of thirteen months. The first, in January 1689, knocked out the radical candidate Peter Gott and led to the unseating of the Tory Thomas Frewen on a petition to the House of Commons. The Commons decided that only resident freemen would have the vote at Rye. The second election, in February 1690, returned Sir John Austen and Sir John Darrell, but this time the two defeated Tory candidates petitioned against the return. They particularly objected against the votes of freemen who had been created by Thomas Tournay, and against the claim to freedom by paternal right of those whose fathers had been ejected under the Corporations Act. The House of Commons had nothing to say about the first problem, but allowed a vote to several Dissenters, including Samuel Jeake senior.[32] The Tory interest seemed to have been squashed in Rye before it had made much of an impact; but this proved not to be so.

The two elections inspired a reconciliation between the old radicals and the new Tories. Both sides recognized that corporate peace would be useful in seeking favours from a mixed administration at Whitehall. The outbreak of war with France increased Rye's need for such favours, especially with regard to the harbour. Rye was still a strategic point on the south coast, and the war gave it unwanted prominence. In July 1690, after their victory at Beachy Head, the French fleet fired on Hastings and considered a landing at Rye. The younger Jeake reported "a terrible alarm in the Towne of Rye of the Frenches coming to land. . . . Nothing seen but fears & consternations; sending of goods out of Towne in Wagons & on horses & the like confusions usuall at such times." Jeake's own family left, carrying his money and his wife's clothes. When the French failed to land, a thankful Jeake reported that the outcome was reflected in the stars: "Behold the face of heaven when the news was first brought me . . . the houses of heaven are disposed as in the Radix, & the Planet Mars on the Cusp of the Ascendant, the Sun as radically in the 12th &c." [33] Others focused their hopes not on the skies but on the commissioners of the navy, who might finance improvements to the harbour for the purpose of national defence. It was no secret that many of the commissioners were Tories.

For these reasons and no doubt for others that remain obscure, Nicholas Mannooch governed with an even hand on becoming mayor in 1690. He chose as his jurats five men who had supported the radicals, including John Spaine and Michael Cadman, and two who had been their bitter opponents in the 1680s, namely Lewis Gillart junior and Joseph Radford.[34] Mannooch and his jurats kept some aspects of the Puritan tradition alive. They fined Sabbath-breakers, allowed the Dissenter Thomas Tutty to sit in the assembly (although Michael Cadman, who owned a rival public house, objected to it), and condemned the 1685 decision to allow the lord warden to nominate one of the town's members of Parliament as "illegally arrived at by violent hands." Yet the godly zeal of the corporation was almost gone. The "day of Rejoycing" for William III's victorious return from

Ireland was marked by the distribution of thirty-six gallons of beer, an act that the Puritans would have deplored.[35] What was missing from the town records is equally significant. No indication can be found of what has been called "the godly revolution," in which William III was imagined as the righteous agent of Providence, who would bring about reformation in church and state. Monthly fast days, intended to solicit divine blessing for the war effort, do not appear to have been observed by the corporation. Finally, there is no sign of the "reformation of manners" movement that emerged in other English towns.[36]

The moderation of the Rye corporation persisted throughout the 1690s. It allowed the mayor and jurats quietly to heal past wounds and to enjoy the profits of their offices. The magistrates had a right to a share of the cargoes of wrecks and prizes or captured enemy ships, which were kept in the customs storehouse at Rye. In May 1695, for example, Nicholas Mannooch withdrew from the storehouse a large quantity of "Scotch cloth," 105 dozen pair of woollen stockings worth twelve shillings a dozen, and seven ells of Holland cloth.[37] Moderation also meant political compromise, which reached a peak in the uncontested parliamentary election in February 1694 that returned the Country Tory Thomas Frewen to replace the deceased Sir John Darrell. The younger Jeake recorded in his diary that he had "contrived with Mr. Jno Spain & Fra: Young to chuse Mr. Frewen." It seems perplexing that the election of a Tory was "contrived" by an old radical and two Whigs, but it probably kept out a more committed Tory candidate and was consistent with the general desire among members of the corporation to avoid conflict. Frewen was re-elected in 1695 along with the court Whig Sir John Austen, again without a contest. Three years later, a general election that produced a strong anti-Court reaction throughout most of England had no such effect in Rye, where Austen, an office-holder or placeman, was returned unopposed.

Apparently, Rye was being spared the "rage of party" that was so widespread throughout England in the late 1690s.[38]

Although the old radicals complied with the moderation of the 1690s, there is evidence of continuing hostility towards them. When the younger Jeake, only three days after Frewen's election in 1694, promised the town £60 to exempt himself from appointment to office, he went on at length "to obviate the malice of all sordid reflections either upon my Profession or my Person. . . . There is no accord but what may be sullied by an invidious minde."[39] He did not name the "invidious minds," but they must have belonged to old enemies such as Lewis Gillart junior. Two years later, an old enemy tried to destroy another Dissenter and radical, Thomas Grebell. An anonymous information was sent to the secretary of state concerning Grebell, a merchant of Rye, who "Corresponds with his majestyes Enemys," according to the writer. One of Grebell's trading partners was William Pigault, the mayor of Calais, who "has been soe busy for King James that he has taken the Title of Intendant of King James Dispatches." Grebell's kinsman John Gee, a mariner and smuggler, was reported to have carried the news of Queen Mary's death to France. The accusation is credible—in fact, there were contacts between radicals and Jacobites at this time. In local terms, however, it can be regarded as an attempt to smear the old radicals with the new taint of Jacobitism. The secretary of state apparently believed the charge, for he ordered Grebell's arrest for high treason.[40]

Thomas Grebell the suspected Jacobite should not be confused with his nephew, the jurat of the same name, who served as mayor ten times between 1699 and 1721. Thomas Grebell the politician, grandson of the Puritan mayor, was neither a radical nor a Jacobite; on the contrary, he was at first associated with Nicholas Mannooch and the conciliatory assemblies of the 1690s. It was then that he began to accumulate the fortune that would make him the most powerful man in Rye. At the end of William III's reign, however, the politics of compromise abruptly fell apart. The causes of its collapse were both national and local. On the national level, a long period of Whig dominance ended in 1700, when William briefly appointed a predominantly Tory ministry before turning again to the more warlike Whigs. The result was increased polarization between the parties. On the local level, the Rye corporation was desperately trying to control the activities of French fishing boats that had begun to frequent the harbour again after the Treaty of Ryswick. The prevention of night fishing and of taking catches out of season was of vital concern. The French fishermen petitioned the Lords Justices about the controls, and Mayor Mannooch had to appear before them in 1698 to give an account of himself.[41] In the same year, the naval commissioners prepared a report on Rye harbour. It concluded "that it is in noe Case proper for a safe Harbour to resort to, nor Capable to be improved by an tollerable Charge for any Services of the Navy."[42] It looked as if truckling with Tories had ultimately brought no positive economic results for Rye.

The result was a dramatic rallying of what can now properly be called the Whig interest, led by Francis Young, who was elected mayor in August 1701. As a mariner, Young was presumably interested in the problems of the harbour and the fisheries. He was also a man of substance who had prospered during the war years by financing privateering voyages. One voyage alone had brought him three small boats, ten guns, and two parcels of old iron, valued at £280. He was rich enough that when a needy Jeake the younger, worried about how to pay for some recently purchased East India Company stock, met him in the streets of Rye, Young "offered me without asking £40 or £50 whithout Interest till Michaelmas."[43] The transaction is a reminder of the "financial revolution" that had taken place in late seventeenth-century England, from which Rye was not isolated. There as in London, the purchasers of shares in joint-stock companies that lent money to the government were mostly Whigs and Dissenters. Thus, through his privateering ventures and joint-stock investments, Francis Young was tied into the "fiscal-military state" of post-Revolutionary England.[44] His financial interests must also have pointed him in the direction of a new war with France, which the Tory party opposed. No wonder he laboured so diligently to elect Whigs to Parliament. For him as for many others in Rye, Whiggism was a matter of bringing national priorities to bear on local affairs.

During his mayoralty, two parliamentary elections took place. The first, in November 1701, returned two Whig landed gentlemen, without a contest. King William's death in March 1702 made another general election necessary. Young had prepared for it by creating five new freemen in order to gain a majority of votes in the Rye assembly, which promptly named eleven more freemen who were his supporters. Young later stated before a committee of the House of Commons, quite disingenuously, that "he understood That the H[ouse]: design'd Increasing the Number of Electors in those Places were [sic] they did not Exceed fifty and therefore thought it a Prudent Precaution in them to make the ffreemen of this Port at least ffifty." The newly created freemen included Jeremiah Grebell, the customs collector of Rye and younger brother of Thomas the jurat, along with at least seven members of the Dissenting congregation that met at Elizabeth Jeake's house. Among the latter was the felicitously named Thankfull Bishopp. Some of the new freemen were initially refused the freedom, but their residential, financial, and religious qualifications were reassessed (or reinvented) and they were then admitted. Two days after Christmas 1701, they turned out in force for an assembly, to the exact number of fifty.[45] Mayor

Young was ready for a political fight, which he must have reckoned would pit him against his colleague Nicholas Mannooch.

Why did Mannooch commit himself to the thankless task of electing a Tory member of Parliament at Rye? The answer lies partly in the strident policies of Mayor Young, which threatened to cut Mannooch out of local affairs, and partly in the economic welfare of the town (which happily coincided with the former mayor's own financial interests). If Rye wanted to revive its sagging fortunes, the Tories may have seemed a better bet than the Whigs, as the latter were bent on the renewal of a costly war with France. Anticipating such a conflict, the corporation had already been obliged to raise £546 in subsidies.[46] The Tories were less bellicose. Moreover, Tory landowners such as the Frewens, Fullers, or Ashburnhams were the wealthiest members of East Sussex society. They owned not only land but also the rights to what was in it, including iron, and many of them were partners in the iron foundries of the Weald. As was mentioned in the previous section, the iron industry was undergoing a small revival at this time, due to the demand for naval ordinance. The Sussex gentry and aristocracy therefore had plenty of money to spend. They were already conspicuous consumers, especially of wine. Wrecks and prize cargoes usually contained wine, which could be sold by the mayor and jurats of Rye without paying duty. Here was a nice opportunity for the ambitious schoolmaster.

The Tory aristocrat to whom Mannooch attached himself was John, 1st Baron Ashburnham, a former member of Parliament for Hastings who owned extensive lands and several iron forges in East Sussex. Ashburnham was a Churchman and a royalist, who exulted in the accession of Queen Anne to the throne in 1702: "since it has pleased Almighty God to give us an English Queene, I doubt not but we are in a true english Bottom and That a stopp will be putt to such proceedings as considered and followed their owne private ends before the Honour and Interest of England." This sort of patriotic rhetoric had seldom been heard at Rye, where England had been viewed more as the fulfillment of biblical prophecy than as a worldly entity with its own "Honour and Interest." Without doubt, those who "followed their own private ends" in Ashburnham's mind were Whigs and Dissenters such as Francis Young, moneyed men who invested in the public funds, supported the Bank of England and were thought by Tories to be guilty of rampant peculation and corruption. They were also men of low birth, and Ashburnham was an unabashed snob. He snorted that "it would look like an affront" if Hastings chose a mere ropemaker as a baron of the Cinque Ports to hold the royal canopy at Queen Anne's coronation.[47]

Ashburnham's letters first mention Nicholas Mannooch in May 1702, when the baron reported to a correspondent in Hastings that "I have heard a very good Character" of him. At the time, Ashburnham was engaged in protecting local fishermen from the press gangs that were carrying them off into the navy. He claimed to be acting out of paternal benevolence, "it not being possible for me to have any selfish ends of my owne in doing you good," but he was also trying to extend his electoral influence at Hastings and Rye. Other than Mannooch, he had connections with Lewis Gillart III, son of the Rye jurat, for whom he solicited a position as surgeon and apothecary at Hastings. Gillart complained that Mayor Young had a "design" against him, but Ashburnham professed not to understand what he meant—a canny ignorance, for he might need Young's support. In June, the baron's plans became clear: his kinsman Edward Southwell was to run for Parliament as a representative for Rye. "And now sir for my Cosin Southwells affaire at Rye," he wrote to Southwell's father, Sir Robert, "I see nothing discouraging I have engaged some Friends that I am persuaded have good interest there and that I thinke will exert it all to serve him freely & honestly."[48] Sir Robert Southwell was secretary of state for Ireland, as his son Edward would later be, and like Ashburnham was a Court Tory. In the early 1690s, he had been president of the Royal Society, when Samuel Jeake the younger had dedicated to him a voluminous tome on arithmetic written by Jeake's late father. The dedication, fulsome but unfawning, noted that "where no Personal Advantages are expected; no imputation of Flattery can be charged."[49] The younger Jeake was not looking for a patron. Would his native town accept one?

Lord Ashburnham worked hard to see that it would. He acted as Edward Southwell's campaign manager, and in spite of his aristocratic status, he did not flinch from doing everything that was required to elect his candidate. Southwell did not go near Rye until the eve of the election, but Ashburnham visited the town in late June 1702, almost a month before the poll. There he "saw the Corporation & discoursed with them concerning the Representatives they would pitch upon for the next parliament," and was pleased to inform Southwell that "I find a good number of them very desirous you should be one, nay indeed warm and earnest to promote your Interest." The visit was a great success, according to Ashburnham, since "I have gained some and offended none for I avoided all distinctions of parties & encouraged them to be unanimous in their choice for the good of their Country the benefit of their Towne, and their own happinesse." Local politicians expected favours, of course. Mr. Mannooch was told "you wold take care of him in what he is now a suitor for," and the mayor Mr. Young "expects something to be done for him which you can doe in the gouvernmt. If when you meete he asks you for it, That may be a means to secure his Interest." Meanwhile, Mannooch "is now alive with heart and head," and had promised eighteen votes "That will vote but one vote [that is, "plump" for a single candidate] if he directs them."

The schoolmaster and wine merchant was evidently Southwell's most devoted supporter.[50]

Members of the Rye corporation later gave their own version of Ashburnham's visit, in testimony to the parliamentary committee on contested elections. They reported that the baron "came to Rye and treated the freemen . . . That he then Recomended the petitioner [Southwell] to them and told them that would be the way to have a good Harbour and to have Convoys and Protections [against impressment] in which the Petitioner being at Court would be more Capeable to Serve than Another, and they said Some of their Neighbours told them afterwards they had Protections."[51] In other words, they had been promised tangible economic benefits for their town if they gave their votes to Southwell. Nobody chose to mention the personal favours that had been requested, and nobody used party labels to describe the candidate, his manager, or his local backers. Yet they must have known that both the manager and his proposed candidate were Tories.

While party affiliations do not figure much in Ashburnham's letters, they were undoubtedly a factor in his calculations. For example, when he wrote to the Earl of Winchelsea to ask him to assist a merchant with an interest at Rye who was finding it difficult to dispose of some timber, Ashburnham was careful to point out that the merchant was being "persecuted by some for his active loyalty," that is, for his Toryism. Help for him would "doe yr. Lordsp allsoe some right against the disaffected," meaning the Whigs. Yet Ashburnham was willing to make overtures to the other side as well. He dined with the Whig candidate Thomas Fagge, and came away with hopes "that he will not appeare virulent against you [i.e. Southwell]." Nicholas Mannooch was also busy. He discerned that Mr. Mitchell of Horsham "has an influence on Morgan Warner his Tenant who is one of the new freemen & his sonne & Brother in Lawe are 2 more of the same, on whom Warner has an influence." Warner had been one of the collectors of the recent subsidies, suggesting that he was a firm Whig. Mannooch advised that the landlord should be instructed to tell Warner that "he shall take him as his ennemy, if he don't grant his request" to vote for Southwell. Ashburnham duly wrote to Mr. Mitchell, whom he did not know, requesting him "to use all yr. power" with Warner "in pressing him earnestly to doe all he can for Mr Southwell."[52] Party ties, self-interest, promises, pressures, and threats—the noble lord employed them all in order to sway a pack of small-town merchants, shipowners, and innkeepers whom he would never have invited to dinner. For their part, the freemen of Rye always showed deference to the baron, but this did not mean they would simply deliver their votes to his candidate. The electoral system at Rye, as elsewhere in England, was neither democratic nor fully representative of the will of voters, but it was unrestrained enough to require constant negotiation and coaxing.

In a situation of increased party conflict, the voters were volatile. On July 14, only a week before the poll, Ashburnham anxiously reported to Southwell that a third Whig gentleman, Phillips Gybbon of Rolvenden in Kent, had declared at the town hall that he would stand for election at Rye. "I believe his Interest very small," noted Ashburnham. Nevertheless, he thought it expedient to meet "alone a full hour with the Mayor persuading him to order matters so as the 20 new freemen might absent themselves & not appear at the day of Election." He warned Young that their qualifications might be challenged before the House of Commons. "The Mayor seemed shaken with my pressing him with these arguments espetially when I added the danger he would be in under the censure of a house of Commons if they found him faulty." A disqualified freeman who had voted would be fined £500. On the day before the election, however, Ashburnham was still not sure of how Young would act.

He advised Southwell, who had finally gone down to Rye, that "if it were possible to prevaile with the Mayor to use his interest with the 20 new Freemen to absent themselves . . . your businesse was sure to your satisfaction."[53]

It was not so sure. On Monday, July 20, the freemen went to the poll at the town hall. Most of the new freemen turned up, in spite of Ashburnham's threats. The result was forty voices for Fagge, thirty-eight for the Whig Joseph Offley and only twenty-five for Southwell. Gybbon had withdrawn from the poll. Assuming that those who supported Offley also tended to support Fagge, then most of those who chose Southwell were "plumpers" who opted to cast only one vote. This was a sign of an extreme partisanship between Whigs and Tories that was not so noticeable in Ashburnham's correspondence. Apparently, party affiliations counted for more among the voters of Rye than they did among the candidates! A petition to the House of Commons against the return was inevitable. The committee of privileges resolved that Rye freemen had to pay scot and lot, that is, local taxes, in order to vote. This meant disqualification for twenty-three freemen who were Dissenters, apprentices, journeymen, non-residents, too poor to pay taxes, or had been rejected and then made free during the same mayoralty. Joseph Radford junior, who had served as a county justice of the peace, "was fallen into decay" and was disqualified for not paying scot and lot. Unlike his father, he had supported the Whigs. Edward Southwell was finally declared elected by the committee, but the decision was not put before the whole House of Commons, leaving it open to reconsideration.[54]

The resolution did not settle much at Rye either. Within a year, Morgan Warner, who had been the object of Ashburnham's pressure tactics, and another rejected freeman had obtained a writ of mandamus restoring them as members of the corporation. Nicholas Mannooch, elected mayor again in 1703, refused to obey the mandamus, leading to a further appeal to the court of Queen's Bench. Cheering Mannooch from the sidelines was Lord Ashburnham, who expressed to the mayor his hope to see "the Bill passed this sessions against occasionall Conformity [taking Anglican sacraments only to qualify for office] which will pull of the Masque from many that have noe good designs in hand [i.e., Dissenters]." Ashburnham consulted with two leading Tory lawyers, Simon Harcourt and Sir Constantine Phipps, who reassured him that the mandamus "is a Parliament businesse to decide and may be too nice a thing for the Courts below to handle roughly." Harcourt was asked to pursue a new writ in favour of the mayor's position. Ashburnham insisted to Mannooch that "these new freemen soe called can never come in but by a new Election & a due Qualification and how that will worke in the Towne in their behalfe I cannot undertake to give an opinion."[55]

Mannooch responded by writing the committee of privilege's recent resolution into the corporation minute book. The names of the disqualified freemen were to be recorded for posterity, along with the testimony of those who tried to defend Mayor Young, such as Thomas Grebell. In February 1705, as another parliamentary election approached, Mannooch took the precaution of demanding that the freemen created by Mayor Young declare whether they had taken the Anglican sacrament within the past year, in accordance with the Corporations Act. Six of them had not, including the former mayor's son John Young, Thankfull Bishopp, and Joseph Breads. Although they were immediately disqualified, three of them appeared as freemen at the next assembly, probably after taking the sacrament.[56] The murderer John Breads's father was baptized as an Anglican in the same month that Mayor Mannooch began his assault on the Dissenters within the corporation, but he did not claim the freedom. He may not have been willing to accept the sacrament.

Lord Ashburnham took no active part in the Rye election of 1705. Perhaps he had tired of his role as campaign manager; perhaps he had realized that Rye would not easily accept a patron. He did keep up connections with Nicholas Mannooch, purchasing from him large quantities of Bordeaux wine, both claret and white, which the mayor was able to import without duty in spite of the war with France. Ashburnham wrote far more letters about wine purchases than about local politics. Edward Southwell, meanwhile, made a very public statement of his political and religious allegiances by donating the large, painted coat-of-arms of Queen Anne that still hangs in the nave of Rye church.[57] According to the corporation minute books, Southwell and another Court Tory, Philip Herbert, were elected in May 1705 without a contest by Mayor Mannooch, nine jurats, the chamberlain, and twenty-seven freemen. In fact, there had been a contest, with Southwell and Herbert pitted against the Whigs Charles Fagge and Phillips Gybbon. The final tally was twenty-one voices for each of the Tories, and nineteen for each of the Whigs—once again, a highly partisan division, with little or no voting across party lines. This time, the Whigs petitioned, and in January 1707 the committee of privileges unseated the two Tories on the basis of Mannooch's unlawful disqualification of the votes of the six Dissenters whom he had identified in February. The Tory-dominated House of Commons, however, overturned the committee resolution and awarded the seats once again to Southwell and Herbert.[58]

Were the Tories building a secure interest at Rye? No, they were not. They owed their success largely to Nicholas Mannooch's efforts, both in persuading moderates to vote for them and in disqualifying Whig freemen. The royal coat-of-arms hanging in St. Mary's does not seem to have swayed or intimidated many. Although the vicar of Rye, Edward Wilson, was undoubtedly a High Churchman and Tory, he had little influence on the town's politics. His unflagging efforts to repair the church, put its accounts in order, and reclaim the vicar's right to first fruits and tenths as well as the tithe on hops, were surprisingly successful, but they cannot have made him popular.[59] In August 1705, the weakness of the Tories at Rye was glaringly revealed, when the Whig Thomas Grebell became mayor, through the votes of the freemen whose qualifications Mannooch had refused to accept. Grebell named the contentious Morgan Warner to the chamberlainship, and even invited Thomas Tournay back from Hythe to serve as town clerk. To placate the moderates, he allowed one of their leaders, Thomas Odiarne, owner of the Mermaid tavern, to lay a pipe from the Strand conduit to his brewhouse, and to "Break and distroy" tubs of clothes that might be brought to the conduit for washing. At the same time, Grebell began to lay the foundations of a new oligarchy: Whig, family-run, committee-based, highly officious, and, above all, lucrative. He named himself, his brother Jeremiah, and his friend Morgan Warner to a nine-man committee that would let out newly imposed duties on the use of the gravel landing place in Rye harbour. Articles for preserving the landing place were pretentiously written on parchment and displayed in the court hall. One of the first lessees of the duties was Jeremiah Grebell.[60]

With the change in local politics came a shift in Rye's parliamentary representation. It preceded the Jacobite attempt of 1708, which caused a reaction in favour of the Whigs throughout England. The appointment of Philip Herbert as commissioner of the sick and wounded meant that he had to vacate his parliamentary seat, and allowed for the election of Phillips Gybbon as a member of Parliament in December 1707. Five months later, the general election of 1708 returned, without a contest, Gybbon and Sir John Norris, a Whig naval captain who was then at sea. It was fitting that Thomas Tournay was one of those who administered the oaths to Norris when he returned to England.

Norris was elected by Mayor Young's Whig freemen of 1701, many of whom were the offspring of Mayor Tournay's radical freemen of 1681.[61]

Edward Southwell made a last, doomed attempt to re-establish the Tory interest at Rye in 1710. He campaigned with John Ellis, a former undersecretary of state, against Gybbon and Norris, but gained only sixteen votes against twenty-nine for the Whigs. The two Tories petitioned Parliament on the grounds that several voters, including the mayor, Walter Waters, had been refused, then readmitted to the freedom. Besides, Waters had lost his freedom again through the 1702 resolution of the privileges committee. Surprisingly, however, neither the committee nor the House of Commons supported the Tory candidates. Both bodies had a strong majority of Tories; but they were mostly fervent back-bench Country members, whereas Southwell and Ellis were moderates and placemen for whom they had little sympathy. Perhaps, too, the national Tory party had simply given up on Rye. The corporation, led again by Thomas Grebell, responded by readmitting all the disputed freemen in August 1711.[62]

Gybbon and Norris were re-elected in 1713, against a high tide of Toryism that swept the nation as a whole. Two obscure Tory gentlemen, Samuel Lynn and John Chamberlain, ran against them without much hope of success, in the town's last contested poll for over a century. A petition was presented to the committee of privileges, for the fifth time in the five general elections of Queen Anne's reign, citing Walter Waters as an illegal mayor who had used bribes and threats to return the Whigs, but it was withdrawn. Gybbon would serve as the member of Parliament for Rye until 1762, fifty-five years after his first election. Norris and his two sons would sit as representative of the port until 1749. Nobody who dared to call himself a Tory would be elected to Parliament at Rye until the nineteenth century. The election of Thomas Grebell as mayor in 1705 had settled Rye's parliamentary history for the next five decades and beyond.[63] The Whiggism that he had established in the town, however, was less ideological than pragmatic. At its heart was economic security for the merchants who profited from the war with France, and religious security for their Dissenting allies. Moroever, Grebell's triumph had been shaped in large part by politics at Westminster, and was not simply a mask for the assertion of local autonomy. The Whigs of Rye, in other words, were Whigs in national as well as in local terms. Unlike their radical predecessors, they saw themselves as members of a party cause that was organized and combative throughout the kingdom.

Cementing the Oligarchy

Between 1710 and 1714, Whig Rye should have been at odds with a Tory national legislature. In fact, no conflict took place between them. This was largely due to the caution of the mayor and jurats, who had entirely given up the explosive radicalism of the Restoration. They might have taken offence when the vicar, Edmund Wilson, gave a sermon on 30 January 1712 commemorating the death of Charles I. It was a High Church occasion, and the sermon had a Tory theme, that obedience to government was necessary. Wilson condemned those whose "Impiety" had led them to "Embrue their Hands in Royal Blood," a topical reference in a town that had once been full of republicans. The vicar went on to praise Queen Anne as "the best of Princes: Her Piety and Zeal for the established Church, has made her the Darling of Heaven, as well as of her People." He lauded the impending peace treaty, which would "free us from the Calamities, of the most bloody and expensive War, that ever *England* was Engaged in." On the other hand, Wilson used language that would have been acceptable to a Whig merchant, describing government not as divinely instituted, but as "necessary to the Welfare of Mankind; because it is the great Band of human Society, the Guard of its Peace, and the Security of a very Man's Person, Goods, and good Name." Rejecting the late attempt at "Arbitrary Power" by James II, he admonished his listeners to pray for "the Establish'd Constitution both in Church and State; because we are thereby protected and secured in our Civil Rights," that is, in the ownership of property, as well as "in the free Exercise of our most holy Religion." As for party differences, "I am confident that we have greater Fears and Jealousies one of another, than we need to have." The Whig jurats of Rye were so pleased with the sermon that they asked for it to be published.[64]

The vicar had achieved a delicate balancing act in this sermon, by presenting a Tory subject in a way that would not be wholly antagonistic to a Whig audience. The Rye magistrates took his advice and quietly waited for a shift in the political winds. It came suddenly in August 1714, when Queen Anne died. The accession of George I, and the subsequent change of ministry from Tory to Whig, must have seemed providential to the magistrates of Rye. Now the national government and that of the ancient port would be in harmony. The Jacobite Pretender may have had admirers in other towns who regarded King George as a usurper, but he had no friends at all in Rye. Francis Jeake, son of the younger Samuel and a law student in London, witnessed Jacobite demonstrations in the capital in 1716. He observed how "the poor deluded Populace" had cut chips of wood from the gallows on which some Jacobite rioters had been hanged, "to keep as Relicts of such pious Martyrs of their Cause."[65] To his Dissenting mind, the Jacobites were no better than superstitious Papists.

The mayor, jurats, freemen, and leading inhabitants of Rye made the same point in a petition addressed to King George in July 1715. Noting that "some of your Subjects regardless of their Oaths, their Faith and their Allegiance have of late dis-

covered such A Spirit of Rebellion in severall parts of this Kingdome as Shews there are many who bid defyance to your Just
and mild Government," the petitioners expressed "Our utmost
Abhorrence of such Tumultuous and Traiterous Proceedings."
Happily, "there yett remains the true Spirit of British Liberty
within this Kingdome, which will always prefere the Clemency
of your Majesty's Governmt., the Enjoyments of the Protestant
Religion and Our Antient Rights to the Arbitrary Reign of a
Popish Impostor tied up with Notions of French Slavery." The
petition was signed by the mayor, Morgan Warner; by Warner's
former antagonist, Nicholas Mannooch; by Thomas Grebell,
his son Allen (who had become a freeman in December 1714)
and his brother Jeremiah; by Ralph Norton, a new freeman and
probably a Tory; and by Walter Waters, Thankfull Bishopp, Bartholomew Breads, Joseph Breads, Francis Jeake, and his brother
Samuel Jeake III. In all, the document carried 158 signatures,
including every one of the leading men of Rye.[66] It was a remarkable statement of unity, a final renunciation of party conflict and
the original contract for forty years of Whig oligarchy.

Their fierce anti-Jacobite feelings represented almost the last
trace of Dissenting radicalism among the Rye oligarchs. The
Puritan moralism of former days had faded away. Although they
continued for a few years to prosecute swearing and drunkenness, the incomplete accounts of fines paid show no more than
three cases each year from 1707 until 1724. Accusations of swearing could be turned against the oligarchs, as was demonstrated in
1717 when the vicar informed against Richard Butler, an ally of
the Grebells, "for prophanely swearing one oath." The incident
may help to explain why prosecutions for swearing soon disappeared. Drunkenness remained an offence as late as 1745, when
two men were presented for being inebriated. One of them was
ordered to sit in the stocks because he was too poor to pay the
five-shilling fine. These isolated prosecutions against obscure

individuals were made for the good order of the town rather than out of lingering Puritanism.[67]

Perhaps the only truly radical act of the Grebell regime was the founding of the non-denominational Sanders School, although it was created by the initiative of an old Dissenter, James Sanders of Winchelsea. At his death in 1709, Sanders left his estate to fund a free charity school at Rye, "for the benefit of the poor Children." After a Chancery suit with Sanders's heirs was resolved in Rye's favour, the estate was allowed to accumulate for ten years, at which point part of it was sold for £720 to Phillips Gybbon and others. The school's articles were drawn up by the mayor, jurats, and town counsel in May 1720. Dissenting as well as Anglican children were to be admitted, and "No Scholler or Schollers shall be required by the Master to go to any certain place of Worship or to learn any Catechism without the Consent and Approbation of his or their parents or Guardians." Students were forbidden "to Use or Speak any Opprobrious or Reprochful Language to or against the other Schollers upon the Account of the said Schollers or their Parents being protestant dissenters." Can we detect here an implicit criticism of Nicholas Mannooch, the Tory master of Peacock's School? The students were to be taught "to Read and Write and particularly Arithmetick & Navigation in all their parts," to train them to be sailors. As for the master, he was to be "a Man well Affected to his Majesty King George and the present Constitution, a man of Sober Conversation good Morals and Manners and Especially one that has not Misbehaved himself or given any just Cause of Offence to this Corporacion of Rye." Again, this may be a barb aimed at Mannooch, who *had* given offence. The corporation was to enjoy more complete control over Sanders' School than over Peacock's. The court of record itself admitted students to the former institution, and it occasionally expelled them.[68]

By the time Sanders' School was founded, the man who would

inherit the Grebell mantle as the leading oligarch of Rye had already entered the local political scene. On 15 October 1717, James Lamb of Shoreham married Martha, daughter of Thomas Grebell. The marriage was by license rather than banns, which may indicate that Martha was pregnant and had to marry in a hurry. Aside from her frequent pregnancies and death in February 1738, very little is known about Martha Lamb, or about the other wives of the Rye oligarchs for that matter. In contrast to some of their Puritan foremothers, they seem to have been silent pawns in the game of political alliance-making. Martha is not even mentioned on her husband's memorial in St. Mary's.

As for James Lamb, his background is obscure. He was most likely one of the Lambs of Udimore, a Wealden village whose lord of the manor was patron of Rye church. Thomas Lamb of Udimore was fined for non-payment of church rates in 1692. He rented the lands attached to Peacock's School during the period of Whig mayoralties from 1690 until 1703. James and Richard Lamb were probably his sons. James entered the customs service in 1713 as deputy collector at Rye, and the following year became collector at both Rye and Shoreham. He and his wife Martha were clearly favoured by her father, Thomas Grebell, who after his death in 1723 left the pair "his Great Deeze" or warehouse and storage vault, along with his property in Kent. This was far more than Thomas left to his son Allen, who received only "the little deeze" along with the remainder of the Kentish properties. Allen should not have been resentful, as he had already been given two houses and extensive lands through the settlement drawn up at his marriage in 1720 to Catherine Hodges of Worshorne, Kent. The inheritance from Thomas Grebell, however, explains how James Lamb became a rich man and was able to extend the big house at the top of Mermaid Street that he had purchased from his brother-in-law Allen. Lamb paid tax on seventeen windows in 1722; within two years, he had added eight more. It was in this house that Lamb entertained King George I for four nights in January 1726, when the monarch was blown into Rye while on his way back from Hannover. The king stood godfather to Lamb's son George and presented the family with a handsome silver christening bowl, the ultimate symbol of having "made it."[69]

Oligarchy in Rye did not survive solely through ties of marriage and inheritance, or by royal favour. It had to be safeguarded by the elimination of rivals, and it had to neutralize potential sources of discontent. It had to find rewards for its supporters, and at least seem to provide general benefits for the town. Finally, it had to be cemented by bonds of sociability that went beyond relatives and in-laws. The remainder of this section will consider the first point; the rest are examined in the next chapter.

To eliminate rivals was always the first priority. The Grebell-Lamb faction was so efficient at it that we can only trace the existence of its enemies through scattered hints in the corporation records and other sources. In February 1718, for example, after the death in office of Mayor Jeremiah Grebell, a contested election raised Richard Higgins to the mayoralty. He chose nine jurats, but aside from Nicholas Mannooch, Thomas Grebell, and two others, "there were no more sworn to the said Mr. Mayor's Assistance." Five junior jurats, including Allen Grebell, were not sworn and so could not act as magistrates. It seems likely that Higgins was trying to put a check on the influence of the Grebells. He was never mayor again. Higgins was succeeded by Thomas Grebell, then by Allen, by Thomas again, by the Grebell ally John Slade, and then in 1723 by James Lamb. Learning from the experience, the Grebell-Lamb faction allowed no new freemen to be elected after 1718. The freedom could only be attained by mayoral choice or by paternal right, as in the case of Samuel Jeake III, who became free in 1719. The number of freemen remained constant at about thirty-five, but they rarely attended assemblies, and only one or two were chosen for committees. With one exception in 1758, no further contested mayoral election is known to have taken place in Rye until 1825. The mayoralty would remain in the hands of the Grebell-Lamb faction until 1833, with only a brief break in 1758–59.[70]

A more formidable rival was the former mayor, Nicholas Mannooch. As the owner of lands on the Wittersham Levels around Rye, he was at odds with the corporation's efforts to force the proprietors of the levels to pay for the construction of a seawall and sluice in the marshes. Mayor Allen Grebell brought a bill in Chancery against Mannooch, Ralph Norton, and three other owners of the levels in January 1721. Their response was a cross bill in Chancery that the corporation minute book denounced as "Scandalous and made up of ffalsities." In August 1722, Mannooch and Norton proposed arbitration by two local gentlemen, one of them the Tory John Fuller of Brightling. The proposal was accepted by the town corporation, and the judgement of the arbitrators appears to have been in its favour; but the threat of a Chancery suit over the levels would continue for another three years.[71]

Meanwhile, as has been seen, the Grebells undermined Mannooch's authority as master of Peacock's School by lending their support to its newly founded competitor. Sanders' School was a broad-minded and liberal project, but as a non-denominational institution, it was an affront to High Churchmen, and especially to the ex-manager of the Tory interest in Rye. In December 1724, Mannooch resigned from the mastership of Peacock's School. Although he probably did this because of ill health, he did not depart happily. He seems to have taken the school records with him (keeping records was always a sign of disgruntlement in Rye). Within a few days, Mannooch was dead. Peacock's School now went into rapid decline, due largely to the neglect of the mayor and jurats. Mannooch's successor, Reverend Lewis Jones, rector of Little Horstead, near Lewes, rented the schoolroom out for storage to Samuel Jeake III, so that by 1741 it "was all Littered with Straw and dirt, and in it were some Gross of empty Bottles and some Dozens of Full ones," alongside hogsheads of wine and "a very large Quantity of Fowl Tobacco pipes." Jeake also kept, in the upper room of the school, an unsuccessful flying machine that he had designed! As for Reverend Jones, he had only one student, whom he taught at his home. The trustees did nothing to alter the situation, and simply ordered another inspection a year later. By 1746, hogs were being kept in the schoolroom. Not until the following year did the trustees decide that Lewis Jones should be "reprehended and Admonished" for being "very ffaulty in not Giveing due Attendance." No scholars then attended the school.[72]

After the death of Nicholas Mannooch in 1724, the Grebell-Lamb faction faced no serious rivals for more than twenty years. Yet the Grebells and Lambs still had to neutralize potential sources of discontent, foremost among them the Church. It was not possible to placate Reverend Wilson in a political sense, because he was an ardent Tory, and no doubt the foundation of Sanders' School infuriated him; but at least he could be allowed to remain unmolested in his own little domain at the top of the hill. Through his efforts, an Anglican charity school for twelve poor boys and girls had been set up at Rye around 1709. It had thirty pupils in 1713, supported by subscriptions, but the contributions were not sufficient to buy the students clothes. The corporation did nothing either to help or hinder the enterprise; indeed, the charity school is never mentioned at all in the town records. It still existed in 1724, but by 1740, after Wilson's death, it was gone. Anglican religious education would remain completely neglected in the town for the rest of the eighteenth century.[73]

The parish church, on the other hand, was saved from ruin by the energetic vicar. According to the 1724 episcopal visitation, St. Mary's was "in good repair," with "a good bible & common prayer book: 2 Silver Cups; 1 patin: 1 plate for Alms Silver; 2 large pewter flaggons; linnen & woollen Cloths for the Communion table; velvet Cloth & cushion for the desk & pulpit: 2 Surplices." The vicarage was "new & built with brick by the present Incumbt." The parish had no glebe land except the garden between the vicar's house and the churchyard, and no benefactions; but the vicar received first fruits and tenths as well as an augmentation of £12.10s per annum, much less than the £20 that was paid to the master of Sanders' School. Wilson offered the sacrament seven or eight times a year, to about fifty communicants. Of two hundred families in the town, only two were reported to be Quakers and ten members of other Dissenting groups. This was doubtless an underestimate, but it shows that many of those who had previously walked in the ways of Dissent had now returned to the conformist fold.[74]

Among those Dissenters who had turned back to the Church was Thomas Grebell. He is buried alongside his family at the east end of St. Clare's chapel. His son Allen first appeared as a churchwarden in 1732. James Lamb held the same office two years later. By that time, Grebell and Lamb both owned pews in the middle aisle of the church, near those of Ralph Norton and the schoolmaster Lewis Jones. Lamb's pew, next to a pillar in an area called "Coblers Hole," measured 10'6" by 3'5" and was one of the largest in the church. The adherence of his generation of Rye Whigs to Anglicanism rather than Dissent certainly lessened religious tensions in the town. It cannot be seen simply as a political move, because it may have reflected personal as much as social motivations. Still, it is not easy to judge how warmly the Grebells and their allies re-embraced the Church of England. As was noted previously, Allen Grebell's memorial contains no reference to his religious life. James Lamb's memorial mentions "the undissembled piety of a true Christian," but this is not very revealing. Neither Grebell nor Lamb left any benefaction to St. Mary's in their wills. It was Lamb's son Thomas, not the patriarch himself, who later ornamented the church with a chandelier and new bells, and probably helped to pay for the two "Quarter-boys" whose fibreglass successors still stand next to the church clock.[75]

The conformity of the Grebells and Lambs never swayed Reverend Wilson from his original Toryism. In the county elections of 1734, he was one of only eight voters at Rye who cast votes for the Tory candidates Sir Cecil Bishopp and John Fuller of Brightling. Among the other seven Tory voices were Francis Mannooch, the late schoolmaster's son, and John Haffenden, a churchwarden at St. Mary's.[76] By the time of Wilson's death in 1739, however, patronage of the living had passed from the Tory earls of Thanet to Spencer Compton, Earl of Wilmington, a prominent Whig. Wilmington appointed as vicar the inoffensive Thomas Hudson, who allowed the angry and unforgiving Grebell monument to be erected, but otherwise left little mark on the parish before his death in 1744.

By the early 1720s, the Grebell-Lamb faction had brought all of its enemies to heel or calmed them with policies of benign neglect. Aided by a fall in population and a decade of peace, it had brought back a semblance of prosperity to the port, and was about to embark on an ambitious reconstruction of the harbour. The next two decades appear to have been a period of tranquility and moderate prosperity, such as the town had not experienced in a century. In all these respects, Rye reflected the experience of many other small towns, and of the kingdom as a whole. The attack of the sanguinary butcher, therefore, struck without warning, from out of nowhere. Yet Breads turned out not to be the only disgruntled man in Rye. In the two decades after the murder, others appeared to challenge the Lamb faction, and for a brief time, they loosened its grip on power. Why had an apparently successful system of governance run into such trouble by the 1740s? To answer that question, and to place the murder of Allen Grebell in its contemporary context, we will have to examine in more detail the workings of oligarchy at Rye in the age of James Lamb.

5

Politeness and Police

Laws, order, police, discipline; these can never be carried
to any degree of perfection, before human reason has re-
fined itself by exercise, and by an application to the more
vulgar arts, at least of commerce and manufacture.
—David Hume, "Of Refinement in the Arts" (1742)

Butchers were more likely than other tradesmen to be hanged
in the eighteenth century—at least the poet John Gay thought
so. In his poem "Trivia: Or, the Art of Walking the Streets of
London," written in 1714–16, Gay advised strollers in the capital to "resign the Way / To shun the surly *Butcher's* greasy Tray, /
Butchers, whose Hands are dy'd with Blood's foul Stain, / And
always foremost in the Hangman's Train."[1] Butchers were used
to blood, and they worked with knives that could be turned to
assault or murder. There may have been a further, more pro-
saic explanation for why the London hangman would have entertained so many butchers: namely, the opening up of the regu-
lated meat markets of the capital. By the early eighteenth
century, the London guilds had lost control of the markets to independent wholesalers and dealers, who engaged in shady practices such as forestalling (keeping meat off the market so as to
increase its price) and regrating (buying up meat in order to sell
it at a higher profit). This drove many of the smaller dealers and
butchers out of business. Some of them took to robbery on the
highways, the same highways by which livestock was brought

into the capital. Thus, the criminality of butchers has been ascribed to the growth of an unregulated free market that benefited the strong and pauperized the weak.[2]

Was John Breads a victim of free-market capitalism? Was he driven to a desperate act of murder by increasing poverty and marginalization? These questions seem to diminish both the shocking brutality of his crime and the possibility of his madness, but we should not dismiss them out of hand. The economy of Rye was certainly changing in the eighteenth century, as was that of England, away from strict regulation, towards less restraint on commerce and exchange. In the Restoration period, nobody could work as a butcher in the town without serving a seven-year apprenticeship. Indentures for apprentice butchers, spelling out the terms of their service, were issued by the Rye court of record and carefully copied out in its register. Each butcher was then annually licensed. A glance at the corporation Assembly Book for 1662–63 shows the magistrates busying themselves with the licensing of four butchers and eighteen victuallers, many of whom practiced butchering. The butchers' money, or fines for licenses, amounted in 1662–63 to 9s.2d, not an inconsiderable part of the £8.4.2 in the corporation's great box. The town imposed religion on the butchers, prohibiting them from practicing their trade on certain holy days and throughout the Lenten season. It also addressed the environmental impact of the meat business. The longest ordinance in the Assembly Book for the late seventeenth century—it may be the longest ever written in early modern Rye—concerned the control of hogs, raw material for butchers. They were creating a nuisance by wandering about the streets unrestrained, presumably eating up the malt used in brewing.[3] Almost every aspect of butchering in Rye was kept under the watchful eyes of the magistrates.

Eighty years later, the tight system of corporate regulation was not gone, but it had frayed at the edges. The sessions court still issued licenses for victuallers, but those for butchers were rarely recorded. The last prosecution of a butcher for lack of a license was in 1715. The process of apprenticeship had also deteriorated. For the whole eighteenth century, only two town apprenticeship bonds have been preserved, neither of them for a butcher. This does not mean that apprenticeship was no longer required, but it suggests that occupational training was not as diligently monitored as in the seventeenth century. Butchers who used short-weights were still occasionally presented at the sessions, as the younger John Breads (not the murderer) was in 1737, but enforcement was haphazard and the penalties were minor. Meanwhile, the Lenten prohibition on butchering, along with other holy day restrictions, had fallen into disuse.[4]

The butchers and victuallers of Rye were not always hurt by this laxity. Regulation of their trade by the corporation added costs to their business and could turn into petty harassment by the magistrates. Even the looser controls of the mid-eighteenth century were sometimes resented. Dame Davis, a victualler of Rye, was so angry when the sessions jury tried to inspect her measuring pots in 1746 that she hit them, abused them, and "Said we had Broke two of her potts that was Measure and had stole another."[5] On the other hand, the stricter regulation of the past had kept out competitors and allowed a small number of licensed retailers to make a good living. In the sixteenth and seventeenth centuries, several families of butchers had attained high status in the town, among them the Grebells and the Bennetts. By the eighteenth century, this had become impossible. No butcher became a jurat under the Grebell-Lamb regime, and apparently none of the freemen was a butcher either.

This may have been galling to John Breads. His father was a butcher, who from 1706 until 1724 stood as surety to numerous other butchers and victuallers when they were taking out licenses. This gave him a certain prestige among the tradesmen of the town. The older Breads was literate, as was his son. His only brush with the law was around 1720, when he was presented for short weights. He supported a large family. His son, the future felon, lived differently. John Breads took up butchering only after working as a freight carrier and keeping an inn. His initial avoidance of the family profession may have been due to its uncertain status. His early career does not seem to have been very successful, however, which brought him back after 1738 to his father's trade of butchering. Breads was involved in four civil lawsuits between 1736 and 1742, arising perhaps from his ownership of the Flushing Inn. In three of these cases he was sued, and he twice had to pay small damages and costs to the plaintiffs. He stood as a surety only twice, for John Igglesdon in 1738 and for a meal-seller in 1741, suggesting that he was less well known or less trusted than his father. He left a small debt amounting to £9.13.8 after his death, but his assets, leaving aside the disputed ownership of the Flushing Inn, were apparently not enough to cover it. Although Breads's fluctuating fortunes cannot simply be ascribed to the decline of regulation in the butchering trade, they were doubtless affected by it.[6]

Another John Breads lived in the town. He was younger, possibly an outsider, and may not have been so distressed by the loosening of regulation in the butchering trade. He seems to have appeared at Rye in the mid-1730s, set up a business in a house near the churchyard, married a local woman, and had two children. If he was from a family that had not previously practiced butchering, then the openness of the trade must have benefited him. There is no evidence that he was licensed, and we would not know his profession at all if it were not for the three short weights for which he was presented to the sessions court in 1737, or the fact that he was described as a butcher when he died in 1745. Judging by his place of residence, he made a good living, but his success should not be overestimated. After his death, his sons were educated at Sanders' School, indicating that they had been left in poverty.[7]

The effects of economic change in the eighteenth century were unpredictable, and we can only speculate as to what their impact was on the mentality of a man like John Breads. We can say that he did not always prosper from them. In any case, he would not have regarded change as a nameless or faceless force that fell on him from the blue. It would have been obvious to him that, if butchers were no longer able to become freemen or enter the highest ranks of local society, it was because the town oligarchs did not want them there. The fault, in other words, lay not with the encroachments of free-market capitalism, but with the Grebells and the Lambs, who by 1740 had established a considerable social distance between themselves and the common tradesmen of Rye. The evidence does not allow us to know how much Breads resented this, but we can at least try to determine what it was he might have resented. How exactly did the Grebell-Lamb domination work, and whom did it benefit?

Profit

Oligarchy depended on profits for its security; and profits were spread through patronage. Money and favours trickled down a hierarchical system. Rye, however, was too poor to provide many perquisites to the oligarchs and their friends. Lacking a property tax, its revenues were drawn mainly from four insecure sources: the renting of town lands; the dues or small-box, levied on goods entering the harbour; market dues on fish and fruit; and various small taxes on shopkeepers and tradesmen that were not regularly collected. Whether members of the Grebell-Lamb faction were systematically given favourable terms on the rental of town lands is hard to determine, although surely James Lamb should have paid more than sixpence a year plus a fine of five guineas for a ninety-nine-year lease on a parcel of wasteland on which he was allowed to build a house in 1726. As for the small-box and market dues, they were leased out to tax-farmers, who paid an annual rent for the right to collect the tax, and pocketed whatever additional money was raised. The small-box rent, which had reached a record £110 in 1626, sunk to only £10 in 1692, a year of war and sunken trade. By 1728, Richard Lamb was paying £80 for it—an improvement over the 1690s, but far less than a century before, especially when inflation is taken into account. The fish and fruit farm, meanwhile, declined from £21 in 1700 to £4.5.0 in 1740.[8]

Nobody can have been enriching himself on such tiny amounts, unless the returns from these taxes were significantly greater than what was paid for them, which is unlikely. In fact, the oligarchs can be seen as helping the town remain solvent by renting lands and farming taxes. Twenty-six years of peace after 1713 greatly assisted them in restoring the town to financial health. By 1739, they could declare that "this Corporacion is now out of Debt and that the Revenues thereof are much increased and in a Flourishing Condition." Balanced budgets did not last long, but it was the outbreak of war, the building of a new town hall and repairs on the harbour, not peculation on the part of the mayor or jurats, that again threw Rye into the red by the early 1740s. Years of borrowing followed: £900 at 3 percent interest from Phillips Gybbon and Sir John Norris in 1742, a debt that was cancelled by the benevolent members of Parliament in 1755; £300 in 1746; £500 from Thomas Lamb in 1754, for the costs of a new bridge to Winchelsea; a further £200 in 1758; and finally, £300 in 1760, at 4 percent annual interest. These were mostly war years, when fewer vessels were entering the harbour. By 1761, according to Phillips Gybbon, the corporation was almost £1,000 in debt.[9] From this perspective, its claim on the estate of John Breads appears to have been made out of necessity rather than greed.

Given the parlous financial situation of the town, the oligarchs were obliged to look outside it to find favours — particularly, to the central administration. For example, James Lamb's early career was promoted not just by his father-in-law, Thomas Grebell, but also by Norris and Gybbon, who recommended him for the customs collectorship at Dover in 1718 (he was unsuccessful). Once he was established, Lamb set up business connections with the great men of Whitehall. In 1726, he sold a shipment of wine to Henry Pelham, the Duke of Newcastle's brother and one of the leading Whigs in East Sussex. In the time-honoured fashion of the landed gentry, Pelham did not pay his debt for several months. The wine was carried to London by "Master Breads," probably the sixteen-year-old John Breads. It was the first of two known occasions when Breads benefited from the patronage of James Lamb. In his last years of power, the mayor was willing to beg for others, as in 1752 when he asked Pelham, who by then was Prime Minister, for something to be done to relieve Thomas Bishop, sometime purser of HMS *Dorset*. Apparently, Bishop owed the government £900 but was destitute.[10] Perhaps nothing was done; by this time, the mayor was not on as good terms as he had formerly been with the prime minister. Meanwhile, the customs officer Nathaniel Pigram senior enjoyed the patronage of Pelham's brother, the Duke of Newcastle, and was apparently less disinterested in using his connections. Newcastle helped to restore Pigram to the customs service after a suspension in 1739, and later recommended that he be allowed to keep his sloop, the *Amelia*, in the employment of the service, although it was larger than the fifty-tons specification.[11]

Perhaps the most assiduous beggar of favours from the government among the jurats of Rye was the attorney Samuel Jeake III, whose father and grandfather had so often refused to court the patronage of great men. Already in 1728, Samuel III had prefaced a treatise by his grandfather on the Cinque Ports charters with a fawning dedication to the Duke of Dorset, in which he begged "Your Protection for a Work that can have no other Patron but Your Self."[12] In 1740, the Duke of Newcastle was solicited by Samuel III and other inhabitants of Rye, who wanted to obtain the position of postmaster for Michael Woollett, a tenant of Jeake who needed the substantial salary of £40 a year to support his eight children. Jeake assured the Duke that "I have always taken Care my Tenants should be in your Grace's Interest." Four years later, Jeake was begging Newcastle to present a petition to the House of Lords, concerning some land rented from the Earl of Thanet that Jeake had enclosed. Thanet opposed the enclosure, and had actually obtained an order for his tenant Jeake to be taken into custody for breach of privilege of the House of Lords. Harassed by the arbitrary power of the nobility, the small-town solicitor had to turn to another noble to find protection. How the affair ended is not clear, but by 1761 Jeake was in Jamaica, writing to Phillips Gybbon about obtaining the position of collector of customs for himself. Alluding to the much-deplored influence of the Scottish Lord Bute on the new king, George III, Jeake maintained that he "will then be the only English Man (except the Atty Genl. the rest are Scotch) in any Imployment worth having on the Island."[13]

The biggest favour that the government could bestow on the oligarchs of Rye was the rebuilding of the harbour. This could also be represented as a general benefit for the town, although it turned out to be a fiasco. The project was initiated by Mayor Mannooch, who sent a petition to Parliament in 1700, asking for an act to provide revenues for harbour repairs. As a result, Rye was given the right to a passing toll of threepence per ton to defray the expenses of restoring the harbour "to its ancient Goodness." Little was done, however, probably because improvements would have infringed on the inning of marshland by landowners such as Mannooch and the Earl of Thanet. These lands were drained by sluices that would have to be removed or redirected by any rebuilding scheme. The duty was nonetheless extended in 1709 and again in 1718. Finally, an act was passed in 1722 that called for the cutting of a canal through Winchelsea. The passing toll was extended to all vessels between twenty and three hundred tons landing at south coast ports, and was to be split between Dover and Rye, with the latter receiving two-thirds of it. The mayor and jurats of Rye were appointed as harbour commissioners, along with twelve proprietors of land in the levels that drained into the harbour.[14]

The commissioners, who met for the first time in May 1724, included Mayor James Lamb, Allen Grebell, and eight other jurats, of whom only Nicholas Mannooch could be regarded at this time as hostile to the ruling oligarchs. Phillips Gybbon, Thankfull Bishopp, and the Whig M.P. John Fane were among the ten marshland proprietors who also sat on the commission, alongside Tory gentlemen such as Thomas Frewen of Brickwall and Sir William Ashburnham. The Grebell-Lamb faction and its allies enjoyed a clear majority. After the first meeting, only the mayor, jurats, and two or three landowners bothered to attend. Within two months, £5,000 had been borrowed from the Bank of England, a sum almost thirty times greater than the £179.18.3 combined revenues of the town of Rye for 1719, the last year in which the accounts were audited. Further amounts were raised by subscription and loans from private individuals. Where all this money went in the next thirty years is impossible to figure out, inasmuch as the accounts were very poorly kept.[15]

What is quite clear is that profit-taking by members of the corporation began almost immediately—and so did the hint of corruption. John Slade was named treasurer in May 1724, with the right to take sixpence in the pound on money collected for the harbour, up to £25 per year. He resigned in August, on the day after the accounts were examined and it was found that more than £300 was owing to the commission. In May 1725, the commissioners decided that the report on Slade's accounts "appears to be a mistake" because the missing £300 was paid to the receiver general of customs, so that Slade owed only £7.16.7 to the commission. Why this information was not available the previous August was nowhere explained. Whatever the actual circumstances, John Slade was a leading merchant of Rye and too important to alienate. Over the next two decades, he and his son Chiswell would sell large quantities of timber and other materials to the harbour commissioners.[16]

Like the Slades, the Lamb family prospered from the sale of building supplies for use in harbour construction. Richard Lamb provided thirty wheelbarrows at 6s.6d apiece, while from James Lamb and Company, the commissioners purchased deals and planks to make walls for the canal. Between 1725 and 1760, James Lamb senior and junior were paid about £1,650 for various services. The mayor's son Thomas was appointed collector of the passing toll. Although returns from this office were meagre at first, between 1746 and 1760 he earned an average of more than £200 a year from the post. The Lamb family was also a source of loans: £267 was borrowed from James Lamb at 5 percent interest from June to September 1725. By 1749, the commissioners owed £1,020 to James Lamb, £800 to Thomas Lamb, and £1,000 to James's daughter Elizabeth.[17] In short, Commissioner James Lamb authorized the borrowing of money at interest from himself and his relations in order to make disbursements to himself and his relations for their services.

The harbour renovations were very much a Lamb family enterprise. The obliging commissioners even reimbursed James Lamb for his losses on a timber contract that could not be filled because the House of Commons failed to provide more money for the project in 1744. The debt on the harbour repairs reached £11,480 in that year, at which point work had to stop. The onset of war with France meant that Parliament was not likely to give much attention to the harbour at Rye, which was not deep enough for naval vessels. Peace brought a revival of construction after 1748, and the revenues from the passing toll peaked at £4,100 in 1752–53.[18] A new infusion of money was still needed, however, and suspicions were raised that a great deal of it had already been squandered. Colonel James Pelham, M.P. for Hastings and second cousin to the Duke of Newcastle, caused a furor when he asserted at a meeting of harbour trustees that "it is universally allowed a thing impracticable to make a Harbour here. . . . And that the People of this Corporation and Town do not desire it should be finished."[19] Just as worrisomely, the potential for conflicts of interest had not gone unnoticed. One exasperated commissioner pointed out in 1751, referring to Thomas Lamb's salary, that "I Cannot think [it] Rite as he is now Mayor of Rye." Responding to the criticism, Lamb temporarily resigned as a jurat the following year.[20]

Profits from the harbour commission even trickled down to John Breads, the future murderer. His name appears in the harbour commissioner's accounts in 1728, when he was paid £5.16.9 for freight on a delivery of deals and spars for James Lamb and Company.[21] The payment is substantial, and it suggests that Breads had good relations with the Lambs at this stage. Something may have altered soon afterwards, however, because Breads's name does not appear again in the accounts.

The renovation of Rye harbour faced constant opposition from neighbouring Winchelsea, whose magistrates wanted trade to be redirected there, as well as from local landowners, who objected to any attempt to prevent them from inning marshland. Under pressure from Parliament, a new harbour plan was drawn up in 1763 by John Smeaton, Fellow of the Royal

Society and builder of the Eddystone Lighthouse, but it was not implemented. The project was finally halted in 1787 when the landowners forced a dam below the Gun Garden to be cut. Whatever its political difficulties, however, the harbour renovation was neither competently planned nor honestly executed. Its history can be summed up by citing a pamphlet by the nineteenth-century reformer John Meryon, brother of the historian Charles Lewis Meryon. Surveying the entire period of the two harbour acts, from May 1724 to October 1787, when more than £200,000 was disbursed by the commissioners, he concluded with evident disgust that "all that was done in all that time, and with all that expense—serviceable at least to navigation—was a canal, short of a mile in length and one hundred and eighty feet wide; two pier heads; a stone sluice and draw-bridge erected; and a channel about three miles in length widened and straitened."[22] He neglected to add that the acts had been very serviceable indeed to the Lambs.

SOCIABILITY AND NATIONAL IDENTITY

The increasing reliance of the Rye oligarchs on the national government meant a definite loss of political independence. No longer was it expedient to scorn the patronage of aristocratic magnates or defy a national administration, as in 1679–82. No longer was it possible to maintain the aura (or the pretence) of political self-determination, except in the most local and petty of affairs. Rye was part of a system of political rewards and obligations that extended into every borough in Britain, no matter how small. It was expected to play its part in maintaining the Whig interest, and in return, its leaders would always find someone at Westminster who was willing to listen to their demands. This does not mean that the Rye oligarchs were slavish minions of the Whig administration. On the contrary, they could still exhibit an independent streak when their interests were perceived to be threatened, as in 1733, when a parliamentary bill to place tobacco and brandy imports under the excise elicited a strong response from the corporation.

"When first We heard the Report of a new or Additional Excise," the corporation fulminated to its parliamentarians, "We looked upon it as a Story invented to create Uneasiness in the Minds of the People. . . . Nor could we suspect a British Parliament would Suffer a Scheme so plainly tending to the Ruine of Trade and Subversion of our Excellent Constitution. . . . These pleasing fflattering Hopes Vanishing, We now alas! See the Monster ready to devour us." The author of this eloquent protest is not named, but it may have been the mayor himself, Allen Grebell. It would not have been recorded in the assembly book without his approval. Whoever wrote it had evidently read some of the anti-excise propaganda that was circulating widely throughout the kingdom. A petition sent from the corporation to the House of Commons complained that the placement of goods in bonded warehouses would put the property of merchants "more at the Will of the Crown officers than is consistent with the Antient Rights ffreedoms and Priviledges of Englishmen." This was the old rhetoric of rights and privileges that had long been heard from the Cinque Ports, but its import was now national rather than local. The liberties of the whole kingdom were threatened.[23]

The bill was dropped, and the Rye oligarchs were heartily satisfied. They had no desire to test the bonds of dependency further. Instead, they held a celebratory dinner at which they toasted the royal family, the town's members of Parliament, "Trade and Navigation, all the honest Gentlemen opposed, & all honest Corporations that petitioned against the Excise Scheme, Sturdy Beggars in their Coaches."[24] They did not raise their glasses to the downfall of the administration. Although

Phillips Gybbon stayed in opposition after the excise bill, he kept up his ties with the Duke of Newcastle, and was considered "reasonable" by Sir Robert Walpole. The other Rye M.P., Admiral Norris, was soon back in the ranks of administration supporters. In the hotly contested county elections of 1734, seventy-nine out of eighty-eight Rye voters chose a straight Whig ticket. Thus, Rye joined the other small boroughs that saved Walpole's majority in the House of Commons.[25]

The celebration of the death of the excise bill may not have marked the return of political independence, but it exemplified the vibrant sociability by which the oligarchs expressed their ties to one another, their civic responsibilities, and their national loyalty. Sociability, in the form of town feasts, drinking bouts, celebrations, and commemorations, cemented the Rye oligarchy as much as did self-interest and party politics. An astounding number of vouchers for these corporate festivities have survived among the chamberlain's accounts. They date back to 1652, when the dinners at the opening of the sessions court were held at Michael Cadman's Mermaid Inn. From the 1660s until the early years of the eighteenth century, most of the bills are for regular corporate events, including the annual meeting with Tenterden, the Corporate Member of Rye within the Cinque Ports. A few national events, like the Restoration or the king's birthday, were also commemorated with feasts or bell-ringings. After the return of Thomas Grebell to the mayoralty in 1705, the number of civic functions and celebrations began to proliferate. Shortly after Grebell's election, the mayor and jurats went to the Mermaid and spent 14s.4d "at the Rejoycing for the Victory at Audenarde." The happy celebration of the Duke of Marlborough's triumph over the French was the beginning of a long series of festive seasons that would keep members of the corporation eating and drinking and carousing for the next six decades.[26]

The mayor, jurats, and freemen went into festive high gear

after 4 August 1714, when they met at the Red Lion to drink punch and wine in joy at "the procliaimein of king georg."[27] Under the first two Georges, they annually celebrated the king's birthday, accession day, and coronation day, the queen's birthday, the Prince of Wales' birthday, the Duke of Cumberland's birthday (after 1753), Charles II's restoration day (surprisingly enough—but it may have been a mock celebration), the sessions dinner, the freemen's dinner, the herring feast, the composition with Tenterden, the militia muster, and the opening of the small-box. They also commemorated national days of thanksgiving, declarations of war, and victories such as the taking of Québec in 1759. Some of these commemorations involved only the ringing of church bells and drinks at a tavern for the ringers, but just as often, punch, wine, and beer were offered to members of the corporation. A few bills of fare from corporate dinners have survived, showing monstrous consumption of food and drink. At the Mermaid on 20 September 1722, for example, the mayor and his guests consumed a rump of beef, fish, two puddings, ducks, tarts, lemons and greens, bread and cheese, beer, wine, and tobacco. The bill came to the enormous sum of £9.2.6.[28]

Interestingly enough, the name of John Breads appears only once in the tavern bills, in a payment of 6s.8d on 4 July 1738, "for the Ringears Drink per 29 May," the anniversary of Charles II's restoration. By contrast, after the Flushing Inn was rented out to John Igglesdon in 1738, the corporation frequently paid for bellringers to drink there.[29] Perhaps the oligarchs had some personal or political reason for not patronizing the tavern more often when Breads was running it. Even the choice of May 29 as an occasion for sending ringers to the Flushing Inn may have been an affront to a man whose family had been Dissenters. Would they have felt very joyful on Restoration Day?

To be left out of the corporate festivities was meaningful, because these events were not just entertaining; they were of great significance in creating a sense of civic solidarity. To attend them was to be recognized as a participant in the political and economic life of the town. The feasts and drinking bouts replaced, after an interval of more than a century, the medieval corporate rituals, most of them religious, that had been eliminated by the Reformation. Unlike those earlier forms of celebration, however, the corporation feasts were entirely secular and not open to the general public. They helped to define an exclusive corporate sphere that was restricted to about forty or fifty men of the middling sort, the magistrates, freemen, and jurymen of the town. Women seem to have been totally excluded, even from victory celebrations, although some of the taverns in which festivities took place were owned and operated by women. Less privileged inhabitants may have had their own associations, like the Rye Benefits Society that loaned £80 to the churchwardens in 1762, but little is known about them.[30]

It was not by chance that the corporate feasts were held in alehouses and taverns rather than the court hall. In the first half of the seventeenth century, alehouses replaced churches as centres of communal ritual and neighbourhood gatherings. By the late seventeenth century, the alehouse was being "improved" into a locale for the more polite activities of clubs and societies for the middling sort.[31] The Rye tavern feasts began to multiply at just this historical juncture. Despite the scenes of drunkenness and gluttony that they must have encouraged, they were signs of an increasing civility and politeness among the town's ruling elite.

The tavern feasts and bell-ringing also reflected an awareness of national politics, strengthening the sense among the Rye oligarchs that they were part of a broader political universe. Rye may have been isolated by bad roads, but its leaders still knew shortly after the event when the rebellion of 1745 was crushed or Quebec had fallen. Newspapers and magazines helped to tie the Rye elite into a national perspective.[32] Periodicals were kept at the court hall, which turned into a sort of circulating library for the magistrates. *The British Merchant,* a multi-part publication of 1713 that attacked the Tory government's proposal for a French commercial treaty, was borrowed by Thomas Grebell, John Slade, and Nicholas Mannooch in 1722–23. Written by a London merchant who was chamber-keeper to the Treasury, *The British Merchant* argued a national case against open commerce with the French. It was clearly of great local interest in a town full of Whig merchants and shipowners who traded with France. Each borrower recorded the lending date in a little daybook that contained sessions court business.[33] Twenty years later, when James Lamb and Thomas Hodges decided to sell the effects of their murdered brother-in-law, Allen Grebell, they advertised the sale in the *Kentish Post.* By that time, having ready access to newspapers was all the more crucial. John Coleman complained to the corporation that the churchwarden John Haffenden was borrowing the newspapers from the mayor's sergeant "before they were brought into the Court Hall and prevented or delayed his reading them." Haffenden was told that "if he Attempts anything of that sort for the Future . . . he shall never afterwards be permitted to come into the Court Hall to read the News."[34]

However parochial their politics, however petty and self-serving their economic goals, the oligarchs of Rye were changing from defenders of narrow civic privileges into the citizens of an expansive nation, founded, as Linda Colley has argued, on the twin pillars of Protestantism and profit. They were becoming "Britons."[35] Yet it is worth adding that they had not broadened their political and economic priorities very much. In their minds, being British was perfectly compatible with a continued allegiance to a local anachronism like the Cinque Ports confederation. The oligarchs never abandoned their fierce defence of Rye's ancient privileges and practices, which so often led to abuses of power, no matter what their views may have been about constitutional propriety on the national level. They never perceived that the interests of Britain might be undermined by quangos like the harbour renovations, which served private ends more than those of the nation. National identity, in short, had to accommodate itself to a persistent provincialism, and to individual greed. In many ways, it grew hand in hand with that provincialism and greed, sharing with them an aggressive Protestantism and a conviction that the pursuit of self-interest would lead to general prosperity.

MUNIFICENCE

If the oligarchs of Rye had been asked to isolate a single accomplishment that demonstrated the congruence of their own self-interest with the general good, they might well have pointed to the court hall, built between 1742 and 1744. The construction of new public buildings was a shining example of what has been called the urban renaissance of the eighteenth century, the recovery of English towns from the economic depression and cultural deprivation of the 1600s.[36] The Rye court hall was not architecturally innovative—like many town buildings of the late seventeenth century, such as the Guildhall at Rochester or the town hall at Abingdon, it consisted of an open-arcaded ground floor with an assembly hall above. Even the cupola at the top of the court hall was a traditional feature. On the other hand, the use of Portland stone on the arches of the arcade, and the addition of "two Rustick Quires at the Ends of the Markett," show some awareness of contemporary taste in architecture. It is notable, moreover, that none of the other Cinque Ports constructed a new town hall in the period 1655–1770. The magistrates of Rye were showing off their own initiative and the influence of the corporation—but not its wealth, for it was evident from the first that the court hall could not be built with civic revenues. In the end, it was financed through a loan of £600 from the two generous members of Parliament, Sir John Norris and Phillips Gybbon.

The court hall building accounts were more meticulously kept than those of the harbour commission, and even the £38.10s that was earned from the sale to James Lamb of the rubble from the dilapidated old hall was carefully recorded. This was done on 2 March 1742, at the last assembly attended by Allen Grebell.[37] Perhaps the sight of profits again being reaped by the oligarchs from public works contributed to the distraction of Grebell's murderer.

The other important civic construction project of the Grebell-Lamb years was the water tower that still stands in a corner of the churchyard. Water had previously been pumped into a town conduit from local wells that were always in danger of being flooded by the sea. The purchase of St. Mary's Marshes by the corporation in 1728 allowed a ready supply of fresh water, and five years later a site was acquired in the churchyard to build a new water tower. Good relations between the Grebell-Lamb faction and the church authorities smoothed the way for this agreement, which had to be approved by the vicar and the patron of the living. The tower itself still stands, a sleek and rather elegant brick building, shaped like a lozenge. The cost of pumping water from the Marshes to the tower was £16.19s in 1736, not a small investment for a money-strapped corporation. Francis Jewhurst was later appointed to work the pump, at a handsome salary of £13 per annum, perhaps as a reward for escorting John Breads to the gallows. The water was conveyed in elm rather than lead pipes, which must have improved the taste and certainly made it less likely to poison its drinkers, although the magistrates of the eighteenth century cannot have known this. The inhabitants of Rye were not as grateful for the new water supply as might be imagined; most of them refused to pay for it to be conveyed to their houses. In 1847, when the charge for water conveyance was only 20s per year, Holloway recorded that "several have availed themselves of the offer," which suggests that most had not.[38] Historians who assume that every eighteenth-century urban improvement was of universal benefit might pay attention to this example.

The court hall and water tower were the only civic buildings constructed in the period of Grebell-Lamb dominance. Both were practical structures. The oligarchs did not invest in costly modern contrivances like street lamps, which were installed at Hastings in 1754 as a gift from Colonel Thomas Pelham. Nor did they build leisure facilities, which may have seemed unnecessary at Rye as it had never been a watering spot for the gentry. The town had no assembly room in the eighteenth century, no place where the local elite, both the gentry and the middle classes, could dance to the latest steps, display themselves in the latest fashions, perfect the politeness of their manners, and arrange marriages for their children. This does not mean that the leading families of Rye were deprived of the civility of assembly-room culture. The fashionable little town of Battle held an assembly in the late 1740s, and there were both assemblies and balls at Hastings in the early 1750s. The first reference to public dancing parties at Rye is in a letter of September 1751 from the lawyer Robert Milward to John Collier of Hastings, who was then taking the waters at Bath: "I have been at many Balls since you have gone, & we have now Established a very good monthly one at Rye, & where we had last Wednesday Ten couple of Good Dames & Sev Agreable Girls."[39] These events were probably held at local inns.

For more sophisticated or more decadent amusements, members of the local elite had to go up to London. Younger men may have done this more often than women or older men. In a 1747 letter to John Collier, William Cranston noted the presence in the capital of two "Rye Beaux," Edwin Wardroper and "Court" Tucker, a nephew of Samuel Jeake III. Cranston had heard "they were last Thursday at the masquerade, & about 4 in the morning unmask'd, by which means a Gentleman, (well intituled to be there) saw 'em, just knew 'em, & told me of it on Tuesday. I can't say but 'tis pretty extra [extraordinary] in both." Cranston was clearly shocked by their presence at a masquerade, where anonymity encouraged scandalous behaviour of all sorts.[40]

The leisure activities of the lower classes were more carefully controlled by members of the Rye corporation, especially if they were perceived as having bad social consequences. A sessions court order of 1731 condemned "a very barbarous Usage in and about this Town in the throwing at Cocks on at about the time of Shrove Tuesday—and Severall Quarrells & Tumults occasioned thereby." Anyone found to be throwing cocks in the future "shall be punished with the Utmost Rigour in Law." Apparently, nobody was. By the end of the eighteenth century, bulls were baited during the town's annual Beggar's Bush fair, but this was done at a field just outside Rye, as it does not seem to have had the approval of the magistrates. When it came to public amusements, however, the magistrates were keepers of good order rather than old Puritans. They had no objection to more sedate activities of a kind their ancestors might have deplored. One year before the court's condemnation of cock-fighting, for example, a company of strolling actors from Canterbury had performed plays at Rye. Their entertainments were probably staged at an inn, as there was no public theatrical space in the town.[41]

One other building testified to the munificence of the Rye elite, although it was neither new nor fashionable. It was the workhouse. The construction of workhouses for the poor, often attached to an infirmary, became more common in English towns after Bristol built one in 1696. The Rye workhouse was a comparatively early example. It followed a parliamentary act of 1722 encouraging their construction by allowing parishes to refuse relief to anyone who declined to enter one. The Rye workhouse was first installed in March 1724 in a deeze or warehouse belonging to Allen Grebell at the upper end of Rope Walk, on the northeast edge of the town. Within a year, a fund had been raised by the parish in order to rent the property as a workhouse and "pest house." Rules were drawn up for its management, and a monthly workhouse committee was organized. Reverend Wilson was given the management of the new facility, and John Hope was appointed as surgeon-apothecary. In 1735, the Grebell warehouse had to be expanded to accommodate the growing number of inmates. A steward was appointed in the following year, and in a measure reminiscent of the 1581 Decree against Whoredom, those receiving parish relief were ordered to wear a badge. In the 1750s, a decade of war and increasing poverty, loans had to be taken out to cover a deficit in the poor rates. There was a sick-chamber in the workhouse, but a separate pest-house was not built until 1762, after a devastating smallpox epidemic. All of this work was carried on by the vestry of St. Mary's Church, not by the corporation, but it would have been impossible without Allen Grebell's initial donation of the premises.[42]

Two contemporary inventories of the workhouse exist in the parish records, dating from 1754 and 1761. In the former year, the building contained sixteen beds, placed in "the Girls Chamber," a parlour and a "Brick'd Room." No men's chamber is mentioned, presumably because male vagrants were not admitted. We do not know how many were expected to sleep in each bed. The shop, where the inmates worked, mainly contained cooking implements. The buttery and brewhouse contained the most expensive set of items in the house, including a copper brewing furnace. To all appearances, the workhouse was a dormitory where indigent young women were employed in butter-making and brewing. Seven years of war and deprivation changed it a great deal. By 1761, the Rye workhouse contained a washhouse, a spinning room with fifteen old spinning wheels, a weaving room with two old looms, a work room, and two butteries. When the inmates were not working, they could eat in a refectory, sit in a community room, and sleep in either a men's chamber with two beds or a women's chamber with three beds. If they were in poor health, they could be sent to a male or female sick room, with two beds in the first and three in the second. The master lived in the facility, to keep a better eye on it. The separation of men from women, healthy from sick, as well as the addition of living and work space, demonstrate that the workhouse was now a community, where the poor were expected to live a respectable and productive existence. Like all communities, it had to be controlled or policed, all the more rigorously because its members could not be trusted to police themselves.[43]

POLICE

Just as the workhouse represented a hidden side of the urban renaissance, so too was police the hidden side of civility. Only an elite of the landed and middling classes could aspire to ideals of politeness; others could not be expected to control their vulgar passions without the imposition of external sources of control. This concern with disciplining the poor may seem like nothing new; but it was. The Puritan conception of civic order in the sixteenth and seventeenth centuries was inspired by religious standards. Anybody who erred might be corrected, no matter what their standing. Puritan civic order might therefore disrupt rather than uphold worldly hierarchies. By contrast, eighteenth-century notions of police concentrated on the preservation of existing social and institutional structures. The wealthy and polite, who dominated those structures, did not have to worry much about falling afoul of police. Moreover, when social institutions came under strain, as they did during the years of war and deprivation from the mid-1740s to the early 1760s, police could become especially severe.

The sessions court, revived during the Breads trial and sitting after 1744 in the new court hall, was the chief instrument of police in Rye during the war years. The crime that it chiefly sought to control was theft. Of the twenty-two people who were reported to the magistrates for felonies between 1746 and 1760, thirteen were accused of theft. Most of them had stolen very little: two silver spoons, some coals, one pair of half-boots, a suit of clothes, a pair of silver shoe buckles, 22s. in silver coins belonging to James Lamb junior, forty pounds of cast iron owned by Nathaniel Pigram junior. A tailor tried in 1758 had taken a gridiron from the workhouse. The only serious criminal was William Pilcher, who stole a horse worth £6 from Francis Jewhurst, the gallows attendant and pump-house operator. Seven of the petty thieves were whipped, a minor but exemplary punishment. William Pilcher was sentenced to hang but was pardoned and transported instead. Among the other alleged felons of Rye were seven men, at least three of them soldiers, who were accused of assault. Five of these men were not even indicted, and only one was punished with a fine, suggesting that personal violence was regarded much less seriously by the court than theft. The most subtle felon was the labourer John Swift, who counterfeited a begging letter to James Lamb in 1750. He was fined a shilling and imprisoned for a month, a lenient sentence. The court was less sympathetic to a woman named only Charlotte, who was found to be a rogue and vagabond and was whipped three times. She must have been considered a much greater threat to good order than the forger Swift.[44]

Police did not simply mean punishment and control. It could

also be compassionate. It bore vestiges of the old values of good neighbourhood, which coexisted with impersonal and bureaucratic attitudes. During times of dearth, for example, the corporation revived the old Assize of Bread, fixing the price of wheat both for shipment and for local consumption. This was done in the terrible year 1740, when "the Extream Cold Season and the necessitys of the Poor within this Town" encouraged the corporation, temporarily released from debt, to donate £10 to the vicar for distribution among the needy. The Assize of Bread was set in the spring of that year at £12 per load, dropped to £8 per load in 1741 and fixed a third time at £6 per load in 1742, as one of the final mayoral acts of Allen Grebell. During the Seven Years' War, the Assize of Bread rose from £7 per load in 1756 to £15 per load in February 1757. Over the next three months, it rocketed to £20 per load; but Rye escaped bread riots, unlike other parts of England, perhaps because its magistrates were perceived as at least trying to address the problem of dearth.[45]

Another example of what might be called compassionate policing in the war years is found in the collection of letters from the Rye overseers of the poor to the overseers of other parishes, relating to indigent people from outside the town who had asked for relief. The letters dealt with nineteen separate cases between 1744 and 1762. With a few exceptions, they were sent to southeastern towns not far from Rye. Ten of the cases involved men who had asked for aid, most of whom were sick. Seven other cases concerned widows or abandoned wives with children, and two dealt with questions of paternity. Only one sick woman without children applied to the overseers. Poverty was apparently less gender and age based in the mid-eighteenth century than it had been in 1698–99, when almost all of those given regular relief were elderly women. Much of the distress of the later period can be explained by the effects of war, which disabled some men, encouraged others to run away from their families, and spread diseases among all groups of the poor. It should also be remembered that the letters of the overseers chronicle problem cases. No doubt the parish was still supporting many elderly women through small payments provided outside the workhouse.

The tone of the overseers' letters is sometimes officious and aloof, but this is often mixed with a measure of human sympathy. Consider the response to Edward Fenn, who wanted to bring his sister's children to Rye for relief in 1750. Immediately suspicious, the overseers demanded proof of his circumstances "from a Substancial Gentleman or two or from the Parish Officers." In a postscript, however, one of the overseers softened, noting that "as the Children are y^r Sisters Children our Parish Loaded with poor & wee to give a strict Acct of our Proceedings & Management I should think it most proper for you to Come yourself. & wee Will be at any Reasonable Charge in part of the Journey or provide for you or you and a Comrade for a Night or two Here." In a 1752 letter to Sidlesham, the overseers painted a pathetic picture of the wife and five children of William Betts, who were "in Deplorable Circumstances. he having not been at home for this Eleven Weeks. his Wife has been with us this day for Relief & Indeed we have been Surprised She has Subsisted so Long, but she has been Very Industrious or the Family Could not have been so long Supported." When one of Betts's children contracted smallpox, the Rye overseers assured their counterparts at Sidlesham that he would be given medical treatment, and "wee will bee as Carefull as of our Own People." When the widow of Gilbert King of Chatham became sick with smallpox in 1762, the overseers wrote how she could not be moved "through the Extreem pain she lays under & being rendred so very weak we thought proper to let you know that the Doct. Has Attended her twice a day for these three weeks past. & we have likewise Releiv'd her with Necessaries without which she must have suffer'd." Of course, they wanted to be reimbursed for their expenses. Compassionate police came with a price attached.[46]

Did anybody resist the corporate police of the eighteenth century? Its most celebrated enemies were the smugglers, for whom policing of any kind was a constant hindrance. By the 1740s, smuggling by organized gangs had become commonplace around Rye. Nathaniel Pigram senior, commander of the customs sloop *Amelia,* assured the Duke of Newcastle in 1741 that "this Station is the most Dangerous of any in England."[47] He may have been correct, but unfortunately, it is very difficult to sort out myth from reality in the history of smuggling. William Holloway cited an aged citizen of Rye in the early nineteenth century, who recalled that the Hawkhurst gang, the most notorious smugglers along the south coast in the late 1740s, had once appeared in arms at the Mermaid Inn, "no magistrate daring to interfere with them." While this memory may be accurate, it is unsubstantiated by contemporary evidence. However, the story may be derived from an actual incident. *The Gentleman's Magazine* for August 1747 reported that two dozen mounted smugglers, "well armed and laden with prohibited goods," had stopped at the Red Lion in Rye "to refresh." There they shot off some guns "to intimidate the inhabitants," and carried off a curious young man, James Marshall, who "has not been heard of since."[48]

Clearly, the control of smuggling was a serious problem. Its dimensions can be glimpsed in the letters and papers of the customs officer and lawyer of Hastings, John Collier, who spent much of his career fighting the contraband trade. In 1742–44, when a French invasion seemed imminent, he became particularly alarmed by contacts between the Transports gang, also known as the Hastings Outlaws, and the French authorities. Two of his subordinates were actually kidnapped by smugglers at Dungeness and taken to Boulogne in 1742. When they were released and returned, their horses were waiting for them at the George Inn in Rye, where the smugglers had thoughtfully sent them! Two years later, it was reported that "one Betts of Rye" had been granted permission by the French king, "to go out and in, at any of the Harbours and Ports of France." This may have been the same William Betts whose wife and family applied for poor relief in 1752. Collier did not want it to be thought at Westminster that he had allowed the situation to get out of hand, and he was sensitive to reports in the national press during the rebellion of 1745 that suggested the smugglers were "associating themselves in a body, regularly arm'd & in Uniforms, & Declaring publicly for the Pretender's Son." He wrote a letter complaining about such stories to the Prime Minister, Henry Pelham. Collier must have known there was some truth in the reports, however, and he apparently never sent the letter. In fact, the defiance of the smugglers soon increased. By the spring of 1747, the customs commissioners in London had become alarmed by information "that the Smuglers from Rye and Hastings have carried to France Sixty or Seventy Swivel Guns, and that they openly carry over Wool." With swivel guns, the contraband boats could defy any customs sloop.[49]

Some local men of substance aided the smugglers. According to Henry Simon, solicitor to the customs commissioners, the notorious Gray brothers, members of the Hawkhurst gang, were assisted by "Mr Lance a brewer at Rye (I think that is his name)." Unfortunately, Mr. Lance cannot be traced. We do not know whether he or the Hawkhurst gang had anything to do with the most alarming smuggling incident in the history of Rye, which happened towards the end of 1750. The ironmaster and landowner John Fuller of Brightling wrote to Collier in November of that year, mentioning that an advertisement had been posted at Battle of a £20 reward for goods stolen from the customs house (presumably at Hastings) by smugglers, "but no

Notice taken of breaking open the Custom house at Rye and taking the Goods from thence." In fact, no further notice of this event has been found anywhere. A notorious attack on a customs house had occurred at Poole in October 1747, and the government had assumed that the hanging of several men connected with that daring episode had provided a deterrent to similar outrages. Apparently, they were wrong.[50]

The attitude of the Rye magistrates towards smuggling was guarded. While they wanted it to be suppressed, they were not willing to antagonize their neighbours in order to accomplish that end. Several leading members of the corporation (James Lamb himself, his son John, the two Nathaniel Pigrams, and Samuel Jeake III) had positions in the customs service, but accusations of smuggling were kept out of the town sessions court. When Samuel Jeake III reported to the court in July 1735 that he had seized forty-nine pounds of tea "clandestinely run or imported" in the house of William Lingfield, a mariner of Rye, James Lamb and Allen Grebell decided that there was not enough proof that the tea had been illegally run and dismissed the case.[51] This was the only time that a prosecution for selling smuggled goods was attempted in the Rye sessions court under the Grebell-Lamb regime. In 1749, the magistrates actually imprisoned an informer named William Harrison, who had barged into a house "with his Pistoll cock'd, which very much frightened a Woman big with Child." He was searching for a Rye man named Prince, "a very great Smugler." "I Suppose Harrison was in Licquor," a discouraged customs officers admitted to John Collier, "and did not behave with the best of Conduct." The informer's name had become detestable at Hastings-indeed, "nine part in Ten thereof wou'd as freely Murder Harrison as they wou'd Eat or Drink when Hungry or Dry." We may assume that he was equally hated at Rye. Harrison's information eventually led to the arrest and execution of Thomas Holman, a member of the Hastings Outlaws who happened to be John Collier's cousin, and whom Collier had tried to protect.[52]

If they were careful not to act too boldly against the smuggling gangs, the Rye authorities were definitely opposed to their activities, which had extended to murder and extortion. It would be misleading to imply that their reluctance to prosecute smugglers meant that they were abetting the contraband trade. When supported by sufficient force, they were willing to act. At the same time that Harrison was languishing in Rye gaol, a much more important prisoner was being held under strong guard in the town: John Evers, a smuggler who was involved in the 1740 killing of a customs officer named Thomas Carswell. He had been captured by a party of dragoons. Eventually, Evers offered to give evidence, and was instrumental in the conviction of several of his former colleagues.[53] The town magistrates were determined that men like these should be tracked down and prosecuted, although they did not have the military or legal resources to carry this out themselves.

In one instance, however, a violent smuggler was allegedly protected by the leading magistrate of Rye. The smuggler was Jeremiah Curtis, alias William Pollard, alias Butler, who was accused of a series of awful crimes. He was first presented at Lewes Assizes in 1737, charged with eight other men of taking part in an armed smuggling incident at Pevensey. Two of his associates confessed, and were transported; but the prosecution against the rest was dropped, "By Warrant from Attorney General." Eleven years later, Curtis was indicted at East Grinstead for the murder of Richard Hawkins of Yapton, who had dared to pilfer some smuggled tea from him. Outlawed for refusing to surrender himself, Curtis took part in an armed robbery in Hampshire before fleeing to France, where he reportedly enlisted in the Irish brigade.[54] In July 1749, a letter about the missing desperado was sent from Rye to the Duke of Richmond, the

West Sussex magnate who was keenly chasing down smugglers throughout the southeast. Curtis was said to be planning a return to England, "to Assist his Wife, in Selling every thing, they have at Hawkhurst, or elsewhere in England." According to the informant, the daring smuggler "still declares, when the Dark Nights come on, that he will Visit his native Country, which if he does, I believe I shall know it, when I will Certainly forthwith, acquaint your Grace, of his Arrival." A postscript to the letter added that "as Curteis, is here looked upon, as the naturall Son of Mr. Lamb our Great Man, I am obliged to Act with the greatest Caution."[55] Who wrote this extraordinary denunciation of James Lamb? It was his old enemy, Henry Dodson. The truth of the rumour about Curtis's paternity is impossible to judge, but Dodson's way of expressing it suggests that he did not give it full credit himself. Curtis was never apprehended. What relation he bore to Jeremiah Curteis, town clerk of Rye from 1756 to 1800, is unknown. Was the respectable civic officer a son of the feared smuggler? Was he a grandson of James Lamb? Those who knew the answers never committed them to posterity.

The treatment of smuggling in Rye during the 1740s demonstrates that police was not a rigid system of social control, imposed from above on an unwilling populace. It had to be applied carefully, and it could be challenged. It was often corrupt, by contemporary standards as well as by ours. The oligarchs could not push police too far in directions that were resisted by the ordinary inhabitants of the town; but they also could not allow themselves to be viewed as weak, either by those whom they governed or by the national authorities. This meant that they had to be constantly on their guard, constantly aware of what was being said about them both in the town itself and at Westminster. It reveals something about the resourcefulness of James Lamb that he was able to steer through these dangers with such success for so many years. At the same time, he had a ruthless side, displayed in the Breads case, that would earn him many political enemies by the late 1740s, as will be seen.

Taste and Refinement

Smuggling may have been an affront to good police, but in a different way it served to promote civility. After 1730, most of the south-coast owlers carried boxes of tea back from France and the Low Countries. Grown in East Asia, this tea had been shipped to Europe by state companies as well as by independent merchants or interlopers. By bringing so much cheap tea into the country, the smugglers were in part responsible for the tremendous increase in tea drinking among every segment of the English population. Taking afternoon tea out of porcelain cups was the height of politeness among the elite, while the poor might enjoy a few leaves steeped in hot water and drunk from an earthenware mug. "Tea is now Grown one Meal in 3 of almost all the people in England especially in the South," wrote John Fuller of Brightling to his friend John Collier in 1750. As a Tory paternalist, Fuller was more understanding towards the tea smugglers than were his Whig associates, and he blamed the East India Company for their crimes, noting that it was because "the India Company have the Monoply & sell it for a third perc dearer than the rest of Europe that this pernitious practice must Continue."[56]

Tea, along with sugar, coffee, and chocolate, was at the heart of the consumer revolution of the eighteenth century.[57] All of these commodities were imported from places in Asia and the Americas, and, with the exception of tea, were grown by slaves in the colonies of the European imperial powers. Thus, the consumers of Rye and of a thousand other small towns in England were linked to a world-wide network of commercial production and trade, much of which depended on unfree labour and imperial domination. At least one individual whose economic activities were very important to Rye also had a hand in this international network: namely, Rose Fuller of Rose Hill, brother of the country gentleman quoted above, who was one of James Lamb's business associates. Rose Fuller took over the family's Jamaican estates in the 1730s, and became one of the most prominent planters on the island. Whatever sympathy his brother may have had for poor smugglers did not prevent Rose from exploiting the unpaid labour of African slaves on his extensive sugar plantations. He was unusual among West Indian planters in that he invested some of the profits from the sugar business into English enterprises, notably the Sussex ironworks and gun foundries that he inherited from his brother in 1755. Rose Fuller also used his vast sugar wealth to sweeten the Lambs, who supported him as member of Parliament for Rye from 1768 to his death in 1777.[58]

Whether or not their taste for consumer items from outside Europe made the Rye oligarchs into ardent supporters of imperial expansion is hard to determine. They certainly applauded British victories overseas, but not until the American Revolutionary War did the corporation express any overt enthusiasm for empire. The expansion of national trade, not the annexation of territory, was their main concern. On the other hand, the oligarchs and their descendants were not loath to seek their own fortunes in imperial ventures. We have already encountered Samuel Jeake III in Jamaica, trying to solicit a customs office and complaining about the Scots. A keener English colonialist could hardly be imagined.

Consumerism depended on changing polite tastes and fashions—on learning to drink tea rather than beer. Rye's relative geographic isolation (the first London coach service began in 1778) meant that its wealthier inhabitants were not always as up-to-date as their counterparts in other towns, but they tried just as hard to keep pace. Local letters provide some insight into their attitudes. As early as 1718, John Collier of Hastings was ready to mock any countryman who failed to keep up with London fashions. "Here's Tom Ellesdon in Towne in a Lace Hat," he wrote to his wife from the capital, "—the brims were in fashion about the 6th year of Queen Anne, & he is in that respect a complete Romney marsh man." Two decades of peace and relatively good economic times bolstered Collier's conviction that one could live politely even in East Sussex. In 1738, he defended the gentility of Hastings against his unhappy wife's complaint that it was "a desolate place." He added that "I can't at all agree with you in the politeness of our Two Neighbouring Towns," presumably Battle and Rye. Unconvinced, Mrs. Collier chose to spend more time in London. From there, she provided a consumer intelligence service for her family. In 1742, her daughter Cordelia wrote to her mother, rejoicing at a recent revolution in headgear that had taken place in the capital: "I am very glad to here Clipt hats are worn, & beg that you will buy me one, for belive I shall like it better than my Bonnet, for Every Boddy is goeing to have one." If everybody was going to have one in Hastings, then we may assume that everybody was going to have one in Rye as well.

John Collier stubbornly defended provincial politeness, but like his wife and daughters, he was not under any illusions as to where the standards of taste originated. Larger urban centres such as Bristol and Newcastle might generate their own versions of middle-class culture (although they may have been less autonomous than some historians care to admit), but in the small towns of the southeast, polite values came directly from London. This was a kind of mild cultural imperialism, by which the centre dominated the peripheries through the mechanism of social anxiety. John Collier was a typical provincial worrier about what was fashionable. He was kept informed by his London tailor, Mr. Gyles, about such matters as the colour and cut of men's coats, or the attractions of "Lac'd Waistcoats," about which he observed, "I Don't find but they are full as much worn as ever by all Degrees of Gentlemen."[59] To appear a gentleman or a gentlewoman in the London mode was the chief sartorial purpose of wealthy, aspiring middling people like the Colliers. This was what set them apart from mere rustics.

Evidently, much had changed since the previous century. It is impossible to imagine Samuel Jeake the elder worrying about whether the lace on his waistcoat made him more or less of a gentleman. He would no doubt have been astonished to discover the extent to which household items had become matters of fashion rather than practicality. The lawyer William Cranston, for example, showed his fine appreciation of silver coffee pots in writing to his friend John Collier in 1748:[60]

> The present taste for Coffee potts is so much different from the old ffashion (& which by the way I think much the Handsomest), that I did not care to speak for one till I had your Directions therein— the old fashion made taper wise, with a Spout from about the middle, chas'd (as the run of all plate is now), is handsome, but the modern ffashion is made exactly in the fform of an old earthen Jugg with a Spout at the Top, much like a Chocolate pott— these I think ugly enough, but many men of many minds—these also are generally more chas'd than the other—so now you have an Account of both, chuse as you please.

In Jeake's day, the purchase of silver had been a form of investment by the rich; but by the mid-eighteenth century, silver was a consumer item like any other, subject to alterations in fashion and available to the middling classes. A system in which commodities had fixed social values had changed to one in which nothing had value unless it was currently desired by the London-based arbiters of taste.

Both male and female members of the Collier family were avid consumers, but matters of fashion occupied a far higher percentage of the correspondence of Collier's wife and daughters than they did that of the patriarch himself. To a large extent, the consumer revolution was led by women. It increased their economic clout and social significance, but if they wanted to be taken seriously, their taste still had to show male *gravitas* rather than female "frivolity." That message is clearly expressed in the memorial inscription to Dorothy, wife of Thomas Lamb, who died in London shortly after her father-in-law. She is described as having had "every amiable quality of her sex, with a manly sense and elegance of taste." Her unfeminine elegance may explain why she is the only wife of an eighteenth-century Rye oligarch to merit a description on a family funeral monument.

Luxury consumer items were usually bought in shops. Sussex was relatively well supplied with shops by 1759, when the accounts of the excise office showed 2,658 shops in the county for a population of approximately 94,000. This compared favourably with Hampshire and Surrey, although Kent, with a population of about 169,000, had more than twice as many shops as Sussex, due to its proximity to London. The capital was a retailing magnet for the whole southeastern region, and the Collier family did most of its clothes shopping there. Comestibles, however, were bought locally, and about one-quarter of the shops in the 1759 excise account dealt in that most desirable of comestible infusions, tea.[61]

The records of shopping at Rye are sketchy. The town had mercer's and chandler's shops from the late sixteenth century. Local merchants sold cloth and other goods out of their warehouses. Nevertheless, many specialty items were still purchased in London, as the Jeake correspondence shows. Trade cards issued after 1735 by the enterprising John Hogben, master of Sanders' School and town chamberlain, advertise books (mostly religious and historical), maps, prints, globes, mathematical instruments (for navigation), spectacles, fishing tackle, and insurance policies from the Sun Fire Office. His son carried on these varied businesses, with their emphasis on pedagogy and security. By the mid-nineteenth century, however, almost anything could be bought at Rye, and the Landgate was a bustling street of shops, without a single private house. This development must have begun earlier, but the only local shop of the eighteenth century whose records have survived is the one at Northiam that existed from 1707 to 1744. Its owner, Stephen Hatch, kept meticulous account books in which were listed his purchases of groceries, haberdashery, laces and ribbons, flannels, fustians, hose, combs, bodices, ironware, earthenware, cutlery, and drugs (including saffron, turmeric, coriander, brimstone, quicksilver, and six bottles of Stoughton's Elixir). He recorded the sale of only one book, *Christ's Famous Titles and a Believer's Golden Chain* by the Puritan minister William Dyer (someone in the area was still reading the godly literature of an earlier age). Most of Hatch's suppliers were in London. His customers included Nicholas Mannooch of Rye, who bought groceries from him.[62] Clearly, a successful general store did not have to be located in an urban area. Hatch made deliveries, but some of his customers were willing to ride or drive out to rural Northiam to visit his emporium. No doubt many of them (although surely not the buyer of *Christ's Famous Titles*) were landed gentry from East Sussex and Kent. In this case, shopping may have diminished the social distance between town and country.

So long as they could draw customers from the vicinity, shops could thrive in a town that was otherwise economically ruined.

Winchelsea, for example, had a general store by 1760, when the shopkeeper Thomas Turner of East Hoathly near Lewes thought of buying it. Turner recorded in his diary for 19 February 1760 how he "set out for Rye in order to take a shop which I heard was to be let in Winchelsea (and a very frosty morning I had to ride in)." Snow and rain slowed his trip, but he arrived in Rye the next morning, only to find "the shop I went after was let." Turner was a general retailer who sold almost everything: beds, bearskins, beehives, sheep bells, bread, brooms, butter, packs of cards, chairs, cheese, chocolate, clogs, cloth, coffee, coffin plates, Dr. Godfrey's cordial, currants, earthenwares, ferrets, fish, flour, gin, gingerbread, gloves, gunpowder, handkerchiefs, hats, hops, horsehair, inkpowder, jewellery, teakettles, lobsters, nails, needles, paper, pencils, pewter, pipes, potatoes, punch bowls, razors, scythes, sheets, shrouds, silk, soap, spatterdashes, spirits, sugar, tea, New Testaments, tobacco, thread, elixir of vitriol, wheat, wine, and wool. If he had moved to Winchelsea, Turner probably would have dominated the retail trade in nearby Rye as well.[63]

The Rye elite did not need to be introduced to good taste by Thomas Turner. They were already well acquainted with it by 1750, judging by the letters that Mary and Jane Collier wrote home to their parents while staying in the vicinity. They were receiving smallpox inoculations at Northiam from Dr. Thomas Frewen, which required them to remain indoors for a couple of weeks. The girls were quite charmed by the attentions of the local people of quality: "we have not been a quarter of an hour without Company since we came." They drank tea and played cards with Dr. and Mrs. Frewen, to whom they taught the new game of "Commett." One evening, during a trip to Rye, a certain Mr. Dorman "entertain'd us with the German Flute, and indeed every Body was prodigious Civil to us. Mr. [Thomas] Lamb came to visit us in his Sexton Green waistcoat & clean

White Gloves, & invited us to his house, but Mr Frewen did not think it was proper to go out much, and we need not have done that to be deverted, for we had quite a running Camp at home, & not one evening without Company to Supper with us. I think Mrs. Lamb a very agreeable Woman."

To the delight of the Collier girls, the gentry and middling classes mixed at Rye in what seemed to be perfect cultural harmony. After another week of confinement back at Northiam, however, the patience of the two girls began to wear thin: "Here is cards, cards, nothing but cards going forward, that we are a most tired of them, but we have now sent to Miss Lamb for the fortunate Country maid, to read that." Mary confessed that "we often fancy ourselves in a Nunnery, as we don't dare go out of the Gate, & have but little Company here, it often Diverts us to see the People run away at the sight of us & hold their noses when we appear, as much as if we were all over Infection." [64]

Evidently, the poorer inhabitants of the Rye district were less enlightened about inoculation than their social superiors. While Frewen had treated three hundred patients by then, it is likely that most were of the upper and middling sort. [65] Yet before we conclude that the lower orders were excluded from the culture of politeness, we should remember that it was their taste for tea, sugar, and tobacco that had given the greatest boost to consumption in eighteenth-century England, and had in turn allowed so many families of the middling classes, like the Colliers and the Lambs, to raise themselves to gentility. A demand for small household luxuries was also growing among the poor. It can be observed in the Delft plates and two teapots found in the workhouse inventory, the property of a female inmate who had died. John Breads himself was no stranger to polite culture. The inventory of Breads's estate drawn up after his execution shows that he owned two violins, which the corporation sold for a profit of £1.10s. The ownership of musical instruments has been seen as a prime indicator of the new civility of the urban middling classes. The violins owned by John Breads may have been intended for use by his two sons, but they were still very young in 1743. It is equally possible that Breads himself played at the Flushing Inn or was a member of a local musical club. Such societies were becoming widespread in the mid-eighteenth century.[66] As a skilled artisan in a trade that did not have much social prestige, Breads stood between the labouring and middling classes, on the edge of the consumer revolution. Yet his ears were not wholly deaf to the seductive music of eighteenth-century politeness.

THE LAMBS UNDER ATTACK

The Grebell-Lamb oligarchy did much for the town and port of Rye. One measure of its success was a modest recovery in population. In 1756, the list of residents required to attend the court leet (and therefore liable to militia duty) included 286 males between the ages of sixteen and sixty, not including freemen, jurats, or clergy. Only 188 adult males had been recorded in 1682, when the population was around 1,000, so by 1756 there may have been 1,500 people in the town. The population continued to increase over the next four decades, reaching 2,145 at the first national census of 1801. In the first year of the nineteenth century, however, 368 inhabitants of Rye had to receive parish assistance in order to keep themselves fed.[67] Understandably, many felt that the oligarchs had done more for themselves than they had for others.

Whether or not John Breads thought so cannot be known for certain. The fragments of his life story that have been cited in this chapter suggest that he had been connected with James Lamb in his younger days, but had somehow fallen afoul of him by the 1730s, perhaps on account of his "pretended madness."

The profits of oligarchy were not showered on him as they were on others. If Breads was resentful, he was not alone. The aftermath of the Grebell murder demonstrated that many people in Rye resented Mayor Lamb. Between 1747 and 1762, they tried hard to overthrow the dominance of his family. While he may have gone peacefully to his death on the gallows, Breads nonetheless helped to unleash a firestorm of anger against the Lambs.

In the wake of his brother-in-law's murder, James Lamb's position was highly insecure. Judging by his involvement with the harbour commission, his promotion of the Assize of Bread, and his assistance in establishing the workhouse, Allen Grebell was a less grasping and more charitable individual than Lamb, which may have made him more popular. He also had longer-standing family ties to the town. With Grebell suddenly removed, Lamb faced potential rivals in Edwin Wardroper, the town clerk who also controlled the corporation of Winchelsea, and Nathaniel Pigram senior. The mayor decided to make the Breads trial into a show of who was the real boss in Rye. The inclusion of Pigram's son on the Breads jury was highly satisfactory to Lamb; it implicated his opponents in Breads's fate and prevented them from accusing the mayor of acting like a tyrant. Putting Ralph Norton, another potential enemy of the Lambs, on the bench was an equally clever stroke. As a means of insuring that the death of Allen Grebell would not bring about the break-up of the Grebell-Lamb connection, the trial was a great success. Even a critic like Henry Dodson felt compelled to keep his negative opinions private rather than risk offending the mayor.

James Lamb's reassertion of authority, however, would not protect him for very long. By 1747, his enemies had become bolder. In that year, John Collier sent to the Duke of Newcastle "Pigrams Scheme abt. Rye," attached to a letter from Edwin Wardroper. The "Scheme" is an extraordinary document. It contains a list of influential persons, divided into two factions. The Lambs have thirteen supporters on the list, including James; his three sons Thomas, James junior, and John; Henry Carleton, along with his son the Reverend George; and the merchant Chiswell Slade. The Pigrams count twenty-one followers, including Samuel Jeake III, who ran unsuccessfully for Parliament at Winchelsea in 1741, Ralph Norton and the Rye customs collector, William Horsfield. Not all the names are those of freemen, and they include a woman, Elizabeth Reeves.[68] Evidently, Pigram and Collier wanted Newcastle to consider the possibility of ditching the Lambs, and had sized up their support in order to convince the Duke that the mayor was not invulnerable. Typically, the cautious Newcastle did not choose to act, but he made Wardroper collector of customs at Rye, and kept him in the position even after the Lambs cast him out as town clerk six years later.[69]

Lamb's anger at the Wardroper-Pigram faction can be measured by the insulting treatment meted out to Ralph Norton's body. The Norton family had been prominent at Rye since the 1630s, as brewers and churchwardens who had supported first the royalist cause, then the Tory party. Norton himself had made peace with the Whigs after 1724. His name appeared on the Wardroper list as a supporter of Pigram, however, and by 1748 he had clearly alienated the Lambs. The result was a peevish refusal by Reverend George Carleton to allow the ageing Norton's body to be buried after his death in the chancel, next to his wife. The Carletons were James Lamb's closest allies besides the Slades, so there could be no doubt as to who was really behind the insult to Norton. When he died in 1750 at the age of eighty-four, his daughters put an angry inscription on his grave, asserting that their parents' request to be buried together had been denied "by the wanton exercise of power." To override the vicar's decision, they had to obtain a faculty from the bishop of Chichester.[70]

One year after her father's death, Catherine Norton put her name to a legal case that was designed to embarrass the Lambs. Along with Nathaniel Pigram senior and junior, Thomas Frewen, Reverend Lewis Jones, and the churchwarden, John Haffenden, she brought an appeal before the sessions court against the parish rate for the relief of the poor. The appellants claimed that, under a recent assessment, they were over-rated, while the justices themselves were under-rated. No more open slap in the face to the Lamb interest could be imagined, especially as the parish overseers had been obliged to borrow money because the poor rate was not raising enough. The appeal was dismissed, but it was repeated in January 1752 and again in April of that year. The final appeal was supported by Catherine Norton's sister Elizabeth, Reverend Jones, Frewen, Haffenden, the two Pigrams, John Parnell, Edwin Wardroper, and Henry Dodson. Now all the enemies of the Lambs, many of them old Tories like the Nortons, Frewen, and Haffenden, had come out into the open. According to Charles Lewis Meryon, writing seventy years later, the appellants made a motion to rule to show cause why an information should not be laid for a misdemeanour in discharging their appeal. In other words, they were asking the sessions court to demonstrate why its own judges were not guilty men. In discharging this brazen attempt to embarrass them, the magistrates tersely replied that "no improper motive was found" to impeach themselves.[71]

The final confrontation between Wardroper and the Lambs began in 1756, when the return of war with France brought the Rye harbour commission into a state of financial crisis. Laden with debt, after spending £7,860 on construction over the past three decades with virtually nothing to show for it, the commissioners had little choice but to try to obtain a new harbour act from Parliament.[72] At that point, Edwin Wardroper saw his moment arrive. He had already infuriated the Lamb faction by allowing non-freemen to ship wool free of duty from the mouth of Rye harbour, which he claimed was in the jurisdiction of Winchelsea.[73] Now, in February 1756, Wardroper went to London to demand his "Share in the Plunder" from the harbour bill, as the lawyer William Cranston bluntly put it in a letter to his friend John Collier. Wardroper wanted the jurats of Winchelsea, whom he controlled, to be written into the new act as commissioners. He managed to convince three or four London merchants, probably the same men who were shipping wool through Winchelsea, to form a committee with the purpose of lobbying the House of Commons in his favour. To support the committee, they raised a subscription of a guinea apiece from no fewer than 150 other merchants of the capital, solicited the support of Sir John Barnard, the well-respected member of Parliament for London, and convinced William Owen, a London bookseller who had been prominent in opposition politics, to publish a treatise pleading the case of Winchelsea against Rye. Cranston wryly observed that "the D-ll that is rais'd, is not likely to be laid."[74]

The real devil that had been raised was political lobbying, which by the mid-1700s had become highly organized and effective. Lobbyists used every means of persuasion, from personal contact to commercial media, in order to make their case. Because it spread information and influence, lobbying was often conducive to broader participation in governance; but it was also expensive and not always distinguishable from bribery or corruption. The harbour commissioners themselves spent no less than £826.8.4 on trips to London, perquisites to officers of the Commons, a survey of the harbour, and maps that were produced by the celebrated London printer Henry Woodfall.[75] In the end, however, everything came down to a decision of the House of Commons, where the efforts of the aged Phillips Gybbon to preserve Rye's privileges were effectively gutted by Sir

John Barnard's demand for an impartial survey of the levels. "I think there is an End of it being made a Jobb of it in future as it has been hitherto," wrote Cranston, showing what he thought of the efforts of the harbour commissioners. By the time the Rye harbour bill was passed in 1762, the committee of London merchants was already making its own survey of the harbour, and Wardroper had been named as a commissioner.[76] It was a bitter pill for the Lamb interest. James Lamb himself died in London in November 1756, while lobbying to defeat Wardroper and his friends. He must have felt great anxiety about the harbour bill, and he would have been uncharacteristically short-sighted if he had not also feared for the continued dominance of his family at Rye.

To protect themselves from further attacks by Wardroper, his sons Thomas and James addressed a fawning letter to the Duke of Newcastle that began by mentioning "Our Dear Deceas'd Parent in whose footsteps we hope always to tread."[77] The duke, facing his own troubles over the formation of a war ministry led by his old foe William Pitt, was not impressed. He did nothing to prevent the temporary collapse of the Lamb interest at the mayoral election of August 1758, when Nathaniel Pigram junior was chosen as mayor of Rye. Like Thomas Tournay in the 1680s, Pigram's political strength rested on the freemen, many of whom were connected to the customs office or were enemies of the Lambs. The response of the Lamb faction to Pigram's victory was to harden their resistance. The following November, the brothers Thomas and James Lamb, Chiswell Slade, William Davis, and Needler Chamberlain Watson signed a secret agreement "to exert themselves for the benefit of each other, for the good and advantage of the corporation in general," by not accepting any place without the consent of the others; by opposing any freeman or candidate for election to Parliament who was not supported by all; by supporting each other for mayor (Slade to serve first, then Thomas Lamb, Davis, James Lamb junior, and Watson); by naming each other as jurats or deputy mayors; by dividing the profits from use of their warehouses or vessels by the customs officers; and by splitting contractual work for the corporation (meaning the harbour repairs) between the companies of Chiswell Slade and James Lamb junior. No more concise summary of oligarchy can be imagined; what is missing is any principle other than self-interest and mutual solidarity. The revelation of this document by the Parliamentary Committee on Elections in 1830 caused a sensation that utterly discredited the Lamb interest and gave a tremendous boost to their reform-minded opponents, the "Men of Rye."[78]

In November 1758, however, the Lambs and their friends were not ruling oligarchs; they had been knocked on the ropes by Pigram and Wardroper. Within four months of the compact being signed, the situation in Rye had deteriorated into a confrontation reminiscent of the 1680s. The Lamb faction wrote to the Duke of Newcastle in the name of the corporation of Rye, accusing Pigram of having "taken with the Assistance of a Constable all the Books, papers & Records belonging to the Corporation, but where he has Carried them or for what purpose is unknown to us." As in earlier instances, the removal of records was a sign of the breakdown of corporate consensus. Pigram had also tried to make Wardroper a jurat, "Contrary to the Law & Custom of this Corporation." The angry petitioners added that "we are Certain from the many Incroachments & Invasions made by Mr. Wardroper on the Libertys of our Neighbouring Town we should be in the Greatest danger of Shareing the same fate." They refused to issue the oath of office to Wardroper, on the flimsy grounds that he should have been named on the first day of Pigram's mayoralty. Like Thomas Tournay before him, Wardroper went to the Court of King's Bench, which issued a mandamus commanding that he be sworn, unless better cause for not doing so could be shown. A lawyer for the jurats pleaded that they were too divided to obey the mandamus, and asked King's Bench to decide on Wardroper's right to be elected a jurat. It finally ruled that Wardroper had not been duly elected.[79] By that time, Nathaniel Pigram's term had ended, and James Lamb had become mayor. The oligarchs were back, more united and determined than ever.

The Duke of Newcastle tried to clean up the mess at Rye by replacing Pigram with John Lamb as captain of the customs sloop, paying £300 of the corporation's legal expenses, and giving a yearly pension of £100 to William Davis.[80] The oligarchs were not satisfied: they wanted Wardroper removed from his customs office. When they heard rumours in February 1761 that Pigram might regain his own customs post, they were furious. Chiswell Slade shot off a passionate letter to Newcastle: "my Self and friends. had Rather die fighting than be any Longer Meanly trampled upon. he [Wardroper] nor no man Living shall Lead me in Triumph Captive to the Conqueror till I have done my Utmost to Resist." With parliamentary elections fast approaching, Thomas Lamb felt he could be even more blunt in writing to the town's M.P., George Onslow: "I am Convinc'd that the Duke of Newcastle will loose this Corporation." The very same day, Lamb sent another letter to Onslow, regretting that "to keep things easy here . . . [will] not be in my Power." A worried George Onslow despatched these two "improper letters" to the duke's London residence immediately, at 10 P.M. on a February night.[81] The duke now had to do something. He promised to remove Wardroper from the Rye collector's office, and may have agreed to pay off the corporation's debt of nearly £1,000. A satisfied Chiswell Slade declared to Newcastle that the corporation was again at his command. In fact, Rye remained faithful to its old patron even after he went into opposition in 1763. Wardroper, whose loyalty to the duke had been wavering before his removal, defected to the new administration. He continued to cause trouble at Rye for another few years, but was never again able to establish himself as a force within the corporation.[82]

In spite of its resemblance to the disorders of the 1680s, the political crisis at Rye in 1756–62 was typical of the eighteenth century, in that it could not be fully resolved without appealing to a patron at Whitehall. Town affairs and national politics had become so closely intertwined that only intervention from the centre could bring an end to the turmoil. The sense of civic autonomy that had infused the radicalism of the late seventeenth century was dead. Mayor James Lamb's brief, self-interested attempt to revive it, by resuscitating the sessions court for the trial of John Breads, had ultimately made no difference. The real arbiters of Rye's political destiny were now the ministers of national government—particularly those who headed the Treasury and named the customs officers. In contemporary parlance, Rye was a Treasury borough. This did not mean that the wishes of local magistrates could be ignored, or that management of the town did not demand a great deal of careful attention; but ultimately, authority came from the centre.

Integration into the national structure of government was economic as much as political. The oligarchs had tied themselves to the structure of government finance, not just through the harbour renovations, but through personal investment. The ledger book of Chiswell Slade for 1761–71 shows that by the mid-1760s, he had purchased £4,545.17.6 of government securities, mostly the 3½ percent annuities that were issued during wartime. This represented a far greater investment, and much larger annual returns, than his share in James Lamb junior's timber business, or his small local dealings in wine or oats. Only the wool trade with the West Country, which was reviving towards the end of the Seven Years' War, was more important to Slade's finances;

but the merchants of Exeter, Crediton and Tiverton often paid him with hogsheads of cider, which had to be sold at Rye before his profit could be realized. Government securities were an easier and safer means of making money. War may not have been profitable for the port of Rye, but it certainly benefited Chiswell Slade and other investors in government securities.[83]

The oligarchs had become culturally integrated as well. Abandoning the Puritan thrift of their forebears, they had embraced conspicuous consumption and the polite values of the middling classes. Slade had a portrait of himself painted in the magnificent embroidered waistcoat that he wore to the coronation of George III. The first known painting of a Rye magistrate is Allan Ramsay's 1753 portrait of a self-satisfied Thomas Lamb, wearing a gorgeous waistcoat like the one that had so impressed Jane Collier. Lamb remained a paragon of civility throughout his life. A pair of comic poems published at London in the 1780s by his friend Major Henry Waller characterized the mayor as a connoisseur of "Musick and Virtu" and a would-be epicure whose pretensions to culinary taste were dashed by the fact that "*Sussex* Cooks, without a jest, / Can only roast, or boil, at best." Waller also praised the musical talents and wit of the town brewer Nathaniel Procter, a jurat whose father built a curious brick observation tower in his garden at the centre of Rye. Procter was described as "a miserable bad Brewer," but "a Brother Fidler, / Perhaps a Rhymer too, or Ridler."[84] One wonders what had become of John Breads's two violins.

Waller wrote of himself that "I glory in the Name of *Whig*," and it is likely that Rye's leaders did as well. Their threats of "resistance" against the "tyranny" of Edwin Wardroper were meant to remind the Duke of Newcastle of their common Whig heritage. By the 1760s, however, Whig rhetoric was wearing thin, and over the next four decades it would gradually be drowned out by a conservative patriotism that focused on the defence of the kingdom against its enemies. In November 1775, the corporation struck a less Whiggish note when it sent an address to the king, assuring him that "he had in the Judgment of this Corporation done his Utmost to Reconcile the Unhappy Troubles and disputes now Subsisting in his Majesty's Colonys in America."[85] This was an endorsement of the coercive policy of Lord North's government, which was generally opposed by Old Whigs. Although Rye still contained a large number of Dissenters, especially Baptists, who tended to sympathize with the Americans, they were not able to sway the corporation.[86] Similarly, during the French Revolution, the mayor and jurats condemned "the wicked citizens and base factions" that had beheaded the king, forgetting how their predecessors had reacted to the beheading of Charles I. They welcomed French émigrés and raised a company of volunteers, commanded at first by a Lamb and later by Nathaniel Proctor, to defend the town against invasion. The pro-French views of the Foxite Whigs found no echo among them. The magistrates must have been outraged when a group of "Jacobins" in the Landgate elected a mock mayor to defy them, a custom that would be annually observed in the early nineteenth century.[87] This was the first sign of a radical revival that would end in the campaign of the "Men of Rye."

The move towards conservatism had much to do with Thomas Lamb, who last served as mayor in 1801–2, fifty-five years after his first mayoralty. His family influence *"no human power can shake,"* according to a Whig electoral agent who visited Rye in 1790. Although Lamb was even then willing to flirt with the Whig opposition, its leaders realized that support from Rye was "quite out of the question." After all, the government had rewarded the town's aged patriarch with the office of tally-cutter in the Exchequer, worth £400 a year, while the Old Whigs, through a 1782 reform, had taken away the votes for Parliament of Treasury placemen, including customs officers.[88] By the time the "Men of Rye" took up the cause of ousting the oligarchs in the 1820s, the Lamb interest was known for its Toryism, meaning simply that it was opposed to any change. That Whigs of the 1760s could become Tories of the 1820s was an indication of a broad ideological shift in English politics since the accession of George III. The memory of Rye's erstwhile radicalism, of the Puritan zeal of the Jeakes and the staunch Whiggism of the Grebells, had been completely buried by the Lambs.

The events that have been recounted in this section might well have happened if John Breads had not killed Allen Grebell, but they would have happened in a different way. The murder weakened the Lambs by removing their chief ally, Allen Grebell, a man whose family had been involved in the governance of Rye for over 150 years. Local respect for the Lambs gradually diminished, which in turn sapped the confidence their patron, the Duke of Newcastle. It did not help that so few of the remaining members of the Lamb faction could claim a paternal connection with the Whigs of the 1690s, as Allen Grebell could. Like James Lamb, most of the oligarchs came from families that had settled and made their fortunes at Rye in the eighteenth century. Such men were easily suspected of putting self-interest ahead of principle. They were perhaps more likely to enter into a purely personal compact like that of 1758, in order to preserve their political dominance; and they may have been more inclined to switch from Whigs to Tories after 1770. From this perspective, the murder of Allen Grebell marked the beginning of the end of the Whig oligarchy, clearing the stage for a more conservative era of personal and familial hegemony. That was not, of course, John Breads's intention. If anything, he seems to have wanted to prevent the Lambs from exercising greater power. His deed made it easier to challenge the oligarchs, but it also forced them to entrench their authority even further. In this manner, Breads set in motion a chain of events that had a considerable impact on the governance of Rye, as surely as if he had intended to carry out a political assassination.

6

Looking for Allen Grebell

And even now at Saltinge, blessed little Saltinge, hateful little Saltinge, sleeping in its hill between the three baby rivers, while the gilded Quarter-Boys on the church clock pivoted in the dark to smite yet another flat-voiced bell, *ting-tang, ting-tang, ting-tang.*

—Conrad Aiken, *Ushant* (1952)

Rye has never been typical. Call it odd or unusual, special or strange; but do not try to force it into the straitjacket of typicality. Its uniqueness is rooted in a long, complicated history. From its foundation as a port in the late eleventh century until today, the town's location and poor land connections have given it a strong maritime character that it still retains in spite of the silting up of the harbour. Its incorporation in the thirteenth century set up a fiercely independent system of local government that endured to the 1830s in practice, long after that in spirit. Confederation with the other Cinque Ports in the early 1300s further separated Rye from its rural setting, giving the town a powerful sense of civic identity. This helped to prevent the local gentry from exercising the influence that they enjoyed in other English towns. In the seventeenth and eighteenth centuries, its dwindling fisheries, lack of naval facilities, and peripheral connections with trans-Atlantic or East Indian trade meant that Rye went through difficulties that were not shared by more prosperous ports. On the surface, then, it had little in common, economically, socially, or politically, with a bustling packet station like Falmouth, a naval bastion like Portsmouth, a booming tobacco town like Whitehaven, or a ship-building centre like Great Yarmouth. Rye might easily be written off as an eccentric pin-prick of a place, an incurable anachronism, an insignificant exception to every rule: except that it was not.

Rye's proud and prickly magistrates were quick to defend the differences that defined their town, but they were always aware of the extent to which it was tied into local and regional economies. The port depended on wool and iron from the Weald and the Marsh. Many of its inhabitants were recent immigrants from rural areas. Its leading citizens were eager to acquire land in East Sussex and Kent and to foster good relations with the local gentry. The merchants of Rye traded through Exeter, Colchester, Newcastle, and above all London, where they kept houses and bought clothes and squirreled away money in investments. Although strong cultural differences in early modern England may have separated town from village, province from capital, region from region, they did not prevent the creation of innumerable links, personal and commercial, that crossed those barriers.

Inward-looking though they may have been, the Rye magistrates would never have wanted their history to be read as a series of radical divergences from national trends. On the contrary, they eagerly sought to place themselves at the forefront of every trend, by mediating between local and national priorities. If they wanted Tudor and early Stuart Rye to be a godly citadel, it was because they believed the whole of the English Israel, not just one little port, could be led back towards godliness. If they slowly abandoned a religiously based conception of order between 1660 and 1710, it was because confessional strife had threatened the peace of the entire kingdom, not simply because it had torn up the harmony of Rye. The magistrates understood that a shift away from godly rule would compromise the much-vaunted independence of their town, but they were willing to accept less control over their own affairs in return for greater social and political tranquility. By taking this step, they left the austerity and self-denial of small-town Puritanism behind, opening Rye up to the cultural revolution of the eighteenth century—the wave of politeness, urban improvement, and luxury consumption that swept out of London and engulfed the whole kingdom. Rye was too small a place for its leading families to ride that wave as if it were under their own control, although they kept up a greater degree of social confidence and self-direction than their counterparts in other boroughs, who bartered their autonomy to the local gentry and aristocracy in exchange for corporate peace.

Like the rest of England, then, Rye experienced first the failed political revolution of the godly, then the successful cultural revolution of the polite. The latter was not a social revolution, although it eventually created the conditions for one. The middling sort gained a broader sense of self-awareness, one that extended beyond their localities, but their leaders ended up more culturally attached to the landed elite than their ancestors, the uncouth burghers of the thirteenth century, had been. Linked to their social superiors by ties of patronage as well as social imitation, the middling sort of Hanoverian England were not likely to seek power beyond the local level, except on the terms of advancement laid down by the landed elite. At the same time, cultural fragmentation between the middling sort and groups lower down the social scale became more acute, as certain trades and occupations, such as butchers and mariners, were effectively blocked from civic participation and the membership in polite society that went with it. Neither in Rye nor anywhere else did the rise of politeness mean greater equality. Instead, polite culture thrived on social distinction.

The cultural revolution of the eighteenth century was limited in its institutional impact as well. The governance of Rye maintained a great deal of its medieval character. This was not a contradiction, because the values of politeness were quite compatible with institutional structures that dated back to before the Reformation. Corporate feasts and commemorations may have taken on a new importance after 1660, but they served to cement the exclusivity of the corporation, not to open it to outsiders; thus, they bolstered the ancient structures of local government. Again, Rye was hardly unique. Virtually every borough in England retained a medieval or Tudor charter throughout the eighteenth century. These charters created a multiplicity of special franchises, administrative procedures, and jurisdictions. Rye may have been unusual in the range of its corporate privileges, but hundreds of small towns could claim a few. Canterbury and Bristol and Derby had their own town courts, just as Rye had. London, with its guild system, byzantine administrative procedures, and incredible patchwork of secular as well as ecclesiastical courts, can be regarded the foremost English example of the survival of a medieval commune into the eighteenth century and beyond. Perhaps the birth of the Bank of England and the rise of the joint stock company should have altered London's way of governing itself, but to all appearances, they did not. The capital of modern politeness was administered much as it had been in the age of Gothic "rudeness."

For all that, the cultural revolution of the eighteenth century made a difference. By increasing the English desire for luxury goods derived from Asia and the Americas, by elevating the status of the middling sort, and by promoting the idea of "improvement," it set in motion economic, social, and political changes that would take a century or more to work out. Moreover, it was not just English; it took place in Scotland, Ireland, the British North American colonies, and other parts of Europe as well.[1] Rye's ancient trading partners, Dieppe and Rouen, were seized by the spirit of politeness, consumerism, and urban improvement in the late eighteenth century. Dieppe became a centre of the tobacco industry, as its harbour, badly damaged by the 1694 bombardment, was gradually reconstructed. By 1773, tobacco processing employed eight hundred workers there. The largely medieval town of Rouen was often criticized by enlightened minds for its architectural "Gothicism," but by 1780 it had an academy of letters, a botanical garden, and a successful theatre. Its first weekly newspaper appeared in 1762. As in Britain, the politeness of the middling sort did not alleviate the misery of the poor, but even those at the bottom of Rouen's society experienced a loosening of traditional social controls, one sign of which was a rising rate of illegitimate births.[2]

In short, Rye was not so very different from the rest of the kingdom, or even from other parts of Europe. It was not an easy place for change to reach, but neither was it an island. The historical experiences of its inhabitants resembled those of the whole kingdom, and mirrored those of people in other small English towns. The themes of good neighbourhood and police, sectarianism and oligarchy, godly rule and urban renaissance, played out against a background of civil and foreign wars, were the same themes that dominated the histories of Dorchester and York, Harwich and Coventry. There too, despite the upheavals of the seventeenth and early eighteenth centuries, existing social hierarchies and institutional structures survived well into the age of tea-drinking and assembly rooms.

It was not until the 1760s, as the Whig administration began to crumble and new cultural as well as political forces were unleashed, that some critical minds throughout Britain began to entertain the thought of reforming the administrative and judicial institutions on which oligarchy rested. At that point, cultural revolution began to merge into political change, with violent consequences in British North America. Rye was not isolated from these developments, but its magistrates took a hostile view of them. Their hostility seemed to be justified by events in France after 1789, where the polite world of salons and clubs gave birth to the "hydra" of democracy. It was only after the fear of political revolution had subsided that Rye entered the vanguard of the reform movement, as has been seen.

Oligarchy had never been universally accepted in England. Before 1760 its opponents were mostly Tories, allied with groups of Country Whigs. In a town like Rye, where the opposition had no broad support, Tories and their allies were reduced to impotent grumbling, as can be seen in Thomas Frewen's family letters. After the accession of George III, with the Whig party hopelessly split and the rhetoric of patriotism trumpeted from every corner of the land, critics of small-town oligarchy could be more open in demanding reform. One of the first published attacks on the judicial system of the Cinque Ports appeared in an anonymous letter sent to the *London Magazine* in 1761. It is worth citing here as the first, ineffective salvo in a long, tortuous campaign that would culminate in the reforms of the 1830s.

The letter writer claimed that he had been present at a meeting of the sessions court of Tenterden, which took place at an inn. Three magistrates sat on the bench, "one of most profound taciturnity, who never uttered a single syllable; the others were very loquacious and dogmatical, men only remarkable for their effrontery, and being professed infidels." Their lack of respect for religion was manifest, according to the writer, when they committed for trial a clergyman who dared to smile at their proceedings. The only person to appear before the court was "a poor, industrious labouring man," accused of taking some old horseshoes from his master. The grand jury was hand-picked by the chief magistrate, and it included the constable who had arrested the defendant. None of the fourteen or fifteen jurors was challenged by the prisoner, as was his right.

The defendant pleaded not guilty, saying he had found the

horseshoes on the road. His former master, however, identified as his property three out of seven horseshoes that had been
sold to a blacksmith by a boy allegedly sent by the defendant.
The witness recognized them because they were crooked—"a
crooked evidence, truly! As if no crooked shoes were to be found
in any other place." The blacksmith was called upon to give evidence; he turned out to be the same constable who had carried
out the arrest, and a member of the jury to boot! The boy who
had brought him the horseshoes admitted under oath that he
did not know what an oath was. The only witness for the defendant was "a person commiserating the unhappy case of the
prisoner," probably the writer himself. He pleaded "that the law
did not intend to punish the seizure and detention of every con-
ceivable article of property, though it should be proved." In other
words, not all property was sacred—a radical point indeed in the
century of consumerism! The witness also pointed out the ir-
regularities in the case, which did him no good with the chief
magistrate. The summation was delivered "in such partial re-
proachful terms, with such bitter invectives, as plainly shewed,
that Mr. President had absolutely forgot, that the judge was
counsel for the prisoner." The jury debated a full hour before ac-
quitting the prisoner, "to the universal joy of the people, which
diffused itself through every countenance."

The writer was outraged by the spectacle of judicial chicanery.
"Now," he asked, "is it fit that our laws should be thus administered, or that such persons should be intrusted with authority?"
English law and liberties were "mere empty names; if the igno-
rant and illiterate, the cruel and the oppressive, are to distribute
the awards of justice." The corporation of Tenterden formed "a
despicable junto, a detestable faction; trampling, with impunity,
upon the laws of their country." His conclusion was unequivocal
and radical: "may all special jurisdictions, the common nurseries
of barbarism and despotism, be abolished; may the course of jus-

tice not be obstructed and polluted, by narrow, dirty channels; but may it flow freely and clear, as a perpetual mighty stream!" To underline his truthfulness, he signed himself "VERAX."

In the national situation of 1761, Verax may well have been a supporter of the patriot cause, perhaps a former Tory, as his sympathy for the clergy and denunciation of judicial "infidels" suggest. Under the new regime of the "Patriot King" George III, Verax may have hoped for the end of "faction" and of political injustice, which meant turning out the Whig oligarchs who had ruled the country on both a national and a local level for almost fifty years. When he wrote of "a despicable junto," using a term that had described the Whig leadership in the 1690s, he meant to point an accusing finger at Whigs like Thomas Lamb or the Duke of Newcastle. He went further in espousing the abolition of all special jurisdictions like the sessions courts of the Cinque Ports. This constituted a direct threat to the foundations of oligarchical power throughout the nation.

Unfortunately for his chances of promoting reform, the veracity of Verax was immediately questioned. Two months after the appearance of his letter, the *London Magazine* was induced to issue an apology for it, "being credibly informed, that some of the facts are absolutely false, others grosly and vilely misrepresented." No further explanation was offered, which makes the retraction suspect. Had someone in a position of authority put pressure on the editor of the *London Magazine*? Verax replied by publishing an advertisement in a Canterbury paper, saying that "he will reveal his real name when called upon, and support every fact he has asserted by undoubted affidavits." Apparently, nobody called on him to do so. The dispute faded into silence.[3]

Judicial prejudice, abuses of power, irregular courtroom proceedings: Verax's report recalls many aspects of the John Breads case. In fact, the trial and execution of Breads was not a unique event. It represented the kind of situation that might easily arise in a small town court where judges were unaccustomed to their role and determined to convict. Breads was denied justice by the machinations of James Lamb, but the problem with his trial went further than this, because the mayor was working within a system that did little to protect defendants from judges. The jury, the only real obstacle to a judge's power, could be hand-picked, instructed, and manipulated. The judicial system in turn reflected a social and political structure in which authority had been concentrated in a few hands, usually by inheritance. Those privileged few, when faced by violence directed at them from below, sought to repress it in the name of the public good, by making an example of those who were responsible. This might be done through measured lenience, but it was just as often accomplished by severity, especially when only a single perpetrator was involved. Intentionally or not, Breads had challenged the whole structure of governance in Rye when he stabbed Allen Grebell. As a result, he had little chance of escaping the most extreme form of retribution: death, followed by the dishonouring of his body.

Why did John Breads murder Allen Grebell? The best explanation is Breads's own: he was distracted or insane. Insanity, however, does not operate randomly. It can shift or rearrange perceptions, but it cannot separate a sufferer from the social context in which he or she exists. As Locke pointed out, madness recreates the known world "wrongly"; it cannot simply form a new one. Even in his madness, Breads was trapped by his own history and that of his native town. His fantasies about devils drew upon a tradition of "thinking with demons" that was particularly strong in Rye and had long been connected with factional struggles. Breads's religious background may have given him a strong sense of connection with Rye's violent political past, and alienated him from the way the town was governed after 1689. The fact that he wanted to vent his rage on the oligarchs James Lamb and Ralph Norton indicates that his perceived enemies were the heirs of those moderates who had once opposed the godly in Rye. To be sure, Breads was not entirely a man of the past. As a one-time associate of the Lambs, his fortunes had at first risen with theirs. He had once held a position of economic prominence in Rye, as proprietor of the Flushing Inn. Yet he had not become settled or rich; and by 1743, the economy was worsening for him as it was for everyone. Breads may then have begun to wonder whether the compromises of his life had benefited or damned him.

Walking the streets of Rye today, it is easy to appreciate the personality of James Lamb. He left buildings and monuments behind him: the town hall, the water tower, Lamb House. Lamb was enterprising, ambitious, determined to make the most out of a difficult economic situation. His strong-armed and self-interested leadership alienated many, although it lent dynamism to a struggling community. It is not easy to like him. He enriched himself in every way he could from town office, especially from the harbour commission, which his greed, and that of his associates, set on the path towards ultimate failure. He dealt ruthlessly with his enemies. The Breads case, in which Lamb acted without much respect for legal precedents, does not reflect much credit on him. Ultimately, it is as an adept political survivor that he most commands respect.

John Breads is more difficult to find in today's Rye, but he lies there in shadows. He seems to sum up the inwardness and isolation of the marshlands, rather than the strident individualism of the Weald. At the same time, however, Breads was unable to hide his despair and madness from his neighbours. In this respect, he represents an aspect of small-town existence that is often hard for outsiders to grasp: namely, its lack of anonymity. Failure or frustration in a place like Rye could never be kept private. If Breads had failed as an innkeeper, everyone would have known it. If he had a grudge against James Lamb, it would have been common knowledge. If he had exhibited signs of madness, they would have been widely discussed among the townsfolk. Yet he was not protected by them, any more than poor "Mad Ned" Arnold was protected from his own destructive impulses by his family. Neighbours still wanted to know one another's business, but the interventionist values of good neighbourhood had declined beyond recovery, and were being replaced by more formal types of policing. At his trial, John Breads could look nowhere for sympathy or assistance. Can he find them today? Sadly, it is the gruesome sight of his skull preserved in the gibbet, not the pathos of a mentally disturbed man's fate, that will continue to attract attention.

The most elusive character in the story is Allen Grebell himself. Neither tortured nor tyrannical, Grebell gives the impression of being a relatively generous and compassionate man, especially when compared with his self-aggrandizing brother-in-law. Henry Dodson, who hated James Lamb, called Allen Grebell "the Unfortunate good Gentleman." His family had ancient roots in the town, but left few marks on it that are still visible. Their greatest monument, Sanders' School, had no permanent site and has disappeared. We do not know where in the churchyard Allen Grebell was stabbed, or where he died. Even his monument is hard to find. Whereas the Lambs continued to rule over Rye throughout the late eighteenth and early nineteenth centuries, Grebell's son Allen lost his freedom in 1776 for non-residence, and no other direct descendant played a part in town government.[4] The Grebells are gone from Rye.

They are gone, yet surely they are still there as well; not as sad ghosts haunting the place, but as the protectors of a civic life that has persisted in spite of so many obstacles. With the Lambs and the Meryons, the Jeakes and the Gillarts, the Bennetts and the Hamons, their efforts kept Rye from falling into irrelevance, or being commandeered by outside forces, particularly the local gentry. In the sweep of national history, these small-town merchants and tradesmen were almost totally irrelevant; but on the local level, they were the crucial middlemen who mediated between Whitehall and the ordinary people of England. Neither aristocrats nor democrats, they owed their positions to personal effort as much as to lineage. Trade and industry depended on them. By instinct inward-looking, their horizons were broadened by the force of economic necessity. Although they may not have created either, they helped to shape an English imperial identity (which they called British) and a thriving culture of consumption. Far more than the orators in Parliament, the courtiers at St. James, or the great merchants of the cities, it was these small town middling men who were responsible for the great achievements of the eighteenth century—the expansion of internal commerce, a national network of roads and canals, a secure financial system, a growing acceptance of the necessity of social welfare. They also profited from the great injustices of the age: exploitation, slavery, and imperialism.

The small towns that they governed endure today and have become for many people an attractive alternative to the anonymous rush of city life. So the Quarter-boys who still smite the church bells with a *ting-tang* are not sounding a death-knell for Rye; they are drawing our attention to a remarkable survival, built on the struggles of generations of local people—fishermen and innkeepers, mariners and merchants, jurats and housewives. Rye changed, and it survived. For that, the Grebell family was more responsible than any other in the early modern period. The safekeeping and promotion of his native town was Allen Grebell's inheritance from all the other Grebells who had helped to govern Rye since the 1550s. Through the harbour renovations, the anti-excise agitation, and the poor-relief measures of the early 1740s, Allen Grebell maintained that legacy, bequeathing it intact to his unappealing brother-in-law, whose heirs handed it over reluctantly to the "Men of Rye" and their successors. Some credit for Grebell's contributions to the town should have been added to the peevish lines of his memorial. Instead, his claim to immortality has rested on the bizarre stories woven around his killing. Perhaps he can now be granted a more active fame, as a watchful guardian of Rye's interests and a merchant who did something for the poor—not a bad record for a small-town politician of the 1700s. The positive part of the man was important, and it should be allowed to live. The cruel blow of the sanguinary butcher cut short the life of the jurat. After almost three centuries, let us hope that it has not wholly succeeded in murdering Mr. Grebell.

NOTES

Abbreviations

BL	British Library
DNB	Leslie Stephen and Sidney Lee, eds., *The Dictionary of National Biography* (63 vols., London, 1885-1900)
ESRO	East Sussex Record Office, Lewes
ASHB	Ashburnham Archives (letter books of John, 1st Baron Ashburnham)
FRE	Frewen Archives; for a list, see Heather M. Warne, ed., *A Catalogue of the Frewen Archives* (Lewes, 1972)
KRA	Kent River Board Archives
PAB	Paine and Brettell Manuscripts
PAR	Parish Records
Rye	Records of the Corporation of Rye; for a full list, see Richard F. Dell, ed., *The Records of Rye Corporation* (Lewes, 1962)
SAY	Sayer Manuscripts (Collier Correspondence)
HMC	Historical Manuscripts Commission
PRO	Public Record Office, Kew
A94	Southeast Circuit Assizes, Indictments
E190	Exchequer, Queen's Remembrancer, Port Books
SP	State Papers, Domestic
Rye Museum	Rye Castle Museum, Rye
SAC	Sussex Archaeological Collections
WSRO	West Sussex Record Office, Chichester
Ep.	Chichester Diocesan Records
Goodwood	Goodwood Archives (correspondence of 2d Duke of Richmond)

ONE

Spook Stories

1. Keith Wrightson, *English Society, 1580–1680* (New Brunswick, N.J., 1982), p. 51. See also Steve Hindle, "A Sense of Place? Becoming and Belonging in the Rural Parish, 1550–1650," in Alexandra Shepard and Phil Withington, eds., *Communities in Early Modern England: Networks, Place, Rhetoric* (Manchester, 2000), pp. 96–114.

2. Anna Bryson, *From Courtesy to Civility: Changing Codes of Conduct in Early Modern England* (Oxford, 1996), p. 150. The idea of civility is largely derived from the writings of Norbert Elias, especially *The Civilizing Process,* trans. Edmund Jephcott (2 vols., New York, 1978, 1982). For politeness, see Lawrence E. Klein, *Shaftesbury and the Culture of Politeness: Moral Discourse and Cultural Politics in Early Eighteenth-Century England* (Cambridge, 1993). The starting point for the "consumer revolution" is Neil McKendrick, John Brewer, and J. H. Plumb, *The Birth of a Consumer Society: The Commercialization of Eighteenth-Century England* (London, 1982). The "urban renaissance" is defined in Peter Borsay, *The English Urban Renaissance: Culture and Society in the Provincial Town, 1660–1770* (Oxford, 1989), and extended in Peter Borsay and L. J. Proudfoot, eds., *Provincial Towns in Early Modern England and Ireland: Change, Convergence and Divergence* (Oxford, 2001).

3. The first successful "microhistory" was Emmanuel LeRoy Ladurie, *Montaillou: The Promised Land of Error,* trans. Barbara Bray (New York, 1979). It was followed by Carlo Ginzburg, *The Cheese and the Worms: The Cosmos of a Seventeenth-Century Miller,* trans. John and Anne Tedeschi (Baltimore, 1980), and by Natalie Davis, *The Return of Martin Guerre* (New York, 1983). Few "microhistories" deal with England, although notable exceptions are Cynthia B. Herrup, *A House in Gross Disorder: Sex, Law and the 2d Earl of Castlehaven* (Oxford, 1999), and Donna T. Andrew and Randall McGowen, *The Perreaus and Mrs. Rudd: Forgery and Betrayal in 18th-Century London* (Berkeley, 2001). Three important English "microhistories" that deal with small communities are Keith Wrightson and David Levine, *Poverty and Piety in an English Village: Terling 1525–1700* (New York, 1979); Keith Wrightson and David Levine, *The Making of an Industrial Society: Whickham, 1560–1760* (Oxford, 1991); and Eamon Duffy, *The Voices of Morebath: Reformation and Rebellion in an English Village* (New Haven, 2001).

4. Henry James, "An English Winter Watering-Place," in *Collected Travel Writings: Great Britain and America* (New York, 1993), pp. 226, 231.

5. Henry James, "Winchelsea, Rye, and 'Denis Duval,'" in *Collected Travel Writings*, p. 236; K. M. E. Murray, *The Constitutional History of the Cinque Ports* (Manchester, 1935).

6. James, "Winchelsea," p. 251.

7. Patric Dickinson, "Tourists of a Sort," in *Poems from Rye* (Rye, 1979), p. 3.

8. Dickinson, "Henry James and Lamb House," in *Poems from Rye*, p. 5.

9. Henry James to Alice James, 1 December 1897, in Henry James, *Letters*, ed. Leon Edel (4 vols., Cambridge, Mass., 1974–84), vol. 4, pp. 62–64. For James's life at Rye, see Leon Edel, *Henry James: The Treacherous Years, 1895–1901* (Philadelphia, 1969), pp. 193–200, 222–31; Leon Edel, *Henry James: The Master, 1901–1916* (Philadelphia, 1972), pp. 21–31; Miranda Seymour, *A Ring of Conspirators: Henry James and His Literary Circle, 1895–1915* (Boston, 1988), chap. 2.

10. Quoted in Geoffrey Spink Bagley, *The Book of Rye* (Buckingham, 1982), p. 113.

11. E. F. Benson, "James Lamp," in *The Collected Ghost Stories*, ed. Richard Dalby (London, 1992), pp. 485–96.

12. Joan Aiken, *The Haunting of Lamb House* (New York, 1991), p. 113.

13. Jim Foster and Kenneth Clark, *Adams' Historical Guide to Rye Royal* (23d ed., Rye, 1988), pp. 55–57; *Rye Colour Guide* (Rye, 1989); H. Montgomery Hyde, *The Story of Lamb House, Rye: The Home of Henry James* (Rye, 1966), pp. 20, 27–28; Kenneth Clark, *Murder by Mistake: Rye's 18th Century Cause Célèbre* (2d ed., Rye, 1989); John Ryan, *Murder in the Churchyard* (Rye, 1997). Richard Horner, *Rye Shipping* (Rye, 2000), pp. 121–26, offers a novel but implausible explanation of the murder as a revenge killing involving smugglers and engineered by Mayor Lamb himself.

14. Graham Mayhew, *Tudor Rye* (Falmer, 1987), pp. 207–212, 214–15; Cynthia B. Herrup, *The Common Peace: Participation and the Criminal Law in Seventeenth-Century England* (Cambridge, 1987), pp. 44, 59–60.

15. ESRO, Rye 60/12, f. 3; Rye 7/35.

16. ESRO, Rye 7/35; Rye 9/5, 9/11; E. F. Hunnisett, ed., *Sussex Coroners' Inquests, 1603–1688* (Kew, 1998); Rye 70/13, town clerk's accounts for 20 January 1737. Non-capital cases of larceny, of goods worth less than a shilling, also disappear from the early 1680s until 1746; see ESRO, Rye 10/2, 8/44.

17. ESRO, Rye 2/8.

18. ESRO, Rye 70/24; Rye 60/12; PAR 467/1/1/5, ff. 12, 18, 72–73. I owe the second reference to Mike Saville.

19. ESRO, Rye 69/47, vouchers to accounts for March–June 1743. For Francis

and Martha Jewhurst, see Rye 7/40, 8/45. For leg irons, see J. M. Beattie, *Crime and the Courts in England, 1660–1800* (Princeton, 1986), pp. 297–98.

20. J. H. Baker, "Criminal Courts and Procedure at Common Law, 1550–1800," in J. S. Cockburn, ed., *Crime in England, 1550–1800* (London, 1977), p. 40; ESRO, Rye 2/7; Rye 14/21 C and D; PAR 467/30/6.

21. ESRO, Rye 1/18, f. 38; Rye 70/13, accounts dated 23 March 1744 (i.e., 1745); Rye 70/34; Romney Sedgwick, ed., *The History of Parliament: The House of Commons, 1715–54* (3 vols., London, 1971), vol. 2, pp. 27–28, 451–52. Mike Saville has helped me with several issues of interpretation concerning the town clerk's accounts.

22. ESRO, Rye 1/18, fs. 39, 40; Rye 70/29; Rye 71/19; Rye 114/10. A. L. Vidler, "The Fifteenth Century House in Rye Now Known as the Flushing Inn," *Sussex Notes and Queries* 5, no. 5 (Feb. 1935), p. 151, wrongly supposes that Richard rented the Flushing Inn.

23. *The General Evening Post*, no. 1484, 22–24 March 1743; *The Daily Post*, no. 7345, 23 March 1743; *The Kentish Post, or Canterbury Newsletter*, no. 2648, 23–26 March 1743. I am grateful to Mike Saville for sending me photocopies of the last paper.

24. ESRO, Rye 70/24. Other coroners' inquisitions for the period are found in ESRO, Rye 32/3–11.

25. ESRO, Rye 467/30/5.

26. *The General Evening Post*, no. 1512, 28–31 May 1743; *The Daily Post*, no. 7406, 31 May 1743; *The Kentish Post*, no. 2668, 1–4 June 1743. *The Kentish Post* also printed two brief reports from Canterbury in no. 2662, 11–14 May 1743 (a notice of the impending trial), and no. 2666, 25–28 May 1743 (mentioning the length of the trial, and the condemnation of Breads).

27. *The Daily Post*, no. 7417, 13 June 1743; *The Kentish Post*, no. 2672, 13–16 June 1743.

28. Norma Landau, *The Justices of the Peace, 1679–1760* (Berkeley, 1984), p. 209n; Baker, "Criminal Courts and Procedure," p. 30.

29. ESRO, SAY 1811. On the Colliers, see Heather M. Matthews, "The Papers of John Collier of Hastings: A Catalogue," unpublished thesis, University of London, 1966, pp. i–xv; W. V. Crake, "The Correspondence of John Collier, Five Times Mayor of Hastings, and his Connection with the Pelham Family," SAC 45 (1902): 62–109.

30. ESRO, Rye 1/18, ff. 53, 64 (Moneypenny); Sedgwick, ed., *History of Parliament*, vol. 1, pp. 508–9.

31. *Victoria History of the County of Sussex* (7 vols., 1898–1940), vol. 7, pp.

172–76; ESRO, SAY 168, 460, 463, 472; T. B. Howell, ed., *A Complete Collection of State Trials* (34 vols., London, 1816–28), vol. 17, col. 909; ESRO, PAB 304. Dodson's clergyman brother married the daughter of Thomas Marchant, a farmer who left an extensive manuscript diary; see Edward Turner, ed., "The Marchant Diary," SAC 25 (1873): 163–203.

32. "Cinque-Port Law in 1742," SAC 18 (1866): 188–89. I have corrected this against a photocopy of the original, which was traced by Mike Saville and Les Bearman.

33. On eighteenth-century trial procedure, see Beattie, *Crime and the Courts in England*, pp. 340–52; Baker, "Criminal Courts and Procedure," pp. 15–48; Douglas Hay, "Property, Authority and the Criminal Law," in Douglas Hay et al., *Albion's Fatal Tree: Crime and Society in Eighteenth-Century England* (New York, 1975), pp. 17–63; Peter King, *Crime, Justice and Discretion in England, 1740–1820* (Oxford, 2000).

34. Beattie, *Crime and the Courts in England*, pp. 352–62; Knowler is mentioned on p. 360. In 1734, Knowler appeared at Kent Assizes as attorney for the crown in a dispute over the mayoralty of New Romney. This may have brought him to prominence as a lawyer familiar with the customs of the Cinque Ports. Howell, ed., *State Trials*, vol. 17, cols. 822–43.

35. William Blackstone, *Commentaries on the Laws of England* (4 vols., Chicago, 1979), vol. 4, pp. 24, 195–96.

36. On the insanity defence, see Nigel Walker, *Crime and Insanity in England*, vol. 1, *The Historical Perspective* (Edinburgh, 1968); Michael Macdonald, *Mystical Bedlam: Madness, Anxiety, and Healing in Seventeenth-Century England* (Cambridge, 1981), pp. 123–6; Joel Peter Eigen, "Intentionality and Insanity: What the Eighteenth-Century Juror Heard," in W. F. Bynum, Roy Porter, and Michael Shepherd, eds., *The Anatomy of Madness: Essays in the History of Psychology* (2 vols., London, 1985), vol. 2, pp. 34–51; Daniel N. Robinson, *Wild Beasts and Idle Humours: The Insanity Defence from Antiquity to the Present* (Cambridge, Mass., 1996); Roy Porter, *Mind-Forg'd Manacles: A History of Madness in England from the Restoration to the Regency* (London, 1987), pp. 114–117; Beattie, *Crime and the Courts in England*, pp. 82–85.

37. Blackstone, *Commentaries*, vol. 4, pp. 198–201; Beattie, *Crime and the Courts in England*, pp. 81–91.

38. Macdonald, *Mystical Bedlam*, pp. 138–42; Howell, ed., *State Trials*, vol. 16, cols. 695–766, vol. 19, cols. 886–980.

39. Beattie, *Crime and the Courts in England*, pp. 527–30; V. A. C. Gatrell, *The Hanging Tree: Execution and the English People, 1770–1868* (Oxford,

1994), pp. 267–69; Randall McGowen, "The Body and Punishment in Eighteenth-Century England," *Journal of Modern History* 59, no. 4 (1987): 651–79.

40. Gatrell, *Hanging Tree,* p. 87; Peter Linebaugh, "The Tyburn Riots against the Surgeons," in *Albion's Fatal Tree,* pp. 65–117.

41. Rev. Thomas Hutchison, "Ditchling," SAC 13 (1861): 247; Rev. Edward Turner, "The Stapley Diary," SAC 18 (1866): 160–61.

42. John Collard, *A Maritime History of Rye* (Rye, 1985), p. 36. For prejudice against Jews in eighteenth-century England, see Frank Felsenstein, *Anti-Semitic Stereotypes: A Paradigm of Otherness in English Popular Culture, 1660–1830* (Baltimore, 1995); but compare this with the milder judgements in David Katz, *The Jews in the History of England, 1485–1850* (Oxford, 1994), chaps. 5–6. Katz discusses murder trials involving Jewish suspects on pp. 261–64.

43. J. A. Sharpe, *Crime in Early Modern England, 1550–1750* (London, 1984), p. 92.

44. ESRO, Rye 2/8, 29 Dec. 1756 and 26 Jan. 1757; Holloway, *The History and Antiquities of the Ancient Town and Port of Rye, in the County of Sussex* (London, 1847), p. 357; Leopold Amon Vidler, *A New History of Rye* (Hove, 1934), p. 106. Assize indictments for Sussex are found in PRO, A94.

45. King, *Crime, Justice and Discretion,* pp. 361–67.

46. *The Compact Edition of the Oxford English Dictionary* (2 vols., Oxford, 1971), vol. 1, p. 234; vol. 2, p. 2636.

47. Similar purposes inspired local historians of the eighteenth century, as shown in Rosemary Sweet, *The Writing of Urban Histories in Eighteenth-Century England* (Oxford, 1997), chap. 6.

48. H. P. Clark, *Clark's Guide and History of Rye, to which is added its Political History. Interspersed with many pleasing & interesting incidents* (Rye, "1861" [1865]), p. 157.

49. The best account of the "Men of Rye" is in Holloway, *History of Rye,* pp. 244–71; also, Clark, *Guide,* pp. 135–58; Vidler, *New History of Rye,* pp. 118–24; Bagley, *Book of Rye,* pp. 57–64. An invaluable complement to Holloway's work has been provided by the Rye Local History Group, *An Index to William Holloway's "History and Antiquities of the Ancient Town and Port of Rye"* (Rye, 1994).

50. Charles Lewis Meryon, "Some Account of the Ancient Town and Port of Rye and of Its Municipal Government," Rye Museum, 21/7a, vol. 1, p. 15; vol. 2, pp. 565–66.

51. Holloway, *History of Rye,* pp. 81–2 (long quote on p. 82).

52. Porter, *Mind-Forg'd Manacles*, pp. 35, 43–44; Andrew Scull, *The Most Solitary of Afflictions: Madness and Society in Britain, 1700–1900* (New Haven, 1993), pp. 56–60. Holloway later asserted that Breads owned no property, an incorrect claim that served to marginalize the killer even further: see William Holloway, *Antiquarian Rambles through Rye* (Rye, 1863), p. 41.

53. Cynthia and Tony Reavell, *E. F. Benson: Mr. Benson Remembered in Rye, and the World of Tilling* (Rye, 1984), pp. 94–95; Alec Vidler, *Scenes from a Clerical Life* (London, 1977), pp. 9–10; Vidler, *New History of Rye*, pp. 119, 123, 124, 128, 133–38, 144.

54. Vidler, *New History of Rye*, p. 102.

55. Vidler, *New History of Rye*, pp. 96–98.

56. ESRO, Vidler Mss., Acc. 50201/1/1, /2, pp. 42–4.

57. L. A. Vidler, "The Murder of Allen Grebell," *Sussex Notes and Queries* 11, no. 3 (1946): 49–51.

58. Edel, *Henry James: The Treacherous Years*, pp. 88–90.

59. On Benson's life and works, see Geoffrey Palmer and Noel Lloyd, *E. F. Benson as He Was* (Hastings, 1988); Brian Masters, *The Life of E. F. Benson* (London, 1991).

60. E.F. Benson, *Final Edition* (New York, 1940), pp. 18–24, 98–100, 135–36; Palmer and Lloyd, *E. F. Benson*, pp. 84–90; Masters, *E. F. Benson*, pp. 164–69, 193–200, 216–17.

61. Benson, *Final Edition*, pp. 156–63, 266–68.

62. Porter, *Mind-Forged Manacles*, p. 281; see also Vieda Skultans, *English Madness: Ideas on Insanity, 1580–1890* (London, 1979), chaps. 2–3.

63. Robert Burton, *The Anatomy of Melancholy*, ed. Thomas C. Faulkner, Nicholas K. Kiessling, and Rhonda L. Blair (6 vols., Oxford, 1989–2000), vol. 1, pp. 132–3, 438; Michael Macdonald, *Mystical Bedlam: Madness, Anxiety, and Healing in Seventeenth-Century England* (Cambridge, 1981), p. 126.

64. Macdonald, *Mystical Bedlam*, pp. 123, 142; Howell, ed., *State Trials*, vol. 17, col. 764.

65. John Locke, *An Essay Concerning Human Understanding* (Harmondsworth, 1997), pp. 151, 157, 354.

66. William Battie, *A Treatise on Madness* (London, 1758), pp. 5–6, 33, 37, reprinted in Richard Hunter and Ida Macalpine, eds., *A Treatise on Madness by William Battie, M.D., and Remarks on Dr. Battie's Treatise on Madness by John Monro, M.D.: A Psychiatric Controversy of the Eighteenth Century* (London, 1962).

67. John Monro, *Remarks on Dr. Battie's Treatise on Madness* (London, 1758),

pp. 3–4, 7–8, reprinted in ibid.; Howell, ed., *State Trials,* vol. 19, cols. 942–43.

68. ESRO, FRE 1295, 1308. J. Andrews and A. Scull, *Undertaker of the Mind: John Monro and Mad-Doctoring in 18th-c. England* (Berkeley, 2001), ch. 3.

69. ESRO, FRE 1296. The doctor's views on inoculation are found in Thomas Frewen, *The Practice and Theory of Inoculation* (London, 1749). For the Frewen family, see Jeffrey S. Chamberlain, "Portrait of a High Church Clerical Dynasty in Georgian England: The Frewens and Their World," in John Walsh, Colin Haydon, and Stephen Taylor, eds., *The Church of England, c. 1689–c. 1833* (Cambridge, 1993), pp. 299–316.

70. Thomas Frewen, *Physiologia, or, the Doctrine of Nature, comprehended in the Origin and Progression of Human Life; the Vital and Animal Functions; Diseases of Body and Mind; and Remedies Prophylactic and Therapeutic* (London, 1780), pp. 142–43, 330–34.

71. Joel Peter Eigen, *Witnessing Insanity: Madness and the Mad-Doctors in the English Court* (New Haven, 1995).

72. Porter, *Mind-Forg'd Manacles,* p. 138; William Parry-Jones, *The Trade in Lunacy: A Study of Private Madhouses in England in the Eighteenth and Nineteenth Centuries* (London, 1972), chap. 2; Scull, *Most Solitary of Afflictions,* pp. 78–79, 199–203, and 268–69 n. 2–3, for the struggle over the establishment of a Sussex county asylum in the 1840s and '50s. For a philosophical critique of the treatment of insanity, see Michel Foucault, *Madness and Civilization: A History of Insanity in the Age of Reason,* trans. Richard Howard (New York, 1965).

TWO

A Parcel of Devils

1. Robert Burton, *The Anatomy of Melancholy,* ed. Thomas C. Faulkner, Nicholas K. Kiessling and Rhonda L. Blair (6 vols., Oxford, 1989–2000), vol. 1, p. 190; Michael Macdonald, *Mystical Bedlam: Madness, Anxiety, and Healing in Seventeenth-Century England* (Cambridge, 1981), pp. 298–217.

2. R. F. Hunnisett, ed., *Sussex Coroners' Inquests, 1558–1603* (London, 1996), pp. 116–17; Graham Mayhew, *Tudor Rye* (Falmer, 1987), p. 211.

3. *The Examination, confession and condemnation of Henry Robson fisherman of Rye, who poisoned his wife in the strangest maner that ever hitherto hath bin heard of* (London, 1598), pp. [1]–[7]. The pamphlet is mentioned in Peter Lake, "Deeds against Nature: Cheap Print, Protestantism and Murder in Early Seventeenth-Century England," in Kevin Sharpe and Peter Lake, eds., *Culture and Politics in Early Stuart England* (Stanford, 1993), pp. 257–

83. Curiously, a real Henry Robson lived in Baddinge ward, where he paid 1s. in rates in 1576: Mayhew, *Tudor Rye*, p. 282.

4. Stuart Clark, *Thinking with Demons: The Idea of Witchcraft in Early Modern Europe* (Oxford, 1997), pp. 683–84.

5. For comparisons, see A. M. Johnson, "Politics in Chester during the Civil Wars and Interregnum," in Paul Slack and Peter Clark, eds., *Crisis and Order in English Towns, 1500–1700: Essays in Urban History* (Toronto, 1972), pp. 204–36; W. T. McCaffrey, *Exeter, 1540–1640* (Cambridge, Mass., 1975); D. M. Palliser, *Tudor York* (London, 1979); Peter Clark, "'The Ramoth-Gilead of the Good': Urban Change and Political Radicalism at Gloucester, 1540–1640," in P. Clark, Alan G. R. Smith and N. Tyacke, eds., *The English Commonwealth* (London, 1979), pp. 167–87; Ian Mason, "'Do You Think the Town will be Governed by a Parcel of Pimping Burgesses?'" Arundel Borough 1586–1677," SAC 128 (1990): 157–76; David Harris Sacks, *The Widening Gate: Bristol and the Atlantic Economy, 1450–1700* (Berkeley, 1991), chap. 10; David Underdown, *Fire from Heaven: Life in an English Town in the Seventeenth Century* (London, 1992); Robert Tittler, *The Reformation and the Towns in England: Politics and Political Culture, c. 1540–c. 1640* (Oxford, 1998).

6. A. J. F. Dudley, "The Early History of the Rye Fishing Industry," SAC 107 (1969): 36–64; Mayhew, *Tudor Rye,* chap. 7; Stephen Andrew Hipkin, "The Economy and Social Structure of Rye, 1600–1660," Ph.D. thesis, Oxford University, 1986, chaps. 1 and 3.

7. Christopher Haigh, *English Reformations: Religion, Politics and Society under the Tudors* (Oxford, 1993), chap. 7.

8. Mayhew, *Tudor Rye,* pp. 59–60, 67; Graham Mayhew, "Religion, Faction and Politics in Reformation Rye, 1530–59," SAC 120 (1982): 139–60; J. R. Elton, *Policy and Police: The Enforcement of the Reformation in the Age of Thomas Cromwell* (Cambridge, 1972), pp. 20–21, 84–90; M. J. Kitch, "The Reformation in Sussex," in M. J. Kitch, ed., *Studies in Sussex Church History* (London, 1981), pp. 81–82.

9. Mayhew, *Tudor Rye,* pp. 67–69; DNB, under "Scambler, Edmund."

10. Mayhew, *Tudor Rye,* pp. 72–75; Roger B. Manning, *Religion and Society in Elizabethan Sussex: A Study of the Enforcement of the Religious Settlement, 1558–1603* (Leicester, 1969), p. 243; Hipkin, "Economy and Social Structure of Rye," p. 9. For Protestantism in Rouen and Dieppe, see Philip Benedict, *Rouen during the Wars of Religion* (Cambridge, 1981), pp. 49–70, 75–77; Stuart Carroll, *Noble Power during the French Wars of Religion: The Guise Affinity and the Catholic Cause in Normandy* (Cambridge, 1998), pp. 97–99, 101, 232.

11. The Southeast Circuit figures are from C. L'Estrange Ewen, ed., *Witch Hunting and Witch Trials: The Indictments for Witchcraft from the Records of 1373 Assizes held for the Home Circuit A.D. 1559–1736* (London, 1929), p. 99. Ewen miscounted one Kentish indictment (no. 473 in his book) as a Sussex one. The relevant Sussex indictments are numbered 53, 92, 110, 111, 112, 132, 139, 152, 274, 334, 383, 452, 472, 542, 718, 719, 776; five other cases are mentioned on pp. 283–85. Three additional cases are detailed in Mary Anne Everett, ed., *Calendar of State Papers, Domestic Series, 1656–57* (London, 1883), p. 424; Anthony Fletcher, *A County Community in Peace and War: Sussex, 1600–1660* (London and New York, 1975), p. 163; and M. A. Lower, "Story of Witchcraft at Brightling," SAC 18 (1866): 111–113.

12. Ewen, ed., *Witch Hunting and Witch Trials*, pp. 117–269; Malcolm Gaskill, "Witchcraft in Early Modern Kent: Stereotypes and the Background to Accusations," in Jonathan Barry, Marianne Hester, and Gareth Roberts, eds., *Witchcraft in Early Modern Europe: Studies in Culture and Belief* (Cambridge, 1996), pp. 257–87.

13. For population trends in this period, see Peter Brandon and Brian Short, *The South East from A.D. 1000* (London and New York, 1990), pp. 190–96; also, C. E. Brent, "Employment, Land Tenure and Population in East Sussex, 1540–1640," D.Phil. thesis, University of Sussex, 1974.

14. David Underdown, *Revel, Riot and Rebellion: Popular Politics and Culture in England, 1603–1660* (Oxford, 1985), chap. 4 (quotes on pp. 88, 104); David Underdown, "The Chalk and the Cheese: Contrasts among the English Clubmen," *Past and Present* 85 (1979): 25–48.

15. Nicholas Tyacke, "Popular Puritan Mentality in Late Elizabethan England," in Clark, Smith, and Tyacke, eds., *The English Commonwealth*, pp. 77–92, quote on p. 81; Annabel Gregory, "Slander Accusations and Social Control in Late Sixteenth and Early Seventeenth Century England, with Particular Reference to Rye (Sussex), 1590–1615," D.Phil. thesis, University of Sussex, 1985, pp. 137 note 14, 282–83.

16. Susan Dwyer Amussen, *An Ordered Society: Gender and Class in Early Modern England* (Oxford, 1988), chap. 4; Susan Dwyer Amussen, "Gender, Family and the Social Order, 1560–1725," in Anthony Fletcher and John Stevenson, eds., *Order and Disorder in Early Modern England* (Cambridge, 1985), pp. 196–217; David Underdown, "The Taming of the Scold: The Enforcement of Patriarchal Authority in Early Modern England," in Fletcher and Stevenson, eds., *Order and Disorder*, pp. 116–36.

17. Clive Holmes, "Women: Witnesses and Witches," *Past and Present* 140 (1993): 45–78; Deborah Willis, *Malevolent Nurture: Witch-Hunting and*

Maternal Power in Early Modern England (Ithaca, N.Y., 1995); James Sharpe, *Instruments of Darkness: Witchcraft in Early Modern England* (Philadelphia, 1996), chap. 7; Marianne Hester, "Patriarchal Reconstruction and Witch Hunting," in Barry, Hester, and Roberts, eds., *Witchcraft in Early Modern Europe,* pp. 288–306.

18. Keith Thomas, *Religion and the Decline of Magic* (New York, 1970), chaps. 16–17; Alan Macfarlane, *Witchcraft in Tudor and Stuart England: A Regional and Comparative Study* (London, 1970).

19. Sharpe, *Instruments of Darkness,* chaps. 2 and 8; Jonathan Barry, "Introduction: Keith Thomas and the Problem of Witchcraft," in Barry, Hester, and Roberts, eds., *Witchcraft in Early Modern Europe,* pp. 1–45; Gaskill, "Witchcraft in Early Modern Kent," pp. 283–87.

20. Mayhew, *Tudor Rye,* pp. 65, 275; P. W. Hasler, ed., *The History of Parliament: The House of Commons, 1558–1603* (3 vols., London, 1981), vol. 1, p. 481; Holloway, *History of Rye,* p. 502. The name Bredes is derived from the town of Brede, a few miles from Rye. Rye Foreign, the land lying just outside the town boundaries, was in the Manor of Brede. John Bredes had no surviving children, so the "Sanguinary Butcher" was not his direct descendant.

21. HMC, *Thirteenth Report, Appendix, Part IV: The Manuscripts of Rye and Hereford Corporations; Capt. Loder-Symonds, Mr. E. R. Wodehouse, M.P., and Others* (London, 1892), p. 5; Holloway, *History of Rye,* pp. 399–401.

22. ESRO, Rye 1/4, f. 68v; Mayhew, *Tudor Rye,* pp. 206, 211.

23. HMC, *Rye,* pp. 45–46, 47, 52; DNB, under "Fletcher, Richard"; Mayhew, *Tudor Rye,* pp. 127–37; Manning, *Religion and Society,* pp. 76–78; Graham Mayhew, "Order, Disorder and Popular Protest in Early Modern Rye," SAC 127 (1989): 167–87.

24. Philip Mainwaring Johnston, "Wall Painting in a House at Rye Formerly Known as the 'Old Flushing Inn,'" SAC 50 (1907): 117–24; Harold Sands, "The House in Which the Painting was Found, Formerly Known as the 'Flushing Inn,'" SAC 50 (1907): 125–37.

25. ESRO, Rye 1/4, f. 345.

26. Richard F. Dell, ed., *Rye Shipping Records 1566–1590,* Sussex Record Society, vol. 64 (1965–66), pp. xxxiv–xxxv, 145; C. E. Brent, "Urban Employment and Population in Sussex between 1550 and 1660," SAC 113 (1975): 42–46; Gregory, "Slander Accusations," pp. 109, 284–86.

27. HMC, *Rye,* pp. 99–100, 109, 121–22; Hasler, ed., *History of Parliament,* vol. 2, p. 559.

28. HMC, *Rye,* p. 108; Thomas, *Religion and the Decline of Magic,* p. 544.

29. Hipkin, "Economy and Social Structure in Rye," pp. 30, 45–46, 50;

Stephen Hipkin, "Buying Time: Fiscal Policy at Rye, 1600–1640," SAC 132 (1995): 241–54.

30. ESRO, Rye 13/1. Swapper's examination is reproduced in Charles Lewis Meryon, "Some Account of the Ancient Town and Port of Rye and of its Municipal Government," Rye Museum, 21/7a, pp. 32A-D, citing BL, Harleian 358, p. 188. See also Gregory, "Slander Accusations," pp. 146–70.

31. ESRO, Rye 13/5–8, 10, 12, 13–19, 21, 23–25. For Robert Bennett, see R. F. Hunnisett, ed., *Sussex Coroners' Inquests, 1608–1688* (Kew, 1998), pp. 15–16, no. 66.

32. HMC, *Rye,* pp. 136–37, 139–40, 147–8; Hasler, ed., *History of Parliament,* vol. 2, p. 244.

33. Annabel Gregory, "Witchcraft, Politics and 'Good Neighbourhood' in Early Seventeenth-Century Rye," *Past and Present* 133 (1991): 31–66.

34. HMC, *Rye,* p. 145; Mayhew, *Tudor Rye,* p. 130.

35. Hipkin, "Economy and Social Structure of Rye," pp. 160–61; F. W. T. Attree, ed., *Notes of Post Mortem Inquisitions taken in Sussex, 1 Henry VIII to 1649 and After,* Sussex Record Society, vol. 14 (1912), pp. 224–25.

36. John Gruenfelder, "Rye and the Parliament of 1621," SAC 107 (1969): 25–35; Derek Hirst, *The Representative of the People? Voters and Voting in England under the Early Stuarts* (Cambridge, 1975), pp. 161–62, 179; John Collard, *A Maritime History of Rye* (2d ed., Rye, 1985), pp. 27–30.

37. HMC, *Rye,* pp. 144, 162, 170, 174; Gregory, "Slander Accusations," p. 138; DNB, under "Twyne, Brian." The complicated historical debate over Arminianism can be followed in Nicholas Tyacke, *Anti-Calvinists: The Rise and Fall of English Arminianism, c. 1590–1640* (Oxford, 1987); Kevin Sharpe, *The Personal Rule of Charles I* (New Haven, 1992), pp. 275–308; Julian Davies, *The Caroline Captivity of the Church: Charles I and the Re-moulding of Anglicanism, 1625–1641* (Oxford, 1992). The importance of local disputes in defining Puritanism is stressed in Peter Lake, "'A Charitable Christian Hatred': The Godly and Their Enemies in the 1630s," in Christopher Durston and Jacqueline Eales, eds., *The Culture of English Puritanism, 1560–1700* (Basingstoke, 1996), pp. 145–83.

38. HMC, *Rye,* 201–2; Fletcher, *A County Community in Peace and War,* pp. 239, 250; Basil Duke Henning, ed., *The History of Parliament: The House of Commons, 1660–90* (3 vols., London, 1985), vol. 2, pp. 516–17.

39. HMC, *Rye,* pp. 195, 203; Vidler, *New History of Rye,* p. 73; Dixon Ryan Fox, *Yankees and Yorkers* (New York, 1940), pp. 128–40.

40. Hipkin, "Economy and Social Structure of Rye," pp. 252–66; Fletcher, *A County Community,* pp. 139, 247, 249–50, 251–52.

41. F. W. Inderwick, "Rye under the Commonwealth," SAC 39 (1894): 1–15; Fletcher, *A County Community*, p. 329; Bernard Capp, "Naval Operations," in John Kenyon and Jane Ohlmeyer, eds., *The Civil Wars: A Military History of England, Scotland and Ireland, 1638–1660* (Oxford, 1998), pp. 173–74.

42. HMC, *Rye*, pp. 215–16; ESRO, Rye 1/13, ff. 159, 164, 168; Fletcher, *A County Community*, pp. 162–63; Sharpe, *Instruments of Darkness*, pp. 73–74, 143–44, 178–81. Rye had a "Tumbreal or Ducking Stoole, for punishing scolding or brawling women," that was remembered in the nineteenth century. H. P. Clark, *Clark's Guide and History of Rye, to which is added its Political History. Interspersed with many pleasing & interesting incidents* (Rye, "1861" [1865]), p. 85; Gregory, "Slander Accusations," p. 204.

43. F. A. Inderwick, "The Rye Engagement," SAC 39 (1894): 24; ESRO, Rye 82/82.

44. Hipkin, "Economy and Social Structure in Rye," p. 263; A. T. Fletcher, "Puritanism in Seventeenth-Century Sussex," in Kitch, ed., *Studies in Sussex Church History*, pp. 145–8; ESRO, FRE 4223 nos. 30, 32.

45. ESRO, FRE 4223 no. 45.

46. ESRO, FRE 4223 nos. 45–47, 49–52; T. W. W. Smart, "A Biographical Sketch of Samuel Jeake, Senr., of Rye," SAC 13 (1861): 57–79; Fletcher, *A County Community*, pp. 117–19; Michael Allison, "Puritanism in Mid-17th Century Sussex: Samuel Jeake the Elder of Rye," SAC 125 (1987): 125–38.

47. ESRO, FRE 4223 no. 81; Allison, "Puritanism in Mid-17th-Century Sussex," pp. 134–38; Fletcher, *A County Community*, p. 31.

48. ESRO, FRE 4223 nos. 90–91; Smart, "Biographical Sketch," pp. 59–60; Fletcher, *A County Community*, pp. 119–20; Allison, "Puritanism in Mid 17th-Century Sussex," pp. 128–29.

49. ESRO, FRE 4223 no. 76; Fletcher, *A County Community*, pp. 292–93; Capp, "Naval Operations," pp. 180–87; Inderwick, "The Rye Engagement," pp. 16–27.

50. Smart, "Biographical Sketch," pp. 60–61; T. W. W. Smart, "A Notice of the Rev. John Allin, Vicar of Rye, A.D. 1653–1662," SAC 31 (1881): 123–56; ESRO, FRE 4223 no. 90.

51. Blackwood quoted in Fletcher, "Puritanism," p. 152; John Bowle, ed., *The Diary of John Evelyn* (Oxford, 1985), p. 148; Taylor poem quoted in Michael Hunter et al., eds., *A Radical's Books: The Library Catalogues of Samuel Jeake of Rye, 1623–1690* (Cambridge and Woodbridge, 1999), p. xix.

A national perspective on this period can be found in Christopher Durston, "Puritan Rule and the Failure of Cultural Revolution, 1645-1660," in Durston and Eales, eds., *Culture of English Protestantism*, pp. 210-33.

52. Derek Hirst, "The Failure of Godly Rule in the English Republic," *Past and Present* 132 (1991): 53; Mayhew, "Order, Disorder and Popular Protest," pp. 171, 184; HMC, *Rye*, p. 223. The witness against Norton was Mark Hounsell, bricklayer, doubtless a relative of the accused witch Anne Hownsell.

53. Hirst, "Failure of Godly Rule," p. 53; ESRO, Rye 7/21; HMC, *Rye*, p. 229.

54. HMC, *Rye*, p. 234. For another town where republicanism remained strong, see Phil Withington, "Views from the Bridge: Revolution and Restoration in Seventeenth-Century York," *Past and Present* 170 (Feb. 2001): 121-51.

55. ESRO, Rye 1/14, ff. 329, 332-33; Felix Hull, ed., *A Calendar of the White and Black Books of the Cinque Ports, 1432-1955*, Kent Records, vol. 19 (1966), pp. 510-11; Ronald Hutton, *The Restoration: A Political and Religious History of England and Wales, 1658-1667* (Oxford, 1985), chap. 4.

56. HMC, *Rye*, pp. 45-46.

57. ESRO, FRE 4223 no. 100. For the context of radical prophesying, see Paul Christianson, *Reformers and Babylon: English Apocalyptic Visions from the Reformation to the Eve of the Civil War* (Toronto, 1978). Other radical and sectarian responses to the Restoration are considered in Christopher Hill, *The Experience of Defeat: Milton and Some Contemporaries* (New York, 1984), and John Spurr, "From Puritanism to Dissent, 1660-1700," in Durston and Eales, eds., *Culture of English Puritanism*, pp. 234-65.

58. ESRO, FRE 4323, 4422, 4611.

59. Michael Hunter and Annabel Gregory, eds., *An Astrological Diary of the 17th Century: Samuel Jeake of Rye, 1652-1699* (Oxford, 1988), p. 87.

60. Rye Museum, Selmes Ms. 16, notes on sermon of 5 March 1664/5.

61. Smart, "John Allin," pp. 123-56.

62. HMC, *Rye*, 236-37. Although not mentioned in Henning, ed., *History of Parliament*, vol. 1, p. 499, a poll was taken at this election, and is in ESRO, Rye 47/165. Spencer and Morley were elected with twenty-three votes each, while a third candidate, the courtier Sir John Jacob, received five votes. With one exception, all of Jacob's few supporters, including Mayor Mark Thomas junior, voted for Spencer, while one other freeman "plumped" for Morley alone.

63. ESRO, FRE 4251, 4254, 4256; HMC, *Rye*, p. 243; Henning, ed., *History of Parliament*, vol. 1, pp. 499-500.

64. ESRO, Rye 1/15, ff. 3, 25, 18, 27, 67.
65. Inderwick, "Rye Engagement," p. 24; ESRO, Rye 82/82, pp. 52, 55.
66. ESRO, PAR 467/1/1/3, p. 181; Rye 47/169, no. 14.
67. Ewen, ed., *Witch Hunting and Witch Trials*, pp. 263-64.
68. Reginald Scot, *The Discoverie of Witchcraft* (Carbondale, Ill., 1964), pp. 2-5, 143, 145.
69. Sharpe, *Instruments of Darkness*, chaps. 9-11; Thomas, *Religion and the Decline of Magic*, chap. 18.
70. Ian Bostridge, *Witchcraft and Its Transformations, c. 1650-c. 1750* (Oxford, 1997), pp. 108-9.
71. Clark, *Guide*, p. 14.
72. [Thomas Church], *An Essay Towards Vindicating the Literal Sense of the Demoniacks, in the New Testament: In an answer to a late Enquiry into the Meaning of them* (London, 1737), p. 41; also, [Thomas Church], *A Reply to the Farther Enquiry into The Meaning of the Demoniacks in the New Testament* (London, 1738), and [Thomas Church], *A Short State of the Controversy About the Meaning of the Demoniacks in the New Testament* (London, 1739). This controversy attracted much attention in the late 1730s.

THREE

The Valley of Humiliation

1. Scholars have debated whether dying words of criminals should be interpreted as generally submissive, defiant, or covering "a whole range of gestures and counter-gestures." See J. A. Sharpe, "'Last Dying Speeches': Religion, Ideology and Public Execution in Seventeenth-Century England," in *Past and Present* 107 (1985): 144-57; Thomas W. Laqueur, "Crowds, Carnival and the State in English Executions, 1604-1868," in A. L. Beier, David Cannadine, and James Rosenheim, eds., *The First Modern Society: Essays in English History in Honour of Lawrence Stone* (Cambridge, 1989), pp. 305-54; Peter Lake and Michael Questier, "Agency, Appropriation and Rhetoric under the Gallows: Puritans, Romanists and the State in Early Modern England," *Past and Present* 153 (1996): 64-107, quote on p. 65.
2. Peter Lake, "Puritanism, Arminianism and a Shropshire Axe-Murder," *Midland History*, 15 (1990), pp. 37-64.
3. Robert Burton, *The Anatomy of Melancholy*, ed. Thomas C. Faulkner, Nicholas K. Kiessling and Rhonda L. Blair (6 vols., Oxford, 1989-2000), vol. 3, pp. 386, 388; Michael Macdonald, *Mystical Bedlam: Madness,*

Anxiety, and Healing in Seventeenth-Century England (Cambridge, 1981), p. 225.

4. *A Brief Narrative of the Harbor of the Ancient Town of RYE in the County of Sussex, with the present State thereof, and Reasons for Preservation of the same* (n.p., [1677]), in Bodleian Library, Ms. Rawlinson A 185, ff. 234–7; also in John Collard, *A Maritime History of Rye* (2d ed., Rye, 1985), pp. 128–31.

5. Stephen Andrew Hipkin, "The Economy and Social Structure of Rye, 1600–1660," Ph.D. thesis, Oxford University, 1986, pp. 54–64; A. J. F. Dudley, "The Early History of the Rye Fishing Industry," SAC 107 (1969): 63; C. E. Brent, "Urban Employment and Population in Sussex between 1550 and 1660," SAC 113 (1975): 45.

6. Dudley, "Rye Fishing," pp. 58–60; ESRO, Rye 82/82; Rye 47/168, /176. For fishing at Dieppe, see Jean-Pierre Bardet et al., "Laborieux par nécessité: L'économie normande du XVIe au XVIII siècle," in Michel de Bonard, ed., *Histoire de la Normandie* (Toulouse, 1970), p. 294.

7. Hipkin, "Economy and Social Structure of Rye," pp. 168, 184; ESRO, Rye 47/167, /172; Rye 149/2; Geoffrey Oxley, *Poor Relief in England and Wales, 1601–1824* (Newton Abbot, 1974), chap. 4.

8. ESRO, Rye 10/27–28.

9. William Carter, *An Abstract of the Proceedings to Prevent Exportation of Wooll Un-manufactured* (London, 1689), pp. 22–24; ESRO, FRE 4532; Rye 9/6, 10/21, 25, 31, 32.

10. T. S. Willan, *The English Coasting Trade, 1500–1750* (2d ed., Manchester, 1967), pp. 1–2.

11. PRO, E 190/768/17 (1661–62), 768/21 (1662–63), 769/16 (1663–64), 769/25 (1664–65), 770/7, 770/15 (1666–67), 771/17, 771/14 (1671–72), 773/9, 773/12 (1674–75), 778/6, 778/14, 778/15 (1680–81), 782/15, 782/9 (1684–85). The following paragraphs are based on these sources.

12. Peter Edwards, *The Horse Trade of Tudor and Stuart England* (Cambridge, 1988), p. 48.

13. A. D. Francis, *The Wine Trade* (London, 1972), pp. 75–77.

14. Ralph Davis, *The Rise of the English Shipping Industry in the Seventeenth and Eighteenth Centuries* (Newton Abbot, 1962), chap. 2; Ronald Hope, *A New History of British Shipping* (London, 1990), chap. 11.

15. Hipkin, "Economy and Social Structure of Rye," pp. 160–61.

16. Philip Benedict, "The Huguenot Population of France, 1699–85," in *The Faith and Fortunes of France's Huguenots, 1600–85* (Aldershot, 2001), p. 42.

17. Willan, *English Coasting Trade*, pp. 98, 149 (all figures for 1632–33 and 1682–83 are from this source); Brian Short, "The De-industrialization

Process: A Case Study of the Weald, 1600–1850," in Pat Hudson, ed., *Regions and Industries: A Perspective on the Industrial Revolution in Britain* (Cambridge, 1989), pp. 156–74; Brian Short, "The South-East: Kent, Surrey and Sussex," in Joan Thirsk, ed., *The Agrarian History of England and Wales*, vol. 5, part 1, *Regional Farming Systems* (Cambridge, 1984), p. 309.

18. Peter J. Bowden, "Agricultural prices, wages, farm profits, and rents," in Joan Thirsk, ed., *The Agrarian History of England and Wales*, vol. 5, part 2, *Agrarian Change* (Cambridge, 1985), p. 77; Short, "The South-East," pp. 282–85, 304, 311.

19. Willan, *English Coasting Trade*, pp. 210–11.

20. ESRO, Rye 145/11; and references to the ledger in Michael Hunter and Annabel Gregory, eds., *An Astrological Diary of the 17th Century: Samuel Jeake of Rye, 1652–1699* (Oxford, 1988), pp. 149, 154, 158, 171, 182, 188.

21. Anne Whiteman and Mary Clapinson, eds., *The Compton Census of 1676: A Critical Edition,* Records of Social and Economic History, vol. 10 (London, 1986), pp. 27–28, 148, 150–51; N. Caplan, "An Outline of the Origins and Development of Nonconformity in Sussex: 1603–1803," unpublished typescript, 2 vols., Lindfield, 1961, vol. 1, part 2, p. 51 (copy in ESRO); Colin Brent, "Lewes Dissenters outside the Law, 1663–86," SAC 123 (1985): 195–211.

22. ESRO, Rye 7/22, /23, /24, /25, /27; Rye 1/17, p. 4; Rye 82/82.

23. WSRO, Ep. II/7/1, ff. 17, 25; Ep. II/7/2, f. 19 (Welsh); Ep. II/7/3, f. 17; Ep. II/15/3, ff. 18–19 (Gillart, J. Crouch, Tournay); Ep. II/15/5, f. 34 (T. Crouch); Hilda Johnstone, ed., *Churchwardens' Presentments (17th Century). Part 2: Archdeaconry of Lewes,* Sussex Record Society, vol. 50 (1948–49), pp. 28, 37; G. Slade Butler, "The Vicars of Rye and Their Patrons," SAC 13 (1861): 287 (Crouch memorial).

24. ESRO, Rye 82/82, 83/1, 83/2.

25. Gary De Krey, *A Fractured Society: The Politics of London in the First Age of Party, 1688–1715* (Oxford, 1985), pp. 99–112, 136–65; David Harris Sacks, *The Widening Gate: Bristol and the Atlantic Economy, 1450–1700* (Berkeley, 1991), pp. 231–37, 288–303, 312–28.

26. T. W. Smart, "A Biographical Sketch of Samuel Jeake, senr., of Rye," SAC 13 (1861): 78–79; Hunter and Gregory, eds., *Astrological Diary,* pp. 267, 269–72; ESRO, FRE 4418, 4421, 4422, 4429.

27. PRO, PROB 11/358, quire 141, f. 274; ESRO, FRE 4698.

28. Rye Museum, Selmes Ms. 6/1.

29. Lorna Weatherill, *Consumer Behaviour and Material Culture in Britain, 1660–1760* (London, 1988). In 1675, among the inventories from East

Kent inspected by Weatherill, 28 percent recorded books and 37 percent pictures.

30. ESRO, FRE 4412; Michael Hunter et al., eds., *A Radical's Books: The Library Catalogue of Samuel Jeake of Rye, 1623–90* (Cambridge, 1999), pp. xxxii–xli; Mayhew, *Tudor Rye*, pp. 189–91; Helen Clifford, "A commerce with Things: The Value of Precious Metalwork in Early Modern England," in Maxine Berg and Helen Clifford, eds., *Consumers and Luxury: Consumer Culture in Europe, 1650–1850* (Manchester, 1999), pp. 147–68.

31. Carole Shammas, *The Pre-Industrial Consumer in England and America* (Oxford, 1990), chap. 4; ESRO, FRE 4225, 4725; Nigel Tattersfield, *The Forgotten Trade* (London, 1991), pp. 203–11.

32. ESRO, FRE 4223/99. The relationship between vegetarianism and religious radicalism is discussed in Keith Thomas, *Man and the Natural World: Changing Attitudes in England, 1500–1800* (London, 1983), pp. 289–92.

33. ESRO, FRE 5278. For Puritanism, widowhood, and marriage, see Sarah Mendelson and Patricia Crawford, *Women in Early Modern England, 1550–1720* (Oxford, 1998), pp. 180–84. Although Hartshorne and Harding were married by an Anglican minister, the Lord Chamberlain's chaplain, their household was godly enough to satisfy Jeake the younger, who married their daughter. ESRO, PAR 467/1/1/3, f. 201.

34. Paul Slack, *From Reformation to Improvement: Public Welfare in Early Modern England* (Oxford, 1999), chap. 2; Mayhew, *Tudor Rye*, pp. 226–302, 306 n16.

35. ESRO, Rye 47/168; Rye 145/11, p. 5; Rye 148/1–4.

36. The recent literature on this topic includes Tim Harris, *London Crowds in the Reign of Charles II: Propaganda and Politics from the Restoration until the Exclusion Crisis* (Cambridge, 1987); Tim Harris, *Politics under the Later Stuarts: Party Conflict in a Divided Society, 1660–1715* (London, 1993); Mark Knights, *Politics and Opinion in Crisis, 1679–1681* (Cambridge, 1991); Steven A. Pincus, *Protestantism and Patriotism: Theologies and the Making of English Foreign Policy, 1650–1668* (Cambridge, 1996); Perry Gauci, *Politics and Society in Great Yarmouth, 1660–1722* (Oxford, 1996), chap. 4; Paul Halliday, *Dismembering the Body Politic: Partisan Politics in England's Towns, 1650–1730* (Cambridge, 1998).

37. The most thorough treatments of party politics at Rye are in Halliday, *Dismembering the Body Politic*, pp. 132–35, and Hunter and Gregory, eds., *Astrological Diary*, pp. 27–35.

38. ESRO, FRE 5055; *Calendar of State Papers: Domestic Series, Charles II*

(hereafter *CSPD, Ch. II*) (28 vols., London, 1860–1939), 1679–80, pp. 487–88.

39. Hunter et al., eds., *A Radical's Books*, p. xlvii. The original register of Jeake's books is in Rye Museum, Jeake Ms. 4/1.

40. Colin Brent, "The Neutering of the Fellowship and the Emergence of a Tory Party in Lewes (1663–1688)," SAC 121 (1984): 95–107.

41. *CSPD, Ch. II*, 1667, pp. 539, 543; Basil Duke Henning, ed., *The History of Parliament: The House of Commons, 1660–90* (3 vols., London, 1983), vol. 1, pp. 572–73.

42. ESRO, Rye 1/17, p. 38.

43. *CSPD, Ch. II*, 1679–80, pp. 467, 487–88, 526, 527–28; ESRO, Rye 1/17, p. 47; Rye 47/176.

44. *CSPD, Ch. II*, 1679–80, p. 529; ESRO, Rye 1/17, p. 49; Rye 7/28, /29.

45. *CSPD, Ch. II*, 1680–81, pp. 173–75, 202, 209–10; Henning, ed., *History of Parliament*, vol. 1, p. 500; Hunter and Gregory, eds., *Astrological Diary*, pp. 155–56.

46. ESRO, Rye 1/17, pp. 58–59.

47. ESRO, Rye 1/17, pp. 59–61; Hunter and Gregory, eds., *Astrological Diary*, pp. 156–57.

48. Halliday, *Dismembering the Body Politic*, pp. 133–34, quote on p. 144; *CSPD, Ch. II*, 1682, pp. 225, 229, 233–34; Hunter and Gregory, *Astrological Diary*, p. 159.

49. ESRO, Rye 1/17, pp. 70–74; *CSPD, Ch. II*, 1682, pp. 366–67.

50. Jones, *First Whigs*, pp. 198–206; Harris, *London Crowds*, pp. 185–86.

51. ESRO, Rye 1/17, pp. 75–78; *CSPD, Ch. II*, 1682, pp. 367–68, 410, 544. For Radford's illiteracy, see ESRO, PAR 967/1, where as churchwarden he marked the parish rate book with an "X."

52. ESRO, Rye 1/17, pp. 97–98 for the declaration that Tournay's freemen were "noe freemen of this Towne."

53. WSRO, Ep. II/15/5, f. 15; Rye Museum, Selmes Ms. 80, note for 14 Dec. 1681.

54. WSRO, Ep. II/15/5, f. 34; ESRO, FRE 5171, 5175; Rye Museum, Selmes Ms. 80; Hunter and Gregory, eds., *Astrological Diary*, pp. 148, 163–66, 169, 170–71, 173–74.

55. ESRO, Rye 10/5-7, /10, /16, /17-18.

56. W. A. Shaw, ed., *Calendar of Treasury Books*, vol. 8, *1685–1689* (4 parts, London, 1923), part 1, p. 469, part 2, p. 523.

57. ESRO, Rye 1/17, pp. 99, 105.

58. ESRO, Rye 7/33; WSRO, Ep. II/15/5, f. 69; Butler, "Vicars of Rye," p. 287.

59. ESRO, Rye 1/17, pp. 94–97, 105–6, 109–11; *Calendar of State Papers: Domestic Series, James II* (hereafter *CSPD, James II*) (3 vols., London, 1960–72), 1685, p. 24, no. 104.

60. Holloway, *History of Rye,* pp. 4–51; Samuel Jeake, senior, *Charters of the Cinque Ports, Two Ancient Towns, and their Members* (London, 1728).

61. ESRO, Rye 1/17, pp. 116, 119, 121; *CSPD, James II,* 1686–87, p. 59, no. 230; Felix Hull, ed., *A Calendar of the White and Black Books of the Cinque Ports, 1432–1955,* Kent Records, vol. 19 (London, 1966), p. 540; Hipkin, "Buying time," pp. 245–53.

62. Holloway, *Dismembering the Body Politic,* chap. 7.

63. ESRO, PAR 467/30/2; Hunter and Gregory, eds., *Astrological Diary,* p. 178.

64. ESRO, Rye 1/17, pp. 135, 138–9; Samuel Jeake, junior, "Astrological Experiments Exemplified," Clarke Library, University of California at Los Angeles, Ms. J43M3/A859, p. 34; J. R. Jones, "James II's Whig Collaborators," *Historical Journal* 3 (1960): 65–73; John Miller, *James II: A Study in Kingship* (London, 1989), chap. 12 and p. 198.

65. ESRO, Rye 1/17, pp. 135, 141; Rye 45/27–33; *CSPD, James II,* 1687–89, pp. 289–90, no. 1575.

66. ESRO, Rye 47/177; Jeake, "Astrological Experiments," p. 4; Miller, *James II,* pp. 206–7.

67. Hunter and Gregory, eds., *Astrological Diary,* p. 195.

68. ESRO, Rye 1/17, pp. 143–49, 153; Hunter and Gregory, eds., *Astrological Diary,* pp. 34, 38.

69. Henning, ed., *History of Parliament,* vol. 1, p. 500. Significantly, there is no record of this election in the assembly book.

70. For recent views on the Revolution settlement, see R. A. Beddard, ed., "The Unexpected Whig Revolution of 1688," in R. A. Beddard, ed., *The Revolution of 1688* (Oxford, 1991), pp. 11–101; Howard Nenner, "Pretense and Pragmatism: The Response to Uncertainty in the Succession Crisis of 1689," in Lois Schwoerer, ed., *The Revolution of 1688: Changing Perspectives* (Cambridge, 1992), pp. 83–94; Harris, *Politics under the Later Stuarts,* pp. 132–42.

71. Halliday, *Dismembering the Body Politic,* pp. 268–76; ESRO, Rye 1/17, p. 153; Hull, ed., *Calendar of White and Black Books,* pp. 546–47.

72. Rye Museum, Selmes Ms. 16, sermon of 16 July 1665; 18/4, sermon of 16 April 1665.

73. ESRO, FRE 4389a, 4490, 4223 no. 98.

74. ESRO, FRE 5076, 5097; Hunter and Gregory, eds., *Astrological Diary,* p. 207.

75. Rye Museum, Selmes Ms. 32, ff. 3–13, 35–37; Jeake Ms. 4/1; Hunter et al., eds., *A Radical's Books,* pp. xliv–xlv; Jeake, *Astrological Experiments,* pp. 1–2, 90; Hunter and Gregory, eds., *Astrological Diary,* pp. 11–21; Patrick Curry, *Prophecy and Power: Astrology in Early Modern England* (Cambridge, 1989), pp. 86–88.

76. For the decline of astrology, see Curry, *Prophecy and Power,* chaps. 3, 5–6; Michael Hunter, "Science and Astrology in Seventeenth-Century England: An Unpublished Polemic by John Flamsteed," in Patrick Curry, ed., *Astrology, Science and Society: Historical Essays* (Woodbridge, 1987), pp. 260–300. For Jeake's astrological reading of James II's fate, see Jeake, *Astrological Experiments,* pp. 3–4.

77. Hunter and Gregory, eds., *Astrological Diary,* pp. 148, 208; John Bunyan, *The Pilgrim's Progress,* ed. N. H. Keeble (Oxford, 1984), pp. 47–50, and on the politics of Bunyan's work, Christopher Hill, *A Tinker and Poor Man: John Bunyan and His Church, 1628–1688* (New York, 1988), chaps. 18, 25.

78. Hunter and Gregory, eds., *Astrological Diary,* pp. 207, 229, 255; ESRO, Rye 1/17, pp. 201, 215.

79. ESRO, FRE 4609, 5335; Hunter and Gregory, eds., *Astrological Diary,* p. 129. On female consumption, see Lorna Weatherill, "A Possession of One's Own: Women and Consumer Behavior in England, 1660–1740," *Journal of British Studies* 25, no. 2 (1986): 131–56.

80. ESRO, Rye 1/17, pp. 195, 202, 205; PAR 467/1/1/3, ff. 84, 202–3, 209; PAR 467/1/1/4, ff. 120 (first foliation: unbaptised children, 1700–1708), 24 (second foliation: births, 1682–1727), 28; WSRO, Ep. II/15/10, f. 28 (Hastings). Seven children were baptized in early eighteenth-century Rye as the sons and daughters of John Breads: Mary (1703), John (1705), Edward (1707), John (1710), William (1714), Thomas (1719), and Sarah (1723). The mother of the first two is not mentioned, but it is a reasonable assumption that she was Mary Breads, who was the mother of the last five.

81. Bunyan, *Pilgrim's Progress,* p. 52.

FOUR

Oligarchs

1. The various incidents mentioned in this paragraph have been culled from David Underdown, *Royalist Conspiracy in England, 1649–1660* (New Haven, 1960); J. P. Kenyon, *The Popish Plot* (London, 1972); Jane Garrett, *The Triumphs of Providence: The Assassination Plot, 1696* (Cambridge, 1980); John Barrell, *Imagining the King's Death: Figurative Treason, Fan-*

tasies and Regicide, 1793–96 (Oxford, 2000); G. W. Keeton, *Guilty but Insane* (London, 1961), chap. 1; and above all, Steve Poole, *The Politics of Regicide* (Manchester, 2000), chaps. 3, 4, and 6. For the love-hate mixture typical of would-be royal assassins, see Arlette Farge, *Subversive Words: Public Opinion in Eighteenth-Century France,* trans. Rosemary Morris (University Park, Pa., 1994), pp. 125–50.

2. Sheila Biddle, *Bolingbroke and Harley* (London, 1975), pp. 200–207; John Brooke, *King George III* (St. Albans, 1972), pp. 498–99; E. P. Thompson, *The Making of the English Working Class* (Harmondsworth, 1963, 1968), pp. 159, 769–80; J. C. D. Clark, *English Society, 1688–1832* (Cambridge, 1985), pp. 109–17; Poole, *Politics of Regicide,* p. 64; Keeton, *Guilty but Insane,* chap. 2.

3. See Alan Marshall, *The Strange Death of Edmund Godfrey: Plots and Politics in Restoration London* (Stroud, 1999).

4. T. B. Howell, ed., *A Complete Collection of State Trials* (34 vols., London, 1816–28), vol. 16, cols. 695–766.

5. E. P. Thompson, "The Crime of Anonymity," in Douglas Hay et al., *Albion's Fatal Tree: Crime and Society in Eighteenth-Century England* (New York, 1975), pp. 255–344.

6. Lawrence Stone, "Interpersonal Violence in English Society, 1300–1980," *Past and Present* 101 (1983): 22–33; J. M. Beattie, "The Pattern of Crime in England, 1660–1800," *Past and Present* 62 (1974): 47–95; J. A. Sharpe, "Domestic Homicide in Early Modern England," *Historical Journal* 24 (1981): 29–48; J. M. Beattie, *Crime and the Courts in England, 1660–1800* (Princeton, 1986), pp. 107–112; J. S. Cockburn, "Patterns of Violence in English Society: Homicides in Kent, 1560–1985," *Past and Present* 130 (1991): 70–106; Cynthia Herrup, *The Common Peace: Participation and the Criminal Law in Seventeenth-Century England* (Cambridge, 1989), pp. 38–41.

7. Graham Mayhew, *Tudor Rye* (Falmer, 1987), p. 214; ESRO, Rye 32/1–9.

8. Peter Clark and Paul Slack, *English Towns in Transition, 1500–1700* (London, 1976), pp. 128–34; Peter Clark, "Introduction," in Peter Clark, ed., *The Transformation of English Provincial Towns* (London, 1984), pp. 35–41. The best study of oligarchy in an English town is Perry Gauci, *Politics and Society in Great Yarmouth, 1660–1722* (Oxford, 1996), chaps. 2–3.

9. J. H. Plumb, *The Growth of Political Stability in England, 1675–1725* (London, 1967), p. 2 and chap. 6; E. P. Thompson, *Customs in Common: Studies in Traditional Popular Culture* (New York, 1991), p. 26.

10. WSRO, Ep. I/26/3, p. 22.

11. ESRO, Rye 1/17, pp. 243–44; A. J. F. Dudley, "The Early History of the

Rye Fishing Industry," SAC 107 (1969): 58; Holloway, *History of Rye*, pp. 360–61, 383.

12. D. W. Jones, *War and Economy in the Age of William III and Marlborough* (Oxford, 1988), p. 104; John Ehrman, *The Navy in the War of William III, 1689–1697* (Cambridge, 1953), pp. 109–38; Daniel Baugh, *British Naval Administration in the Age of Walpole* (Princeton, 1965), pp. 150–62; ESRO, Rye 100/1–6.

13. ESRO, Rye 149/3. For similar payment of "pensions" in a different part of England, see Lynn Botelho, "Aged and Impotent: Parish Relief of the Aged Poor in Early Modern Suffolk," in Martin Daunton, ed., *Charity, Self-Interest and Welfare in the English Past* (London, 1996), pp. 91–111.

14. The secondary literature on Sussex smuggling mostly relates to the period after 1740, and is considered in the notes to Chapter Five.

15. ESRO, SAY 266–67.

16. ESRO, SAY 281–83, 339.

17. PRO, E 190/786/20, 786/24 (1690–91), 787/3, 790/22 (1694–95), 795/10, 795/17 (1699–1700), 801/2, 801/26 (1704–05), 805/4, 805/9, 806/11 (1709–10), 809/24, 809/25 (1713–14), 811/25 (1723–24), 812/3 (1724–25), 812/6 (1725–26), 812/12 (1726–27), 812/14 (1727–28). The following paragraphs are based on these sources.

18. Patrick Crowhurst, *The Defence of British Trade, 1689–1815* (Folkestone, 1977), pp. 18–19, 25–27, 54–58; J. S. Bromley, "The French Privateering War, 1702–13," in H. F. Bell and R. L. Ollard, eds., *Historical Essays, 1600–1750, Presented to David Ogg* (London, 1963), pp. 203–31.

19. Jones, *War and Economy*, chaps. 4–5. For the more straightforward view that war generally stimulated the English economy, see A. H. John, "War and the English Economy, 1700–1763," *Economic History Review* 7 (1954–5): 329–44.

20. Ralph Davis, *The Rise of the English Shipping Industry in the Seventeenth and Eighteenth Centuries* (Newton Abbot, 1972), pp. 33, 43; Ronald Hope, *A New History of British Shipping* (London, 1990), pp. 220, 223; Kenneth Morgan, "Atlantic Trade and British Economic Growth in the Eighteenth Century," in Peter Mathias and John A. Davis, eds., *International Trade and British Economic Growth from the Eighteenth Century to the Present Day* (Oxford, 1996), p. 15; Phyllis Deane and W. A. Cole, *British Economic Growth 1688–1959: Trends and Structures* (Cambridge, 1962), pp. 41–50.

21. Célestin Hippeau, ed., *L'Industrie, le commerce et les travaux publiques en Normandie au XVIIe et au XVIIIe siècles* (Paris, 1870), pp. 8, 197–207.

22. David Ormrod, "Industries, 1640–1800," in Alan Armstrong, ed., *The*

Economy of Kent, 1640–1914 (Woodbridge, 1995), p. 89; Peter Brandon and Brian Short, *The South East from A.D. 1000* (London, 1990), pp. 229–30; Howard C. Tomlinson, "Wealden Gunfounding: An Analysis of Its Demise in the Eighteenth Century," *Economic History Review* 29 (1976): 383–400.

23. Lorna Weatherill, *Consumer Behaviour and Material Culture in Britain, 1660–1760* (London and New York, 1988), p. 40; Jones, *War and Economy*, pp. 125–26. The commercial transformation of another Sussex town can be traced in Colin Brent, *Georgian Lewes, 1714–1830: The Heyday of a County Town* (Lewes, 1993), chaps. 1–3.

24. Rye Museum, Selmes Ms. 59/2.

25. T. S. Willan, *The English Coasting Trade, 1500–1750* (Manchester, 1967), pp. 210–11.

26. Willan, *English Coasting Trade*, pp. 220–222, reproducing BL, Add. Ms. 11,255. In this tabulation, the tonnage of each vessel is counted only once.

27. Richard Grassby, "English Merchant Capitalism in the Late Seventeenth Century: The Composition of Business Fortunes," *Past and Present* 46 (1970): 87–107. Another example of the consolidation of mercantile wealth in this period is York; see Perry Gauci, *The Politics of Trade: The Overseas Merchant in State and Society, 1660–1720* (Oxford, 2001), pp. 48–55. For the consolidation of business networks, see Shanil D'Cruze, "The Middling Sort in Eighteenth-Century Colchester: Independence, Social Relations and the Community Broker," in Jonathan Barry and Christopher Brooks, eds., *The Middling Sort of People: Culture, Society and Politics in England, 1550–1800* (New York, 1994), pp. 181–268.

28. Jones, *War and Economy*, p. 92.

29. David Crossley and Richard Saville, eds., *The Fuller Letters 1728–1755: Guns, Slaves and Finance*, Sussex Record Society, vol. 76 (1988–89), pp. 26, 101, 127, 222. The survival of the Wealden iron industry is discussed in Jeremy S. Hodgkinson, "The Decline of the Ordnance Trade in the Weald: The Seven Years' War and Its Aftermath," SAC 134 (1996): 155–67.

30. John Caffyn, *Sussex Schools in the 18th Century: Schooling Provision, Schoolteachers and Scholars*, Sussex Record Society, vol. 81 (1995–96), p. 227; Holloway, *History of Rye*, pp. 401–3; Vidler, *New History of Rye*, pp. 73–74; ESRO, Rye 112/4, 6–10, 112/11; Rye 114/1, f. 1 (second pagination); Michael Hunter and Annabel Gregory, eds., *An Astrological Diary of the 17th Century: Samuel Jeake of Rye, 1652–1699* (Oxford, 1988), p. 220 n. 1;

G. Slade Butler, "The Vicars of Rye and Their Patrons," SAC 13 (1861): 281.

31. ESRO, Rye 1/17, p. 141; Rye 20/1.

32. Basil Duke Henning, ed., *The History of Parliament: The House of Commons, 1660–90* (3 vols., London, 1983), vol. 1, p. 500; Thomas Walker Horsfield, *The History, Antiquities and Topography of the County of Sussex* (2 vols., Lewes, 1835), vol. 2, p. 64; Charles Lewis Meryon, "Some Account of the Ancient Town and Port of Rye and its Municipal Government," Rye Museum, 21/7a, vol. 2, pp. 526–34. Eveline Cruickshanks, Stuart Handley, and D. W. Hayton, eds., *The History of Parliament: The House of Commons, 1690–1715* (5 vols., Cambridge, 2002), appeared too late to be consulted for this chapter.

33. Hunter and Gregory, eds. *Astrological Diary,* pp. 303–5; John Collard, *A Maritime History of Rye* (2d ed., Rye, 1985), pp. 30–31.

34. ESRO, Rye 1/17, p. 153; Hunter and Gregory, eds., *Astrological Diary,* p. 208.

35. ESRO, Rye 1/17, pp. 154, 157, 171, 190; Rye 7/34.

36. Tony Claydon, *William III and the Godly Revolution* (Cambridge, 1996), p. 105; David Hayton, "Moral Reform and Country Politics in the Late Seventeenth-Century House of Commons," *Past and Present* 128 (1990): 48–91; D. W. R. Bahlman, *The Moral Revolution of 1688* (New Haven, 1957); John Spurr, "The Church, the Societies and the Moral Revolution of 1688," in John Walsh, Colin Haydon and Stephen Taylor, eds., *The Church of England, c.1689–c.1833: From Toleration to Tractarianism* (Cambridge, 1993), pp. 127–42.

37. Holloway, *History of Rye,* pp. 74, 91–92; PRO, E190/787/3.

38. ESRO, Rye 1/17, pp. 198, 218, 232, 250; Hunter and Gregory, eds., *Astrological Diary,* p. 228. For the "rage of party," see Plumb, *Growth of Political Stability,* chap. 5; Tim Harris, *Politics under the Later Stuarts: Party Conflict in a Divided Society, 1660–1715* (London, 1993), chap. 7; Henry Horwitz, *Parliament, Policy and Politics in the reign of William III* (Manchester, 1977), chaps. 11–12; G. S. Holmes and W. A. Speck, eds., *The Divided Society: Parties and Politics in England, 1694–1716* (New York, 1968), pp. 8–26.

39. ESRO, Rye 1/17, p. 201.

40. BL, Add. 28940, f. 280 (a copy is on ff. 278–79); William John Hardy, ed., *Calendar of State Papers: Domestic Series, William and Mary* (13 vols., London, 1895–1924), 1696, p. 422. For Jacobitism in this period, see Paul Monod, "Jacobitism and Country Principles in the Reign of

William III," *Historical Journal* 30 (1987): 289–310. The Jacobite smuggling system is considered in Paul Monod, "Dangerous Merchandise: Smuggling, Jacobitism and Commercial Culture in Southeast England, 1690–1760," *Journal of British Studies* 30 (1991): 150–82.

41. ESRO, Rye 1/17, pp. 236, 243–44, 263.
42. BL, Sloane Ms. 3233, "A Survey of Ports on the South West Coast of England From Dover to Lands-end," 1698, p. 3.
43. PRO, E190/787/3; Hunter and Gregory, eds., *Astrological Diary*, p. 246.
44. John Brewer, *The Sinews of Power: War, Money and the English State, 1688–1763* (New York, 1989), chaps. 2–4; P. G. M. Dickson, *The Financial Revolution in England: A Study of the Development of Public Credit* (London, 1967); Gary Stuart De Krey, *A Fractured Society: The Politics of London in the First Age of Party, 1688–1715* (Oxford, 1985), pp. 106–12.
45. ESRO, Rye 1/17, pp. 258, 260, 275; PAR 467/1/1/4, f. 120; BL, Add. Ms. 28,948, f. 161.
46. BL, Add. Ms. 42,075, f. 88.
47. ESRO, ASHB. 4464, pp. 342–43; [G. E. Cokayne], *The Complete Peerage of England, Scotland, Ireland, Great Britain and the United Kingdom, Extant, Extinct or Dormant* (14 vols., London, 1910–59), vol. 1, p. 271. For the establishment of a Whig aristocratic interest at Great Yarmouth in this period, see Gauci, *Politics and Society*, chap. 7.
48. ESRO, ASHB. 4464, pp 364–65; ASHB. 4465, pp. 8, 11–12, 14, 18, 22–23.
49. DNB, under "Southwell, Sir Robert"; Samuel Jeake senior, *Logistikelogia, or Arithmetick surveighed and Reviewed: In Four Books* (London, 1696), dedication.
50. ESRO, ASHB. 4465, pp. 26–27.
51. ESRO, Rye 1/17, p. 275.
52. ESRO, ASHB. 4465, pp. 30–33; BL, Add. Ms. 42,075, f. 88. Electoral politics in this period is more fully discussed in W. A. Speck, *Tory and Whig: The Struggle in the Constituencies, 1701–1715* (London, 1970).
53. ESRO, ASHB. 4465, pp. 33–34, 36.
54. ESRO, Rye 1/17, pp. 270, 273–76; Horsfield, *History and Antiquities of Sussex*, vol. 2, p. 64; Narcissus Luttrell, *A Brief Historical Relation of State Affairs from September 1678 to April 1714* (6 vols., Oxford, 1857), vol. 5, p. 245; Holloway, *History of Rye*, pp. 229–31; Meryon, "Some Account of Rye," vol. 2, pp. 536–49. The elder Joseph Radford had died in August 1701; see ESRO, PAR 467/1/1/4, f. 51.
55. ESRO, ASHB. 4465, pp. 230, 233–34, 239; BL, Add. Ms. 28,948, f. 161.
56. ESRO, Rye 1/17, pp. 273–76, 280, 281.
57. ESRO, ASHB. 4465, pp. 300, 309, 328–29, 334–35; ASHB. 4466, pp.

132–33, 138–39; ASHB. 4446, pp. 150, 154, 181, 173–74, 180, 181–83; ASHB. 4447, p. 96; ASHB. 4448, pp. 31, 36; Holloway, *History of Rye,* pp. 508–9.

58. ESRO, Rye 1/17, p. 282; PAR 467/1/1/4, f. 24; Horsfield, *History and Antiquities of Sussex,* vol. 2, p. 64; Luttrell, *Brief Relation,* vol. 6, pp. 127, 131; BL, Add. Ms. 28,946, f. 161; Holloway, *History of Rye,* pp. 231–32; Meryon, "Some Account of Rye," vol. 2, pp. 549–66.

59. ESRO, PAR 467/1/1/4, f. 54; Butler, "Vicars of Rye," p. 275; Holloway, *History of Rye,* pp. 508–9, 510–11. High Church clerical politics in Sussex is discussed in Jeffrey Chamberlain, *Accommodating High Churchmen: The Clergy of Sussex, 1700–1745* (Urbana, Ill., 1997), chap. 2.

60. ESRO, Rye 1/17, pp. 288–89, 297–300, 304, 308.

61. Holloway, *History of Rye,* p. 232; ESRO, Rye 1/17, pp. 305, 308.

62. Horsfield, *History and Antiquities of Sussex,* vol. 2, p. 64; BL, Add. Ms. 28,948, f. 161 (misdated 1707); Meryon, "Some Account of Rye," vol. 2, pp. 556–62; Luttrell, *Brief Relation,* vol. 6, pp. 686, 688; ESRO, Rye 1/17, pp. 313, 318, 322–23, 329.

63. Holloway, *History of Rye,* p. 233; Meryon, "Some Account of Rye," vol. 2, p. 562; Romney Sedgwick, ed., *The History of Parliament: The House of Commons, 1715–1754* (2 vols., London, 1970), vol. 1, p. 368.

64. Edward Wilson, *A Sermon Preach'd in the Parish-Church of Rye in Sussex, on Wednesday, Jan. 30th, 1711/12* (London, 1712), pp. 3–5, 9–10, 18, 20; Chamberlain, *Accommodating High Churchmen,* p. 41.

65. ESRO, FRE 5379, 5381. For these riots, see Nicholas Rogers, "Popular Protest in Early Hanoverian London," *Past and Present* 79 (1978): 70–100; Paul Kléber Monod, *Jacobitism and the English People, 1688–1788* (Cambridge, 1989), chaps. 6–7.

66. PRO, SP 35/3/776.

67. ESRO, Rye 84/1, ff. 9–10, 13, 46, 72–73.

68. Caffyn, *Sussex Schools,* pp. 229–30; ESRO, Rye 114/1, ff. 1–9; 114/5–6; Holloway, *History of Rye,* pp. 408–13.

69. ESRO, PAR 467/1/1/4, ff. 91, 113; PAR 467/30/2; WSRO, Ep. II/15/7, f.62; ESRO, PAB 300, 302–4; Horsfield, *History and Antiquities of Sussex,* vol. 1, p. 511; H. Montgomery Hyde, *The Story of Lamb House, Rye* (Rye, 1966), pp. 15–16, 19.

70. ESRO, Rye 1/17, p. 355; Holloway, *History of Rye,* pp. 239–40; Vidler, *New History of Rye,* p. 93; Sedgwick, ed., *History of Parliament,* vol. 1, p. 368.

71. ESRO, Rye 1/17, pp. 363, 364, 372, 374; BL, Add. Ms. 42,589, ff. 111–12, 116, 124, 126, 176; Collard, *Maritime History,* p. 37.

72. ESRO, Rye 114/1, ff. 1-7 (second pagination); PAR 467/1/1/4, f. 78; Holloway, *History of Rye*, p. 519.

73. Caffyn, *Sussex Schools*, p. 228.

74. WSRO, Ep. I/26/3; Holloway, *History of Rye*, pp. 533-34.

75. ESRO, PAR 467/8/1; WSRO, Ep. II/25/2, pp. 19-23; Butler, "Vicars of Rye," pp. 277, 287; Holloway, *History of Rye*, pp. 512-13, 520.

76. *A Poll Taken by Henry Montague Esq; (Sheriff of the County of Sussex) at the City of Chichester on Thursday and Friday the Ninth and Tenth Days of May 1734. For the Election of Two Knights to serve for the said County in this present Parliament* (London, 1734), pp. 70-72; Chamberlain, *Accommodating High Churchmen*, pp. 124-25, 147. The Edward Wilson who attended an opposition meeting at Lewes in May 1741 cannot have been the Rye vicar, who died in January 1738.

FIVE

Politeness and Police

1. John Gay, *Poetry and Prose*, eds. Vinton E. Dearing and Charles E. Beckwith (2 vols., Oxford, 1974), vol. 1, p. 144.

2. Peter Linebaugh, *The London Hanged: Crime and Civil Society in the Eighteenth Century* (Harmondsworth, 1991), chap. 6.

3. ESRO, Rye 1/15, ff. 5-8, 11-15, 46-47; Rye 33/21.

4. ESRO, Rye 2/6-8; Rye 29/201.

5. ESRO, Rye 7/37.

6. ESRO, Rye 2/6-8; Rye 7/51; Rye 33/23.

7. ESRO, PAR 467/1/1/5, ff. 12, 83, 151; Rye 7/35; Rye 114/1, ff. 27, 30, 114/10.

8. Holloway, *History of Rye*, pp. 359-94; ESRO, Rye 1/17, p. 391; Rye 1/18, f. 4.

9. ESRO, Rye 1/18, ff. 26, 37, 42-43, 55-56, 68-69, 72-73, 85, 89, 92-93; BL, Add. Ms. 32,852, ff. 320-21; Add Ms. 36,920, f. 366.

10. BL, Add. Ms. 61,603, f. 127; Add. Ms. 33,085, ff. 310-11, 340; Add. Ms. 32,724, f. 40. Lamb imported French, Spanish, and Portuguese wine in 1726: PRO, E190/812/12.

11. BL, Add. Ms. 32,692, ff. 27-28; Add. Ms. 32,694, f. 167; Add. Ms. 32,697, ff. 19-20. For Newcastle's management of another Sussex borough, see Colin Brent, *Georgian Lewes, 1714-1830: The Heyday of a County Town* (Lewes, 1993), chap. 9.

12. Samuel Jeake senior, *Charters of the Cinque Ports, Two Ancient Towns, and*

their Members (London, 1728), dedication by "S. Jeake." Dorset was then lord warden of the Cinque Ports.

13. BL, Add. Ms. 32,694, ff. 216, 218, 316, 318, 474–75, 476, 480; Add. Ms. 32,703, ff. 470, 472; Add. Ms. 32,921, ff. 422, 424. See also BL, Add. Ms. 32,693, ff. 5–6, for a dispute over customs duties involving Nathaniel Pigram senior and Samuel Jeake's half-brother Joseph Tucker; and BL, Add. Ms. 32,714, ff. 89–90, for a snippy legal letter from Jeake to Andrew Stone about a petition to the crown.

14. BL, Egerton 2087, f. 83; Add. Ms. 32,691, ff. 87–88; John Meryon, *An Account of the Origin and Formation of the Harbour of the Ancient Town of Rye* (n.p., [1845]), p. 29; John Collard, *A Maritime History of Rye* (2d ed., Rye, 1985), p. 37. An excellent discussion of statutory commissions in the eighteenth century is found in Paul Langford, *Public Life and the Propertied Englishman, 1689–1798* (Oxford, 1991), pp. 207–64, although he too readily assumes that such bodies tended to undermine the rights of corporations.

15. ESRO, KRA 1/1/1, pp. 1, 10; Holloway, *History of Rye,* p. 373; BL, Add. Ms. 33087, f. 149 (a 1751 letter from James Lamb to Thomas Pelham, future Earl of Chichester, asking for a donation to a subscription).

16. ESRO, KRA 1/1/1, pp. 16, 32, 52, 73, 82, 95, 101, 125, 133, 134, 141, 172, 184, 185–86, 188, 195, 198–200.

17. Payments to the Lambs appear in ESRO, KRA 1/1/1, pp. 35, 38–39, 42, 45, 48–49, 54, 59, 69, 81–82, 87, 92, 96–97, 119, 129, 131–32, 135, 137, 138, 140, 148, 152, 153, 157–58, 160–64, 166, 169, 176, 179, 182, 184–86, 188, 195–96, 197–200. Thomas Lamb's salary was only £20 per year from 1743 to 1746 and £10 in 1748–49, but his remuneration escalated thereafter due to higher returns from the duty. When his revenues from Dover are added to those stated in the commission records, he earned about £360 annually between 1750 and 1755, dropping to £140 between 1755 and 1760.

18. ESRO, KRA 1/1/1, pp. 152, 160, 163–64.

19. ESRO, Rye 1/18, ff. 60–61; BL, Add. Ms. 32,724, f. 40.

20. ESRO, KRA 1/1/1, p. 170; Rye 1/18, f. 64.

21. ESRO, KRA 1/1/1, p. 82. I assume that this is not the murderer's father because "Master Breads" was mentioned as a carrier two years earlier.

22. Meryon, *An Account of the Harbour of Rye,* p. 44; Collard, *Maritime History of Rye,* pp. 38–41, 132–36; also, the newspaper clipping found in Bodleian Library, Gough Sussex 3 (3), containing a letter of 1776 by the schoolmaster George Jewhurst, relating to disputes about the harbour. William Holloway, in *The History of Romney Marsh from Its*

Earliest Formation to 1837 (London, 1849), pp. 171–72, was generous to the commissioners. He mainly blamed the landowners for the failure of the renovations.

23. ESRO, Rye 1/18, ff. 12–13.

24. ESRO, Rye 70/23, 16 April 1733. The last toast referred to Sir Robert Walpole's remark that opponents of excise were "sturdy beggars."

25. Romney Sedgwick, ed., *The History of Parliament: The House of Commons, 1715–54* (2 vols., London, 1970), vol. 2, pp. 93, 298–99; *A Poll Taken by Henry Montague Esq; (Sheriff of the County of Sussex) at the City of Chichester on Thursday and Friday the Ninth and Tenth Days of May 1734. For the Election of Two Knights to serve for the said County in this present Parliament* (London, 1734), pp. 70–72; Paul Langford, *The Excise Crisis: Society and Politics in the Age of Walpole* (Oxford, 1975), pp. 50, 112, and chap. 8.

26. Two groups of bills exist, the first in ESRO, Rye 70/14–50, the second in Rye Museum, file marked "Inns of Rye." The only study of them is Geoffrey S. Bagley, *Old Inns and Ale-Houses of Rye,* Rye Museum Publications no. 6 (St. Leonards-on-Sea, 1965).

27. ESRO, Rye 70/23, 4 August 1714.

28. Rye Museum, file marked "Inns of Rye."

29. The voucher is on display in the Rye Museum. The post-1743 vouchers are in ESRO, Rye 70/34.

30. A classic study of medieval civic ritual is Charles Phythian-Adams, *Desolation of a City: Coventry and the Urban Crisis of the later Middle Ages* (Cambridge, 1979). See also Ronald Hutton, *The Rise and Fall of Merry England: The Ritual Year, 1400–1700* (Oxford, 1994), esp. chap. 7. For urban sociability in the eighteenth century, see Jonathan Barry, "Bourgeois Collectivism? Urban Association and the Middling Sort," in Jonathan Barry and Christopher Brooks, eds., *The Middling Sort of People: Culture, Society and Politics in England, 1550–1800* (New York, 1994), pp. 84–112. The Benefits Society is mentioned in H. P. Clark, *Clark's Guide and History of Rye, to which is added its Political History. Interspersed with many pleasing & interesting incidents* (Rye, "1861" [1865]), p. 129.

31. Peter Clark, *The English Alehouse: A Social History, 1200–1830* (London, 1983), chap. 7 and pp. 284–85; also, Peter Clark, *Sociability and Urbanity: Clubs and Societies in the Eighteenth-Century City* (Leicester, 1986), and by the same author, *British Clubs and Societies, 1580–1800: The Origins of an Associational World* (Oxford, 2000).

32. For the London press in this period, see Jeremy Black, *The English Press*

in the *Eighteenth Century* (Philadelphia, 1987); Michael Harris, *London Newspapers in the Age of Walpole: A Study of the Origins of the Modern English Press* (Rutherford, N.J., 1987); Robert Harris, *A Patriot Press: National Politics and the London Press in the 1740s* (Oxford, 1993); Hannah Barker, *Newspapers, Politics and English Society, 1695–1855* (Edinburgh, 2000).

33. ESRO, Rye 84/1, f. 73; Charles King, *The British Merchant; or, Commerce Preserv'd* (3 vols., London, 1721); and for the French commercial treaty, see Perry Gauci, *The Politics of Trade: The Overseas Merchant in State and Society, 1660–1720* (Oxford, 2001), chap. 6.

34. *The Kentish Post, or Canterbury Newsletter*, no. 2665, 21–25 May 1743; ESRO, Rye 1/18, f. 41.

35. Linda Colley, *Britons: Forging the Nation, 1707–1837* (New Haven, 1992).

36. Peter Borsay, *The English Urban Renaissance: Culture and Society in the Provincial Town, 1660–1770* (Oxford, 1989), pp. 101–13, 325–28; also, E. L. Jones and M. E. Falkus, "Urban Improvement and the English Economy in the Seventeenth and Eighteenth Centuries," in Peter Borsay, ed., *The Eighteenth-Century Town: A Reader in English Urban History, 1688–1820* (London, 1990), pp. 116–58; Rosemary Sweet, *The English Town, 1680–1840: Government, Society and Culture* (London, 1999), chap. 7; C. W. Chalklin, *The Rise of the English Town, 1650–1850* (Cambridge, 2001), chap. 4; Brent, *Georgian Lewes*, chap. 11. For private building in towns, see C. W. Chalklin, *The Provincial Towns of Georgian England* (London, 1974), parts 2–3.

37. Holloway, *History of Rye*, p. 377; Rye Museum, "Property: Corporation: Repairs: Correspondence;" ESRO, Rye 1/18, ff. 32–35, 37; Rye 70/1; A. F. de P. Worsfield, "The Court Hall, Rye," SAC 66 (1925): 208–18.

38. Holloway, *History of Rye*, pp. 333–36, 375; Vidler, *New History of Rye*, p. 95; ESRO, 1/18, ff. 5, 16, 36; and on water supplies, Sweet, *The English Town*, pp. 86–88.

39. Charles Lane Sayer, ed., *Correspondence of Mr. John Collier (Deceased), and his Family, 1716–1780* (2 vols., London, 1907), vol. 1, p. 496; vol. 2, pp. 86, 117, 144; Borsay, *English Urban Renaissance*, pp. 150–62; Michael Reed, "The Cultural Role of Small Towns in England, 1600–1800," in Peter Clark, ed., *Small Towns in Early Modern Europe* (Cambridge, 1999), pp. 136–37; Brent, *Georgian Lewes*, chap. 7. The roles of women at these assemblies are discussed in Amanda Vickery, *The Gentleman's Daughter: Women's Lives in Georgian England* (New Haven, 1998), pp. 224–60.

40. Sayer, *Collier Correspondence*, vol. 1, p. 394; Terry Castle, *Masquerade and*

Civilization: The Carnivalesque in Eighteenth-Century English Fiction and Culture (Stanford, 1986).

41. ESRO, Rye 2/7; Clark, *Guide*, p. 75; Reed, "Cultural Role of Small Towns," p. 136.

42. ESRO, PAR 467/12/1/1, pp. 107-111, 116, 125, 128, 145-46, 159-60; Holloway, *History of Rye*, pp. 439-40; Geoffrey Oxley, *Poor Relief in England and Wales, 1601-1834* (Newton Abbot, 1974), pp. 81-82.

43. ESRO, PAR 467/37/1.

44. ESRO, Rye 2/8; 8/42-51; 9/10-17, /20, /21, /23, /24, /26, /29.

45. ESRO, Rye 1/18, f. 26; Rye 2/8; E. P. Thompson, "The Moral Economy of the English Crowd in the Eighteenth Century," in *Customs in Common: Studies in Traditional Popular Culture* (London, 1991), pp. 185-258.

46. ESRO, PAR 467/37/1. A Kentish comparison can be found in Norma Landau, "The Regulation of Immigration, Economic Structures and Definitions of the Poor in Eighteenth-Century England," *Historical Journal* 33 (1990): 541-72.

47. BL, Add. Ms. 32,697, f. 19. Information about smugglers in this period can be found in Cal Winslow, "Sussex Smugglers," in Douglas Hay et al., eds., *Albion's Fatal Tree: Crime and Society in 18th Century England* (New York, 1975), pp. 119-66, and Mary Waugh, *Smuggling in Kent and Sussex, 1700-1850* (Newbury, Berks., 1987).

48. William Holloway, *Antiquarian Rambles through Rye* (Rye, 1863), p. 40; *Gentleman's Magazine* 17 (August 1747): 397.

49. Customs and Excise Library, Collier Papers, pp. 471, 613; Sayer, ed., *Collier Correspondence*, vol. 1, pp. 330-31.

50. ESRO, SAY 311, 456. For the Poole attack, see *A Full and Genuine Account of the Inhuman and Unparalleled Murders of Mr. William Galley, A Customs-House Officer, and Mr. Daniel Chater, A Shoemaker, With the Trials and Executions of Seven of the Bloody Criminals, at Chichester,* (6th ed., Chichester, n.d. [c. 1749]).

51. ESRO, Rye 9/8-9.

52. Sayer, ed., *Collier Correspondence*, vol. 1, pp. 474-77; Winslow, "Sussex Smugglers," p. 141 n. 1.

53. Sayer, ed., *Collier Correspondence*, vol. 1, pp. 474-76; Winslow, "Sussex Smugglers," pp. 128-29, 164-65.

54. PRO, A94/617; WSRO, Goodwood 154/J9-J11, 155/H17, 155/H24, 155/H52, 155/H83, 155/H113. Described as a "yeoman" and possibly a farmer, Curteis was not a poor man, as he kept a servant: Goodwood 155/H23.

55. WSRO, Goodwood 156/G47. Dodson also offered to look out for Thomas Stringer and Daniel Perryer, two smugglers wanted for murdering an informant.

56. ESRO, SAY 456. For tea drinking and smuggling, see W. A. Cole, "Trends in Eighteenth-Century Smuggling," *Economic History Review* 10 (1958): 396–407; Hoh-cheung Mui and Lorna M. Mui, "Smuggling and the British Tea trade before 1784," *American Historical Review* 84 (1968): 44–73; Hoh-cheung Mui and Lorna M. Mui, "'Trends in Eighteenth-Century Smuggling' Reconsidered," *Economic History Review* 28 (1975): 28–43; W. A. Cole, "The Arithmetic of Eighteenth-Century Smuggling: A Rejoinder," *Economic History Review* 28 (1975): 44–49.

57. Neil McKendrick, "The Consumer Revolution in Eighteenth-Century England," in Neil McKendrick, John Brewer, and J. H. Plumb, eds., *The Birth of a Consumer Society: The Commercialization of Eighteenth-Century England* (London, 1982), pp. 9–33; Carole Shammas, *The Pre-Industrial Consumer in England and America* (Oxford, 1990), chap. 5; Maxine Berg, "New Commodities, Luxuries and Their Consumers in Eighteenth-Century England," in Maxine Berg and Helen Clifford, eds., *Consumers and Luxury: Consumer Culture in Europe, 1650–1850* (Manchester, 1999), pp. 63–85.

58. Crossby and Saville, eds., *Fuller Letters,* pp. xxiv–xxvii; Kenneth Morgan, "Atlantic Trade and British Economic Growth in the Eighteenth Century," in Peter Mathias and John A. Davis, *International Trade and British Economic Growth from the Eighteenth Century to the Present Day* (Oxford, 1996), pp. 20–21.

59. Sayer, *Collier Correspondence,* vol. 1, pp. 23, 48, 139, 190, 153–54. Coach services to London are mentioned in Clark, *Guide,* p. 87. For consumption by genteel women, see Vickery, *Gentleman's Daughter,* chap. 5.

60. Sayer, *Collier Correspondence,* vol. 1, p. 408. The changing significance of gold and silver is discussed in Helen Clifford, "A Commerce with Things: The Value of Precious Metalwork in Early Modern England," in Berg and Clifford, eds., *Consumers and Luxury,* pp. 147–68.

61. Hoh-cheung Mui and Lorna H. Mui, *Shops and Shopkeeping in Eighteenth-Century England* (Kingston, 1989), pp. 191, 295.

62. John Feather, *The Provincial Book Trade in Eighteenth-Century England* (Cambridge, 1985), pp. 25, 74; Holloway, *History of Rye,* pp. 413, 419; Clark, *Guide,* p. 69; ESRO, FRE 528–32, esp. 530.

63. David Vaisey, ed., *The Diary of Thomas Turner* (Oxford, 1984), pp. 201–2, 380 (list of commodities bought and sold).

64. Sayer, *Collier Correspondence,* vol. 2, pp. 9–14.

65. Thomas Frewen, *The Practice and Theory of Inoculation* (London, 1749), p. 41. In 1767, however, the corporation of Rye paid Dr. Frewen to inoculate 329 poor persons of the town; Holloway, *History of Rye,* p. 440.

66. ESRO, PAR 467/37; Rye 71/19; Reed, "Cultural Role of Small Towns," p. 135; Carl Estabrook, *Urbane and Rustic England: Cultural Ties and Social Spheres in the Provinces, 1660–1780* (Manchester, 1998), pp. 133–36.

67. ESRO, Rye 15/18–19, 23; Vidler, *New History of Rye,* p. 113.

68. BL, Add. Ms. 32711, f. 458.

69. Sir Lewis Namier and John Brooke, eds., *The History of Parliament: The House of Commons, 1754–1790* (3 vols., London, 1963), vol. 1, p. 452.

70. Butler, "Vicars of Rye," p. 283.

71. ESRO, Rye 2/8; Charles Lewis Meryon, "Some Account of the Ancient Town and Port of Rye and of its Municipal Government," Rye Museum, 21/7a, vol. 2, p. 568.

72. ESRO, KRA 1/1/1, p. 186. An earlier attempt to pass a new harbour act was made by Phillips Gybbon in 1737; see BL Add. Ms. 32691, ff. 85–90.

73. ESRO, Rye 1/18, pp. 72–79, 82–83.

74. ESRO, SAY 1198, 1199.

75. ESRO, KRA 1/1/1, pp. 184–85. Discussion of lobbying in this period can be found in Sheila Lambert, *Bills and Acts: Legislative Procedure in Eighteenth-Century England* (Cambridge, 1971), chap. 8; John Money, *Experience and Identity: Birmingham and the West Midlands, 1760–1800* (Manchester, 1977), chap. 7; John Brewer, *The Sinews of Power: War, Money and the English State, 1688–1783* (New York, 1988), chap. 8.

76. ESRO, SAY 1200–1207 (quote from 1200), 1252, 1256.

77. BL, Add. Ms. 32872, f. 157.

78. Horsfield, *History of Sussex,* vol. 1, p. 65.

79. BL, Add. Ms. 32883, ff. 112–13.

80. Lewis Namier, *The Structure of Politics at the Accession of George III* (2d ed., 1957, 1975), p. 459 and note 1.

81. BL, Add. Ms. 32919, ff. 48, 78, 80–82. Onslow was cousin once removed to the Lord Onslow who was shot by "Mad Ned" Arnold in 1723.

82. Namier and Brooke, eds., *History of Parliament,* vol. 1, p. 453; BL, Add. Ms. 32919, f. 412; 32920, f. 366; 32921, f. 53; Meryon, "Some Account of Rye," vol. 2, pp. 570–72. Wardroper's attitudes in 1761 can be gauged from BL, Add. Ms. 32918, f. 57.

83. Rye Museum, Chiswell Slade Ledger Book.

84. Henry Waller, *A Familiar Poetical Epistle to Thomas Lamb, Esq., Mayor*

*of Rye, in Sussex; Supposed to be WRITTEN about THREE YEARS ago,
and occasioned by a WAGER concerning the present John, Earl of Sandwich* (London, 1784), p. 24; Henry Waller, *A Rump and a Dozen; being
the Conclusion of a Letter to Thomas Lamb, Esq., Mayor of Rye* (London,
[1784]), pp. 12, 73. Ramsay's portrait of Lamb is in the National Gallery
of Scotland.

85. Waller, *A Rump and a Dozen*, p. 34; ESRO, Rye 1/18, 10 Nov. 1775; James
Bradley, *Religion, Revolution and English Radicalism: Non-conformity in
Eighteenth-Century Politics and Society* (Cambridge, 1990), pp. 74, 361–62.

86. For Baptists at Rye in the late eighteenth century, see Roger Homan,
"Mission and Fission: The Organization of Huntingtonian and Calvin-
istic Baptist Causes in Sussex in the 18th and 19th Centuries," SAC 135
(1997): 271, 280; A. R. Bax, "Notes and Extracts from Non-Parochial
Registers of Sussex," calendared by Michael J. Burchall, transcript in
ESRO, pp. 184–92; Reverend Morgan Edwards, *A Farewell Discourse Delivered to the Baptist Meeting in Rye* (Dublin, 1761). The revival of Dissent
in the late 1700s is discussed in Brent, *Georgian Lewes*, chap. 8.

87. Vidler, *New History of Rye*, p. 111; Clark, *Guide*, pp. 89–90. Vidler's great-
grandfather was a commander of the Volunteer Company, which helps to
explain his very lenient view of the Lambs.

88. Donald Ginter, ed., *Whig Organization in the General Election of 1790:
Selections from the Blair Adam Papers* (Berkeley and Los Angeles, 1967),
pp. 167–74, 177–8 (quotes on pp. 169, 173); R. G. Thorne, ed., *The History
of Parliament: The House of Commons, 1790–1820* (5 vols., London, 1986),
vol. 2, pp. 471–73; vol. 4, pp. 358–59.

SIX
Looking for Allen Grebell

1. See Stana Nenadic, "Middle-Rank Consumers and Domestic Culture in
Edinburgh and Glasgow, 1720–1840," *Past and Present* 145 (1994): 122–56;
Patrick Fagan, *Catholics in a Protestant Country: The Papist Constituency
in Eighteenth-Century Dublin* (Dublin, 1998); T. H. Breen, "'Baubles of
Britain': The American and Consumer Revolutions of the Eighteenth
Century," *Past and Present* 119 (1988): 73–104; and generally, John Brewer
and Roy Porter, eds., *Consumption and the World of Goods* (London, 1993).

2. Célestin Hippeau, ed., *L'Industrie, le commerce et les travaux publiques en
Normandie au XVIIe et au XVIIIe siècles* (Paris, 1870), pp. 9, 14–15, 345–
66; Jacques Bialek, *Evolution du port de Dieppe du XVIIe siècle à nos jours*

(Dieppe, 1996), pp. 19–27; Jean-Pierre Bardet, *Rouen aux XVIIe et XVIIIe siècles: Les mutations d'une espace social* (2 vols., Paris, 1983), vol. 1, pp. 160, 251–52.

3. *The London Magazine: or, Gentleman's Monthly Intelligencer* 30 (1761): 314–16, 404, 505. For reform in a nearby town, see Colin Brent, *Georgian Lewes, 1714–1830: The Heyday of a County Town* (Lewes, 1993), chap. 10.

4. ESRO, Rye 1/19, 6 Aug. 1776.

Index

Lamb, James senior: as Anglican, 181–82; background of, 177–78; business interests of, 154–55, 190, 193–95, 202, 216; counterfeit letter to, 207; death of, 228; and Grebell murder, 5, 10–11, 20, 36, 41, 48, 137, 141, 200, 245; house of, 7–8, 9, 10, 11, 43, 177–78; as oligarch, 12, 24–31, 143, 177–78, 188–89, 190, 214–15, 223–25, 234, 245, 246, 248; and smuggling, 212, 214; and trial of John Breads, 3, 11, 14, 17, 22, 24–31, 40, 41–42, 44, 45, 49–50, 51, 52, 57, 73, 79, 231, 244

Lamb, John, 10, 41, 212, 225, 230

Lamb, Martha, 41, 42

Lamb, Richard, 177, 189, 193

Lamb, Thomas, 25, 182, 193, 194, 221–22, 225, 228–30, 232, 243; as mayor, 233–34

Lamb family, 37, 40, 143, 155, 177, 188, 193, 195, 216, 222, 224, 226, 228–35, 245, 246, 248

Lennox, Charles, 2nd Duke of Richmond, 213–14

Lewes, 34, 60, 61, 65, 106, 107–8, 116, 123, 180, 220

Lightfoot, Francis, 118

Lingfield, William, 212

Lobbying, 97–98, 100, 227–28

Localism, 19, 59, 75, 96, 123, 125, 126, 162, 173, 195–96, 200–201, 217–18, 231, 236–38, 240, 246–47

Locke, John, 47–48, 244

London, 24, 25, 31, 56, 88, 104, 110, 113, 116, 119, 122, 131, 135, 138, 151, 152, 162, 174, 184–85, 203–4, 227, 237, 239; as center of taste, 217–18, 219, 220, 238

Lydd, 100, 146–47

Lynn, Samuel, 172

Mackley, John, 110

Madness, 12, 22, 27, 29–31, 39, 43, 44, 46–53, 93, 138–39, 140

Magical Beliefs, 33, 44, 58, 65, 68–69, 70–74, 79–80, 86, 91–93, 131–32, 135

Mannooch, Francis, 182

Mannooch, Mercy, 157

Mannooch, Nicholas, 156–60, 163–71, 175, 176, 178, 179, 191, 192, 200, 220

Margery, Mother, 63–64, 79

Markwicke, Thomas, 110, 123–24, 157

Marten, Alice, 89, 90, 117

Marten, Benjamin, 105, 117, 120

Marten, Henry, 89, 90

"Men of Rye," 37, 229, 233, 234, 248

Mermaid Inn, 109, 171, 197, 198, 210

Meryon, Charles Lewis, 37, 38, 45, 195, 226

Meryon, John, 195

Meryon family, 37, 246

Millenarianism, 83, 86–87, 130–31, 132–33, 135–36

Miller, Elisa, 134

Miller, Thomas, 103, 105, 108, 110, 123–24, 130

Milward, Robert, 203

Moneypenny, Robert, 24, 25

Monro, Dr. John, 49–50

Morley, Herbert, 88